WOMEN'S AMERICAN ORT
SOUTHEAST DISTRICT

Published by

WOMEN'S AMERICAN ORT
SOUTHEAST DISTRICT
2101 East Hallandale Beach Boulevard
Hallandale, Florida   33009

Cover illustration-Arthur J. Sarlin
Section illustrations-Rhoda Gould and Arthur J. Sarlin
Cookbook editor-Betty Sarlin

Library of Congress Catalog Card Number
90-70051

ISBN 0-9624696-1-0

Printed by
WIMMER BROTHERS
Memphis-Dallas

Manufactured in the United States of America

For more than a century, ORT (Organization For Rehabilitation Through Training) has trained the hands and minds of the Jewish people throughout the world. Today, ORT is more than a network of fine vocational and technical schools for teenagers and adults in 35 countries, including the United States. It is a program with a purpose and philosophy which provides marketable skills for tomorrow's technological world, while playing an important role in the lives of its students, their families and their communities.

Chef's EscORT is dedicated to the 26,000 members of the Southeast District of Women's American ORT with sincere appreciation for their generosity in sharing their favorite recipes. The proceeds from this book will help escort nearly 200,000 students annually through their technological training. This training, and the students' exposure to ORT's ever-increasing world-wide program of democratic and social action, will enable these graduates to be among the most productive members of the 21st century.

Chef's EscORT contains favorite recipes from the personal files of members of Women's American ORT, Southeast District, comprised of Alabama, Florida, Georgia, North Carolina, South Carolina, Tennessee and Mississippi. Although the organization has no reason to doubt the accuracy of ingredients and instructions, neither Women's American ORT, Southeast District, nor its contributors, publisher, printer, distributors or sellers of this book is responsible for the originality, errors, omissions or degrees of recipe success.

TABLE OF CONTENTS

Indicates Microwave

Indicates Food Processor

MEASUREMENTS AND EQUIVALENTS

Dash			less than ⅛ teaspoon
Trace			less than ¹⁄₁₆ teaspoon
3 teaspoons			1 tablespoon
2 tablespoons		1 liquid ounce	⅛ cup
4 tablespoons		2 liquid ounces	¼ cup
5 tablespoons + 1 teaspoon			⅓ cup
8 tablespoons		4 liquid ounces	½ cup
16 tablespoons		8 liquid ounces	1 cup
2 cups		16 liquid ounces	1 pint
2 pints		32 liquid ounces	1 quart
Beans		16 ounces dry	cooked 6-7 cups
Butter or margarine		¼ pound stick	½ cup
Cheese	hard	4 ounces, shredded	1 cup
	cottage	8 ounces	1 cup
	cream	8 ounces	1 cup
Chocolate		1 ounce	1 square
	morsels	6 ounces	1 cup
	substitute	3 tablespoons cocoa + 1 tablespoon butter	1 square
Coconut		3 ounces shredded	1 cup
Coffee		1 pound brewed	40 cups
Cranberries		12 ounces fresh	3 cups
Cream		1 cup unwhipped	2 cups whipped
	sour	8 ounces	1 cup
Crumbs (fine, dry)		3 slices bread	1 cup
		28 saltines	1 cup
		22 vanilla wafers	1 cup
		14-15 graham crackers	1 cup
Dates or candied fruit		8 ounces chopped	1 cup
Egg	whites	8 to 10	1 cup
	yolks	12 to 14	1 cup
Flour	sifted	1 pound	4 cups
	unsifted	1 pound	3½ cups
Garlic		1 clove	powdered ⅛ teaspoon
Gelatin, unflavored		1 envelope	1 tablespoon
Herbs	fresh	1 tablespoon	dried 1 teaspoon
Lemon (juice)		1 medium	3 tablespoons
Lime (juice)		1 medium	2 tablespoons
Macaroni		1 cup	cooked 2 cups
Meat		1 pound chopped cooked	3 cups
		1 pound ground cooked	2 cups
Mushrooms		4 ounces canned	fresh 8 ounces
Mustard	prepared	1 tablespoon	dried 1 teaspoon
Noodles		1 cup	cooked 1¾ cups
Nuts		4 ounces	1 cup
Onion	fresh	¼ cup	dried 1 tablespoon
Orange (juice)		1 medium	½ cup
Raisins		16 ounces	3 cups
Rice		1 pound	2 cups
		1 cup	cooked 3 cups
Spaghetti		1 pound	cooked 8 cups
Sugar	granulated	1 pound	2½ cups
	packed brown	1 pound	2¼ cups
	confectioner's	1 pound	4-4½ cups
Zest			colored part of lemon peel

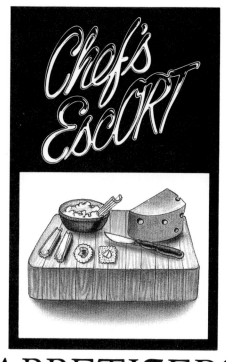

APPETIZERS

ARTICHOKE PARTY DIP

Serves: 4 to 6

1 (15-ounce) can artichoke hearts,
    drained
1 cup mayonnaise
1 cup grated Parmesan cheese

2 teaspoons minced garlic
1 (16-ounce) round loaf onion rye
    bread

- Preheat oven to 350°.
- In medium-sized mixing bowl, chop artichokes.
- Stir in mayonnaise and cheese. Season with garlic.
- Cut thin slice from top of loaf. Hollow out loaf by removing the bread in chunks, leaving sides about ½-inch thick; cut bread chunks in dipping-sized pieces.
- Spoon dip into bread "bowl" and place on baking sheet lined with aluminum foil.
- Bake, uncovered, for 30 minutes. Dip will be lightly browned on top.
- Place on serving tray and surround with bread chunks for dipping. Serve hot or within 30 minutes of baking.
- Dip may be mixed in advance and stored in mixing bowl in refrigerator until ready to bake.

Dawn Weiser
Parkland, Florida

HOT ARTICHOKE DIP

Yield: 2½ cups

1 (15-ounce) can artichoke hearts,
    drained

¾ cup mayonnaise
¼ cup grated Parmesan cheese

- Preheat oven to 350°.
- In small mixing bowl, combine artichoke hearts, mayonnaise and cheese.
- Spread mixture in 1-quart casserole.
- Bake for 20 minutes.
- Serve hot with wheat crackers.

Rhoda Gould
Parkland, Florida

ANCHOVY DIP

Serves: 12 to 15

1 small onion, cut in chunks
1 (2-ounce) can flat anchovies,
drained
½ teaspoon hot sauce

¼ teaspoon paprika
1 (8-ounce) package cream cheese, cut
in chunks

- Using electric blender, place onion, anchovies, hot sauce and paprika in blender container.
- Add part of cream cheese and blend well; add remaining cream cheese in several additions, blending after each.
- Spoon dip into serving bowl. Sprinkle with additional paprika, if desired.
- Serve with crackers and raw vegetables.

Mina Goldberger
Boca Raton, Florida

CAPONATA

Yield: 6 cups

1 unpeeled eggplant, diced
1 small onion, diced
1 (4-ounce) can mushrooms, diced
1 red pepper, diced
⅓ cup olive oil
1 clove garlic, crushed
1 cup stuffed green olives, sliced
1 tablespoon capers, drained

Pignoli (optional)
1 (6-ounce) can tomato paste
2 tablespoons wine vinegar
1 teaspoon sugar
1 teaspoon salt
½ teaspoon pepper
1 teaspoon dried oregano

- In large saucepan, combine eggplant, onion, mushrooms, red pepper, oil and garlic. Cook until vegetables are soft.
- Add olives, capers, tomato paste, pignoli, vinegar, sugar and seasonings. Simmer for 25 minutes.
- Serve as relish with crackers or as salad. May be prepared and frozen.

Anne Baron
Boca Glades, Florida

EGGPLANT CAPONATA

Yield: 4 to 5 cups

1 medium-sized onion, diced
½ green pepper, sliced
1 medium eggplant, diced
2 cloves garlic, crushed
¼ pound mushrooms, sliced
½ cup olive oil
1 (6-ounce) can tomato paste

2 tablespoons wine vinegar
½ cup sliced stuffed green olives
1½ teaspoons sugar
½ teaspoon salt
Dash of pepper
½ teaspoon dried oregano

- In large skillet, cook onion, green pepper, eggplant, garlic and mushrooms in oil until soft.
- In small mixing bowl, combine tomato paste, vinegar, olives and seasonings. Add to vegetable mixture in skillet.
- Simmer, covered, for 20 minutes.
- Serve with crackers. May be prepared a day in advance.

Bernice Goodman
Longboat Key, Florida

TABBOULEH

Serves: 8

1 to 2 cups cracked wheat (bulgar)
Warm water
2 cups tightly-packed chopped parsley
½ cup minced onion
1 green pepper, chopped
1 clove garlic, minced

Salt and pepper to taste
⅓ cup lemon juice
⅓ cup olive or peanut oil
1 large tomato, chopped
Green onion, chopped

- In small bowl, soak wheat in water for 15 minutes; drain.
- In medium-sized mixing bowl, combine parsley, onion, green pepper and garlic; season with salt and pepper.
- Add wheat, tossing gently until just mixed. Add lemon juice and oil and toss until mixed.
- Just before serving, add tomato.
- Spoon mixture on lettuce leaves and garnish each serving with green onion.

Patti Hershorin
Sarasota, Florida

HOUMMUS

Yield: 2 cups

1 (20-ounce) can chickpeas, drained
1 small clove garlic
¼ cup fresh lemon juice
¼ teaspoon salt

¼ cup olive oil
1 teaspoon dried mint
½ teaspoon chopped fresh parsley
1 tablespoon olive oil (optional)

- Using electric blender, purée chickpeas, garlic, lemon juice and salt together.
- Gradually add ¼ cup olive oil, blending thoroughly. Chill, covered. May be prepared a day in advance.
- Serve cold, sprinkled with mint and parsley and drizzled with 1 tablespoon olive oil, with toasted pita wedges.

Kala B. Norton
Coral Gables, Florida

SPINACH DIP

Yield: 3½ cups

1 bunch scallions
1 cup mayonnaise
1 (10-ounce) package frozen chopped
spinach, thawed

1 (1-ounce) package ranch salad
dressing mix

- Using food processor, chop scallions.
- Add mayonnaise, spinach and salad dressing mix to scallions and process until well blended.
- Serve with fresh zucchini strips, carrot and celery sticks or other vegetables.
- May be prepared a day in advance and stored in refrigerator.

Phyllis R. Levin
Palm City, Florida

TEHINA

Yield: 2 cups

1 cup tehina (sesame seed paste)
⅔ cup water
⅓ cup lemon juice
2 cloves garlic, mashed
1 teaspoon salt

⅛ teaspoon pepper
1 tablespoon snipped parsley
Paprika for garnish
1 tablespoon olive oil

- Place tehina in food processor bowl. Add water in a slow stream, processing until all water is added. Paste may turn white and separate.
- Add lemon juice. Paste will become smooth and velvety with consistency of mayonnaise. Add small amount of water or paste if necessary.
- Stir in garlic, salt, pepper and parsley; mix thoroughly.
- Spoon paste into serving bowl and sprinkle with paprika. Make small indention in center of paste and fill with olive oil.
- Serve with pita bread.

Patti Hershorin
Sarasota, Florida

TACO SALAD

Serves: 6

1 (16-ounce) can refried beans
1 small head lettuce, shredded
2 cups diced tomatoes
1 (16-ounce) carton sour cream
1 (4-ounce) package shredded Cheddar cheese

1 (10-ounce) jar chunk-style salsa
1 small onion, chopped
1 (4-ounce) can black olives, sliced
1 or 2 (16-ounce) packages tortilla chips

- If available, place ring of springform pan on serving platter to help contain edges of salad layers.
- Near serving time, spread refried beans in circle on platter. Spread lettuce on beans, then add layers, in order, of tomato, sour cream, cheese, salsa, onion and olives.
- Carefully remove springform ring and serve salad with tortilla chips.

Note: Refried beans may contain lard; lard-free natural refried beans may be obtained at health food stores. A layer of diced avocado may also be used in the salad.

Nancy Gillen Doyle
North Miami Beach, Florida

TACO DIP

Serves: 10

2 (8-ounce) packages cream cheese, softened
1 (6-ounce) jar hot taco sauce
1 medium-sized onion, minced
¼ teaspoon garlic powder
¼ teaspoon lemon pepper
½ head lettuce, shredded

1 large tomato, cut in very small wedges
1 (6-ounce) package sharp Cheddar cheese, crumbled
12 black olives, sliced
1 (16-ounce) bag round taco chips

- In medium-sized mixing bowl, combine cream cheese, taco sauce, onion and seasonings; beat with electric hand mixer until smooth. Mixture will be thick.
- Spread sauce in bottom of shallow serving bowl. Top with layers, in order, of lettuce, tomato, cheese and olives.
- Place some taco chips upright around inside rim of bowl, overlapping slightly.
- Serve with remaining chips.

Note: May be prepared several hours in advance.

Merle E. Mash
Coral Springs, Florida

MEXICAN DIP

Yield: 1½ cups

3 scallions
1 (5¾-ounce) can pitted black olives
1 medium tomato

1 (4-ounce) can chopped green chilies
Salt and pepper
Garlic powder

- Using food processor, separately chop scallions, olives and tomatoes.
- In small mixing bowl, combine all vegetables and mix thoroughly. Season to taste.
- Chill overnight, stirring occasionally.
- Serve with tortilla or other Mexican-style chips.

Arlene Solomon
Atlanta, Georgia

CHEESES—HOT AND COLD

Serves: 10 to 12

4 (3-ounce) packages cream cheese, softened
1 (16-ounce) package shredded sharp Cheddar cheese
1 (16-ounce) package Muenster cheese, shredded
¼ cup Dijon mustard

4 cloves garlic, pressed
2 medium-sized onions, minced
¼ teaspoon red pepper sauce (optional)
½ cup chopped parsley
½ cup chopped chives
1 round loaf whole rye bread

- In large mixing bowl, combine cheeses, mustard, garlic, onion and red pepper sauce; mix thoroughly.
- Place half of mixture in serving bowl. Sprinkle with half of parsley and chives. Chill, covered, until ready to serve.
- Cut thin slice from top of loaf. Hollow out loaf by removing bread in chunks, leaving sides about ½-inch thick. Spoon chilled cheese spread into bread bowl to serve.
- Preheat oven to 375°.
- Place remaining cheese mixture in 1-quart casserole. Add remaining parsley and chives.
- Bake for 15 minutes.
- Serve with apple slices and crackers.
- May be assembled several hours in advance and heated through just before serving.

Lanee Reicher Friedel
Fort Lauderdale, Florida

BAKED BRIE APPETIZER

Serves: 4

1 (4½-ounce) round package Brie cheese
2 tablespoons mango chutney
¼ cup slivered almonds

- May be prepared in conventional or microwave oven. Preheat oven to 325°.
- Place cheese on baking sheet or microwave-safe plate. Spoon chutney evenly on top and sides of cheese; cover with almonds.
- Bake for 10 minutes or microwave on medium (50%) for 2 minutes.
- Serve with crackers or toasted bread rounds.

Carolyn Stein
North Miami Beach, Florida

BAKED BRIE

Serves: 10 to 12

1 (8-ounce) package frozen puff pastry sheets, thawed
1 (8-inch) round Brie cheese
1 (8-ounce) jar apricot preserves
¾ cup chopped pecans or walnuts

- Preheat oven to 350°.
- Place one sheet pastry in 9-inch piepan, allowing pastry to overlap pan edge.
- Place cheese in center of pastry-lined pan. Spread preserves on top of cheese; sprinkle nuts on preserves.
- Cover cheese with second pastry sheet. Trim edges to fit perimeter of piepan. Press pastry sheet edges together and fold inward to seal.
- Bake for 30 minutes or until golden brown.

Ava Feldman
Dunwoody, Georgia

BOURSIN CHEESE SPREAD

Yield: 4 cups

½ (16-ounce) package whipped salted butter, softened
2 (8-ounce) packages cream cheese, softened
2 cloves garlic, pressed
1 teaspoon finely crushed oregano
¼ teaspoon white pepper
¼ teaspoon basil
¼ teaspoon thyme
¼ teaspoon marjoram

- In medium-sized mixing bowl, cream butter and cheese together.
- Blend in seasonings, mixing until smooth.
- Spoon into containers with tightly-fitting lids.
- Store in refrigerator or freezer; spread may be refrozen.
- Serve with crackers.

Linda Kahn
Miami, Florida

PINEAPPLE CHEESEBALL

Yield: 2½ cups

1 (8-ounce) package cream cheese, softened
½ cup drained crushed pineapple
1 cup chopped pecans, divided

2 tablespoons finely chopped green pepper
1 tablespoon minced red onion
1½ teaspoons seasoned salt

- In medium-sized mixing bowl, combine cream cheese and pineapple.
- Stir in ¾ cup pecans, green pepper, onion and salt; mix well.
- Shape mixture into ball. Roll in remaining pecans.
- Chill. Serve with crackers.

Marsha Pollock
Jacksonville, Florida

I CAN'T BELIEVE IT'S NOT CHOPPED LIVER

Serves: 8

1 (16-ounce) can green peas
2 large onions, chopped
1 beef-flavored bouillon cube
2 tablespoons vegetable oil
1½ teaspoons butter or margarine

1 slice toasted pumpernickel bread
2 hard-cooked eggs
½ cup chopped walnuts
Salt to taste

- In small saucepan, bring peas to a boil, cook for 3 minutes and drain.
- Sauté onion with bouillon cube in oil in small skillet until onion is golden brown. Stir in butter.
- Using food processor, process peas, bread, eggs, walnuts and salt until blended. Add onion and process for 2 seconds.
- Spoon mixture into a mold. Chill.
- To serve, remove from mold. Serve with crackers or squares of pumpernickel bread.

Daye S. Glassman
North Palm Beach, Florida

IMITATION CHOPPED LIVER

Serves: 5 to 6

½ cup walnuts
½ cup cooked lentils
2 medium-sized onions, chopped

¼ cup margarine
2 hard-cooked eggs, separated
Salt and pepper

- Using food processor, blend walnuts well. Add lentils and process.
- Sauté onion in margarine in skillet until onion is translucent. Add to walnuts and lentils and process.
- Add egg yolks to onion mixture and process.
- Chop egg whites and fold into onion mixture (do not process).

Lisa Epner
Cary, North Carolina

VEGETARIAN CHOPPED LIVER

Serves: 8 to 12

3 large onions
2 tablespoons vegetable oil
3 hard-cooked eggs
1 (8-ounce) can green peas, drained
1 (8-ounce) can French-cut green
  beans, drained

Salt and pepper to taste
1 cup chopped walnuts
2 tablespoons dry breadcrumbs

- Using food processor, chop onions. Sauté onion in oil in large skillet.
- Return onion to food processor and add eggs, peas, green beans and seasonings. Blend thoroughly.
- Add walnuts and mix well. Mix in breadcrumbs by hand.
- Spoon mixture into mold or shape into mound on serving plate. Chill.
- Serve with crackers or rye bread.

Joan L. Friedman
Delray Beach, Florida

CAVIAR EGG MOUSSE

Serves: 10 to 12

1 tablespoon unflavored gelatin
2 tablespoons sherry
2 tablespoons lemon juice
6 hard-cooked eggs
1 cup mayonnaise

1 teaspoon anchovy paste
1 teaspoon Worcestershire sauce
Pinch of onion powder
1 (2½-ounce) jar black caviar

- In small heatproof mixing bowl, soften gelatin in sherry and lemon juice. Place bowl over boiling water and stir until gelatin is dissolved.
- Press eggs through coarse sieve into medium-sized mixing bowl.
- Add gelatin liquid, mayonnaise, anchovy paste, Worcestershire sauce, onion powder and caviar; mix well.
- Spoon mixture into greased 4-cup mold, pressing lightly to compact ingredients. Chill several hours before serving.
- Invert mold on serving plate. Serve cold as appetizer with crackers or for lunch with lettuce, tomatoes and other vegetables.

Arlene Klinger
Roswell, Georgia

SALMON PÂTÉ

Yield: 2 cups

1 (15½-ounce) can salmon, drained,
   or 1 pound fresh cooked salmon
1 (8-ounce) package cream cheese,
   softened

2 tablespoons minced green onion
¼ teaspoon salt (optional)
1 tablespoon lemon juice
1 teaspoon horseradish (optional)

- Remove skin and bones from salmon. In medium-sized mixing bowl, flake salmon with fork to separate.
- Add cream cheese, onion, salt, lemon juice and horseradish; mix well.
- Spoon mixture into 2-cup mold. Freeze, covered, for several hours or up to 2 weeks.
- To serve, invert mold on serving dish and allow to thaw for 15 minutes. Serve with crackers or toast rounds.

Fay K. Penn
Bay Harbor Island, Florida

SALMON BALL

Yield: 2½ cups

1 (15½-ounce) can salmon, boned and well drained
1 (8-ounce) package cream cheese, softened
2 tablespoons chopped onion

1 tablespoon white horseradish
1 teaspoon lemon juice
¼ teaspoon liquid smoke
Chopped fresh parsley
Chopped nuts

- In medium-sized mixing bowl, combine salmon, cream cheese, onion, horseradish, lemon juice and liquid smoke; mix thoroughly. Chill overnight.
- Shape salmon mixture into ball.
- Roll lightly in mixture of parsley and chopped nuts on waxed paper.
- Serve with a variety of crackers.

Sue Botwinick
Boca Raton, Florida

TUNA PÂTÉ

Yield: 4 cups

1 (8-ounce) package cream cheese, softened
3 tablespoons sour cream
2 tablespoons chili sauce
2 tablespoons chopped fresh parsley

1 teaspoon minced onion flakes
½ teaspoon red pepper sauce
¼ teaspoon curry powder
2 (6½-ounce) cans oil or water packed tuna, drained

- In medium-sized bowl, combine cream cheese, sour cream and seasonings; mix thoroughly.
- Stir in tuna and mix until well blended.
- Spread mixture in 4-cup mold, pressing to pack firmly.
- Chill, covered, for 3 hours.
- Serve with crackers.

Lori Pomerantz
Longwood, Florida

TUNA ANTIPASTO

Yield: 8 cups

2 carrots
2 green peppers, cut in chunks
1 large white onion, diced
2 stalks celery, sliced
Vegetable oil

1 cup catsup
Juice of ½ lemon
1 (6½-ounce) can tuna, drained
¼ pound mushrooms, sliced

- Cut carrots lengthwise and cut in thin slices.
- In large skillet, cook carrots, green pepper, onion and celery in small amount of oil for 10 to 15 minutes.
- Stir in catsup, lemon juice, tuna and mushrooms. Cook, stirring often, for 5 minutes.
- Cool, then store in refrigerator, preferably for 24 hours before serving. May be frozen.
- Serve with crackers.

Florence Gilbert
Coconut Creek, Florida

ITALIAN ANTIPASTO

Yield: 8 quarts

2 cups vegetable oil
3 cups wine vinegar
1 teaspoon ground cloves
1 tablespoon sugar
4 (8-ounce) cans tomato sauce
3 (6-ounce) cans tomato paste
4 (2-ounce) cans anchovies, drained
1 cup water
2 cups cut fresh green beans
2 cups diced fresh carrots
2 green peppers, diced

2 cups thinly sliced Kosher pickles
4 (3¼-ounce) jars cocktail onions
1 medium head cauliflower, cut in
   chunks
3 (5¾-ounce) jars green stuffed olives
2 (6½-ounce) cans tuna, undrained
2 (3¼-ounce) cans sardines, drained
3 (15-ounce) cans artichokes, drained
   and rinsed
4 (4-ounce) cans chopped or sliced
   mushrooms, drained

- In large stockpot or soup kettle, combine oil, vinegar, cloves, sugar, tomato sauce and paste, anchovies and water; bring to a boil.
- Add beans, carrots, peppers, pickles, onions, cauliflower; boil until vegetables are tender.
- Stir in olives, tuna, sardines, artichokes and mushrooms; heat thoroughly.
- Cool mixture. Pour into containers for freezer or refrigerator storage. May be kept several months in freezer or refrigerator.
- Serve at room temperature with crackers or cocktail rye bread.

Frani Imbruno
Sarasota, Florida

COCKTAIL BLINTZES

Serves: 10 to 12

12 to 14 slices white bread
1 (8-ounce) package cream cheese,
   softened
1 egg yolk

1 cup plus 2 tablespoons sugar, divided
2 teaspoons ground cinnamon
½ cup butter or margarine, melted

- Trim crusts from bread and roll each slice until thin.
- In small mixing bowl, combine cream cheese, egg yolk and 2 tablespoons sugar (slightly more if desired); blend well.
- Spread mixture on bread slices, then roll up.
- Combine 1 cup sugar and cinnamon in shallow bowl. Dip each roll in butter, then roll in sugar-cinnamon mixture. Chill.
- To complete preparation, preheat oven to 350°.
- Slice each roll in 3 or 4 pieces. Place on baking sheet.
- Bake for 15 minutes or until lightly browned.
- Serve plain or with sour cream.
- Blintzes may be assembled in advance and frozen.

Carrie Silver
Boynton Beach, Florida

FRIED CHEESE APPETIZERS

Yield: 30

⅓ cup unsifted all-purpose flour
⅓ cup fine dry breadcrumbs
Vegetable oil
1 (10-ounce) package Cheddar,
   Romano, kasseri or goat cheese, cut
   in 1x½x½-inch pieces

2 eggs, lightly beaten with fork

- Combine flour and breadcrumbs on waxed paper sheet.
- In large, deep skillet preheat 2-inch depth of vegetable oil to 350° on deep-fat thermometer.
- With fork, dip each cheese piece into egg, drain slightly and roll in crumb mixture until coated on all sides.
- Fry for 1 minute or until golden brown. Drain on paper towel.
- Serve hot.

Sari F. Rutt
Fort Myers, Florida

MINI-STUFFED POPOVERS

Yield: 18

3 eggs
1 cup milk
1 cup all-purpose flour
3 tablespoons melted margarine

½ teaspoon salt
⅛ teaspoon celery salt
Sesame seeds
1 (3-ounce) package Brie cheese

- Preheat oven to 400°.
- In medium-sized mixing bowl, thoroughly beat eggs with fork.
- Add flour, milk, margarine, salt and celery salt; beat just until blended.
- Grease miniature muffin pans with margarine and place in oven, heating until margarine sizzles.
- Spoon batter into muffin cups, filling half full. Sprinkle with sesame seeds.
- Bake for 40 minutes or until golden brown.
- Remove popovers from pan and cut small opening in side of each. Insert 1 teaspoon cheese in each popover.
- Serve hot or cold.

Frani Imbruno
Sarasota, Florida

CHEESE SNACKS

Yield: 21

1 (4-ounce) package Cheddar cheese, shredded
¾ cup all-purpose flour
¾ cup coarsely crushed crispy rice cereal

½ cup chopped walnuts
½ teaspoon garlic salt
⅓ cup butter, softened
2 tablespoons cold water

- In large mixing bowl, combine cheese, flour, cereal, walnuts, garlic salt, butter and water. Mix with fork until dough forms.
- Lightly butter a circle on each of 3 microwave-safe plates. Drop 7 level tablespoons of dough to form ring on plates.
- Microwave on high for 2¾ to 3½ minutes, rotating dish a quarter turn after 1½ minutes. Dough will be slightly puffed but will crisp on drying.
- Remove immediately from plate and serve.

Arlene Gelber
Boca Raton, Florida

JOAN'S SPICY CHEESE SQUARES

Serves: 12 to 15

12 eggs, beaten until frothy
1¼ teaspoons chili powder
1¼ teaspoons oregano
1 teaspoon paprika

2 (4-ounce) cans green chilies, liquid
reserved and chilies chopped
2 (16-ounce) packages sharp Cheddar
cheese, grated

- Preheat oven to 350°.
- In large mixing bowl, combine eggs, seasonings and liquid drained from green chilies.
- Sprinkle half of cheese in 15x10x1-inch jellyroll pan or 17x12x1-inch baking sheet. Spread with peppers and top with remaining cheese.
- Pour egg mixture over cheese.
- Bake for 40 minutes or until knife inserted near center comes out clean.
- Cut into squares to serve.

Betty Sarlin
Sarasota, Florida

CHEESE PINWHEELS

Yield: 26

1 (8-ounce) package frozen puff
pastry, thawed
1 (8-ounce) package sharp Cheddar
cheese, grated

2 small eggs
Salt and pepper to taste
½ teaspoon dry mustard
¼ teaspoon paprika

- On lightly-floured board, roll pastry to 10x16-inch rectangle.
- In medium-sized mixing bowl, combine cheese, eggs and seasonings; mix with fork until blended. Spread mixture over pastry.
- Loosely roll up pastry, place on baking sheet and freeze for 2 hours.
- To complete preparation, preheat oven to 400°.
- Cut pastry roll in ¼-inch slices, carefully pressing slightly with spatula. Place on parchment-lined baking sheet.
- Bake for 15 to 20 minutes or until crisp and golden.
- Serve immediately.

Shirley Sutter
West Palm Beach, Florida

PINWHEELS

Yield: 60 to 75

1 (8-ounce) package cream cheese, softened
2 tablespoons mayonnaise
1 (4-ounce) can green chilies, chopped

2 teaspoons minced onion
Dash of salt
Dash of hot pepper sauce
5 flour tortillas

- In small mixing bowl, combine cream cheese and mayonnaise; mix until smooth. Stir in chilies, onion and seasonings.
- Spread each tortilla evenly with cream cheese mixture. Roll, wrap in aluminum foil and chill overnight.
- Just before serving, cut tortilla rolls in ⅜-inch slices.

Linda Neel
Boca Raton, Florida

ROASTED BELL PEPPER AND FONTINA SANDWICHES

Yield: 24

¼ cup olive oil
1 clove garlic, crushed
1 (12 to 13-inch) French or Italian bread baguette or thin loaf
1 (16-ounce) package Fontina or provolone cheese, shredded

2 (12-ounce) jars roasted red peppers in oil, drained and rinsed
48 leaves fresh basil or crumbled dried basil

- Preheat oven to 425°.
- In small mixing bowl, combine oil and garlic. Lightly brush some of mixture on 2 baking sheets lined with aluminum foil or nonstick baking sheets.
- Place half of bread slices on prepared baking sheets. Spoon half of cheese on slices, pressing slightly.
- Top with roasted peppers, trimming to fit bread slice if necessary. Top with remaining cheese, then add 2 basil leaves or sprinkle with dried basil.
- Cover with remaining bread slices. Brush tops with remaining oil.
- Bake for about 10 minutes or until bottoms of sandwiches are golden brown. Using metal spatula, invert sandwiches. Remove any melted cheese from baking sheets. Bake for about 5 minutes or until second side is golden brown.
- Serve hot or at room temperature.

Frani Imbruno
Sarasota, Florida

FLORENTINE CRÊPE CUPS

Serves: 6 to 12

Crêpes

3 eggs, lightly beaten
⅔ cup all-purpose flour

½ teaspoon salt
1 cup milk

- In medium-sized mixing bowl, combine eggs, flour, salt and milk. Beat until smooth. Let stand 30 minutes.
- Pour 2 tablespoons batter into hot lightly-greased 8-inch skillet. Cook until underside is lightly browned and top appears dry. Remove from skillet, set aside, and repeat with remaining batter to make 12 crêpes.

Filling

1 (6-ounce) package shredded sharp
  Cheddar cheese
3 tablespoons all-purpose flour
3 eggs, lightly beaten
⅔ cup mayonnaise

1 (10-ounce) package frozen chopped
  spinach, thawed and drained
1 (4-ounce) can chopped mushrooms,
  drained
½ teaspoon salt

- Preheat oven to 350°.
- In large mixing bowl, toss cheese with flour. Stir in eggs, mayonnaise, spinach, mushrooms and salt.
- Carefully fit prepared crêpes into cups of greased muffin pan.
- Spoon spinach filling into crêpe cups.
- Bake for 40 minutes or until filling is firm.

Eleanor Malamuth
Pembroke Lakes, Florida

MARGARET'S RED ENCHILADAS

Serves: 6

12 corn tortillas
½ cup vegetable oil
2 (10-ounce) cans enchilada sauce
1 clove garlic, minced
1 bay leaf

1 (4-ounce) package Monterey Jack cheese, grated
1 (4-ounce) package longhorn Cheddar cheese, grated
1 medium onion, chopped

- Preheat oven to 350°.
- Soften tortillas in oil and drain well.
- In medium-sized saucepan, combine enchilada sauce, garlic and bay leaf. Simmer until very warm.
- Dip each tortilla in sauce, fill with cheese and onion, then roll. Place rolls in 2 layers in 11x8x2-inch baking dish.
- Sprinkle extra cheese and pour excess sauce over tortilla rolls.
- Bake, uncovered, for 10 to 15 minutes or until cheese is melted.

Linda Neel
Boca Raton, Florida

SPINACH PIE

Serves: 6

1 (10-ounce) package frozen chopped spinach, thawed and drained
3 eggs, beaten
1 (8-ounce) carton sour cream
1 (8-ounce) package Swiss cheese, cubed

1 (3-ounce) can fried onion rings
1 teaspoon salt
Pepper to taste
1 unbaked 9-inch deep-dish pastry shell

- Preheat oven to 350°.
- In large mixing bowl, combine spinach, eggs, sour cream, cheese, onion rings and seasonings; mix thoroughly.
- Pour spinach mixture into pastry shell.
- Bake for 30 minutes.
- Serve hot.
- Pie may be assembled, then frozen. Bake unthawed pie at 350° for 30 minutes plus additional time until knife inserted near center comes out clean.

Cecelia H. Fink
Sarasota, Florida

RICK'S QUICHE

Serves: 12

⅓ cup minced onion
1 (8-ounce) package Swiss cheese, finely diced
2 unbaked 9-inch deep-dish pastry shells
6 eggs

1 pint whipping cream
1 (10¾-ounce) can cream of mushroom soup, undiluted
2 (10-ounce) packages frozen chopped spinach, cooked and well-drained
Salt and pepper to taste

- Preheat oven to 350°.
- Sprinkle half of onion and cheese in each pastry shell.
- In large mixing bowl, combine eggs, cream and soup; beat until smooth.
- Add spinach to egg mixture. Season with salt and pepper.
- Pour spinach mixture into pastry shells. Place each piepan on sheet of aluminum foil on oven rack.
- Bake for about 1 hour or until knife tip inserted near center comes out clean. If crust edges begin to overbrown before quiche is baked, cover edges with strips of aluminum foil.
- Serve hot. Baked quiches may be frozen.

Carol Sue Press
Hollywood, Florida

ENGLISH MUFFIN APPETIZER

Yield: 48

1 cup chopped ripe olives
½ cup minced onion
1½ cups grated cheese
½ cup mayonnaise

½ teaspoon salt
1 teaspoon curry powder
6 English muffins, split

- Preheat oven to 400°.
- In medium-sized mixing bowl, combine olives, onion, cheese, mayonnaise, salt and curry powder. Spread mixture on cut surface of muffin halves and place on baking sheet.
- Bake for about 15 minutes or until cheese is melted.
- To serve, cut into fourths. May be assembled, then frozen unbaked. Bake at 350° for about 20 minutes.

Barbara Ratnofsky
Royal Palm Beach, Florida

MINI QUICHE MUFFINS

Yield: 24

1 (8-ounce) can refrigerated butter-
flake dinner rolls
1 egg, beaten
½ cup half and half
½ teaspoon salt

Dash of pepper
2 (8-ounce) cans sliced mushrooms,
drained and diced
4 (8-ounce) packages Gruyère cheese

- Preheat oven to 375°.
- Separate roll dough into 24 pieces. Press each into cup of greased miniature muffin pan, shaping to form shell.
- In medium-sized mixing bowl, combine egg, half and half, salt, pepper, mushrooms and 2 packages cheese cut in very small pieces. Spoon mixture evenly in dough-lined muffin pans.
- Slice remaining cheese into 24 triangles; place 1 piece on each filled muffin cup.
- Bake for 20 minutes or until golden.
- Serve hot. Muffins may be baked, cooled, wrapped in aluminum foil and frozen. Place frozen muffins on baking sheet and bake at 375° for 10 to 12 minutes.

Pat Kimmel
Plantation, Florida

MOCK STUFFED DERMA

Serves: 18 to 24

1 (12-ounce) package round butter
crackers, crushed
1 stalk celery
2 large carrots, cut in chunks

1 large onion, cut in chunks
1 tablespoon water
Salt and pepper to taste
½ cup margarine, melted

- Using electric blender, blend crackers and vegetables until finely chopped. Pour into mixing bowl.
- Add water and seasonings, then stir in margarine and mix well.
- Divide mixture into 3 portions and shape each into roll. Wrap each roll in aluminum foil and freeze.
- To complete preparation, preheat oven to 350°.
- Place foil-wrapped frozen roll on baking sheet. Bake for 50 minutes, remove foil, and bake for additional 10 minutes.
- Slice and serve. Slices may be lightly broiled.

Ann Linden
Miami Beach, Florida

HERBED SPINACH BALLS

Yield: 75 to 80

2 (10-ounce) packages frozen chopped
spinach, cooked and well drained
2 cups herb seasoned stuffing mix
¾ cup grated Parmesan cheese
¾ cup butter or margarine, melted

1 medium-sized onion, minced
4 eggs, well beaten
Salt and pepper to taste
Dash of garlic powder
Dash of ground thyme

- Preheat oven to 350°.
- In large mixing bowl, combine spinach, stuffing mix and cheese. Add butter, onion and eggs. Season with salt, pepper, garlic powder and thyme.
- Shape mixture into small balls (about 1 tablespoon each) and place on greased baking sheets.
- Bake for 15 minutes.
- Spinach balls may be baked in advance, frozen on baking sheets until firm, placed in freezer container or plastic bag and stored until needed. Reheat in oven preheated to 400° for about 10 minutes.

Belle F. Suskin
Tamarac, Florida

HERB STUFFED MUSHROOMS

Yield: 18

1 pound mushrooms, stems removed
and reserved
¼ cup butter or margarine, melted

¼ cup finely chopped green onion
¼ cup white wine, sherry or water
1 cup herb-seasoned stuffing mix

- Preheat oven to 350°.
- Dip mushroom caps in butter and place in 13x9x2-inch baking pan.
- Finely chop part of mushroom stems to measure ¼ cup.
- In small skillet, sauté with green onion in remaining butter, adding more butter if necessary. Stir in wine, sherry or water. Add stuffing mix and mix gently.
- Spoon mixture into mushroom caps.
- Bake for about 10 minutes or until very hot.
- Serve hot.

Mimi Gardner
Fort Lauderdale, Florida

MUSHROOM ROLL-UPS

Yield: 42

½ pound fresh mushrooms, chopped
¼ cup margarine or butter
3 tablespoons all-purpose flour
¾ teaspoon salt

½ pint half and half
2 teaspoons minced chives
1 teaspoon lemon juice
1 (24-ounce) loaf sliced white bread

- In large skillet, sauté mushrooms in margarine for 5 minutes.
- Stir in flour and salt. Add half and half and cook over medium heat, stirring often, until mixture is thickened.
- Add chives and lemon juice. Set aside to cool.
- Remove crusts from bread and roll each slice until thin. Spread with cooled mushroom filling; roll up.
- Chill or freeze roll-ups.
- To complete preparation, preheat oven to 400°.
- Cut each roll-up in half; place on baking sheet.
- Bake until lightly browned.

Miriam Weisberg
Lake Worth, Florida

STUFFED MUSHROOMS

Yield: 16 to 20

1 (8-ounce) package Rondele cheese, softened
1 (8-ounce) package reduced-calorie cream cheese, softened

1 pound medium to large mushrooms, stems removed
1 cup pecan halves

- Preheat oven to 350°.
- In medium-sized mixing bowl, blend cheeses.
- Fill each mushroom cap with cheese and top with pecan half.
- Bake for 10 minutes.
- Serve hot or cold.

Barri L. Sherman
Atlanta, Georgia

MUSHROOM CROUSTADES

Yield: 48

24 slices white bread
2 tablespoons butter, softened
3 tablespoons finely chopped shallots
¼ cup butter
½ pound mushrooms, chopped
2 tablespoons all-purpose flour
1 cup whipping cream

1 tablespoon finely chopped parsley
1½ tablespoons finely chopped chives
½ teaspoon salt
⅛ teaspoon cayenne pepper
½ teaspoon lemon juice
2 tablespoons grated Parmesan cheese

- Preheat oven to 400°.
- Using 2-inch cutter, cut 48 rounds from bread slices. Brush each cup of miniature muffin pans with butter. Press bread round into each.
- Bake for 10 minutes or until browned. Remove from pans.
- In 10-inch skillet, sauté shallots in ¼ cup butter for 4 minutes. Stir in mushrooms, sauté until moisture is evaporated and cook for 15 minutes, stirring frequently.
- Add flour and cream to mushroom mixture. Bring to a boil, then simmer for 2 minutes. Remove from heat and add parsley, chives, salt, pepper and lemon juice. Cool.
- Reduce oven temperature to 350°.
- Spoon mushroom filling into bread cups, sprinkle with Parmesan cheese and place on baking sheet.
- Bake for 10 minutes, then broil for a few minutes.
- Serve hot. Bread cups can be frozen or stored in refrigerator; cups can be filled in advance and baked just before serving.

Pearl Schwarz
North Miami Beach, Florida

COCONUT CHICKEN WITH CURRY SAUCE

Yield: 36

6 chicken breast halves (about 2
   pounds), skin removed and boned
⅓ cup lemon juice
1 teaspoon salt
2 teaspoons hot curry powder
¼ teaspoon ground ginger
2 cups all-purpose flour

2 teaspoons baking powder
1½ cups non-dairy creamer
All-purpose flour
1 (12-ounce) package desiccated
   coconut or 2 (7-ounce) packages
   shredded coconut
1 cup vegetable oil

- Cut each chicken breast into 6 pieces.
- In medium-sized mixing bowl, combine lemon juice and seasonings. Add chicken, stir to coat well and marinate for 30 minutes.
- In medium-sized mixing bowl, combine flour, baking powder and creamer; beat until smooth. Batter will be thick.
- Drain excess marinade from chicken, adding marinade to batter.
- Dredge chicken in flour, dip in batter and roll in coconut.
- Heat oil in large skillet to 375° (or when pinch of coated chicken dropped into hot oil sizzles and rises to surface). Oil should not be so hot it burns the coconut.
- Fry chicken pieces for about 2 minutes, turn, and fry 2 minutes, or until golden brown. Drain on brown paper.
- Serve with warm curry sauce.
- Chicken may be prepared, frozen in a single layer on a baking sheet, placed in plastic bag and frozen. Thaw in single layer on baking sheet and bake at 350° for 15 minutes.

Sauce

1 medium-sized onion, minced
1 small red or green pepper, finely
   chopped
2 tablespoons margarine

1 tablespoon hot curry powder
½ teaspoon salt
¼ cup all-purpose flour
2 cups chicken broth

- In medium-sized skillet, sauté onion and pepper in margarine for 5 minutes or until onion is tender. Stir in seasonings and flour.
- Gradually add broth and cook, stirring constantly, until mixture bubbles and is thickened. Simmer, covered, for 15 minutes, stirring occasionally.
- May be prepared up to 4 days in advance and stored, covered, in refrigerator. Reheat over low heat, stirring frequently.

Carol Glazer
Cape Coral, Florida

PARTY CHICKEN WINGS

Yield: 28

⅓ cup catsup
¼ cup soy sauce
2 tablespoons firmly-packed brown sugar
3 tablespoons lemon juice
¼ teaspoon garlic powder or 1 clove garlic, minced
⅛ teaspoon red pepper
3 pounds chicken wings, cut at joints and tips discarded
Paprika

- In small mixing bowl, combine catsup, soy sauce, brown sugar, lemon juice, garlic and red pepper; mix well.
- Arrange chicken pieces in 12x8x2-inch microwave-safe baking dish. Pour sauce over chicken and mix lightly to evenly coat pieces.
- Chill, covered, for 8 hours or overnight, occasionally turning pieces.
- Just before cooking, turn chicken to coat with sauce, then sprinkle with paprika.
- Microwave on high for 16 to 18 minutes or until chicken is tender, stirring once.
- Drain excess marinade and place wings on serving plate.

Faye B. Weiner
Delray Beach, Florida

SWEDISH TURKEY BALLS

Serves: 6 to 8

1 (12-ounce) jar grape jelly
1 (12-ounce) jar chili sauce
2 tablespoons lemon juice
¼ cup catsup
2 to 4 tablespoons ice water
2 pounds ground turkey
2 eggs
½ cup breadcrumbs
Pepper to taste
Onion powder to taste

- In large saucepan, combine jelly, chili sauce and lemon juice. Cook over medium heat, stirring frequently, until jelly is melted and mixture is hot.
- In medium-sized mixing bowl, dilute catsup with ice water.
- Stir in turkey, eggs, breadcrumbs and seasonings and mix well. Shape into 1-inch balls for appetizer servings or 1½- to 2-inch balls for main dish servings.
- Simmer meatballs in sauce for 2 to 3 hours.
- Serve as appetizer or as main dish over rice.

Renee Weintraub Feldman
Apopka, Florida

CHICKEN SESAME

Serves: 4 to 6

1½ pounds boned chicken breast
2 eggs
2 tablespoons soy sauce
6 tablespoons water
1 cup dry breadcrumbs
½ cup sesame seeds
1 teaspoon paprika
½ teaspoon garlic powder

½ teaspoon salt
¼ teaspoon pepper
1 (8-ounce) jar apricot preserves
1 clove garlic, minced
2 teaspoons soy sauce
All-purpose flour
Vegetable oil

- Cut chicken in bite-sized pieces.
- In small mixing bowl, combine eggs, 2 tablespoons soy sauce and 2 tablespoons water.
- In shallow bowl, combine breadcrumbs, sesame seeds, paprika, garlic powder, salt and pepper.
- In small saucepan, combine preserves, garlic, 2 teaspoons soy sauce and ¼ cup water; simmer for 15 minutes or until preserves are melted and mixture well blended.
- Heat oil in skillet.
- Dip chicken in flour, in egg mixture and in crumb mixture. Fry until golden brown and tender. Place in sauce.
- Serve hot. May be prepared a day in advance and reheated to serve or frozen, then thawed and reheated. For entrée, chicken may be left in breast halves.

Fay Wildman
Fort Lauderdale, Florida

GRANDMA DIAMOND'S CHOPPED HERRING

Serves: 6 to 10

2 fillets pickled herring
½ cup chopped onion
1 small apple, pared and cored
2 hard-cooked eggs

1 slice rye bread
1 teaspoon sugar
2 tablespoons vegetable oil
Vinegar to taste

- In large mixing bowl, combine all ingredients.
- Press through food grinder. Mixture should be chopped and blended.

Dana Gilbert
St. Petersburg, Florida

DANISH HERRING

Serves: 18 to 24

1 cup firmly-packed brown sugar
⅓ cup vegetable oil (may use less)
1 cup apple cider vinegar
½ cup sweet wine
1 cup tomato purée
1½ cups diced apple

1 cup diced onion
1 diced pickled cucumber
½ cup chopped green pepper
¼ teaspoon pepper
1 teaspoon prepared mustard
8 to 12 herring fillets in wine sauce

- In large mixing bowl, blend sugar and oil thoroughly. Add vinegar, wine, tomato purée, apple, onion, cucumber, green pepper, pepper and mustard.
- Dice herring and add to vegetable mixture.
- Place in bottle or bowl, cover, and chill for 48 hours before serving.

Hilly Panovka
Atlanta, Georgia

WATER CHESTNUT MEATBALLS

Serves: 8 to 10

2 slices white bread
½ to ¾ cup water
1 pound ground beef
1 (5-ounce) can water chestnuts,
  finely chopped

1 teaspoon garlic salt
½ teaspoon onion powder
½ teaspoon seasoned salt (optional)
1 tablespoon soy sauce
½ teaspoon hot pepper sauce

- In medium-sized mixing bowl, soak bread in water. Press to remove excess moisture.
- Mix beef with bread. Add water chestnuts and seasonings; mix well.
- Shape mixture into 1-inch balls. Cooking a few at a time, brown meatballs in oil in skillet.
- Serve hot. Meatballs may be assembled in advance and frozen, then thawed and browned or cooked, frozen, thawed and reheated.

Cele Baron
North Miami, Florida

ROSÉ PUNCH

Serves: 60

4 (6-ounce) packages frozen
  strawberries, thawed
1 cup sugar
4 (6-ounce) cans frozen lemonade
  concentrate, undiluted

3 (1 fifth) bottles rosé wine
2 (1-liter) bottles club soda

- In large mixing bowl, combine strawberries and sugar. Let stand for 1 hour. Using electric blender, blend until smooth. Return to mixing bowl.
- Add lemonade and wine to strawberries; mix well. Chill.
- Add club soda just before serving.

Irma Rosenzweig
Orlando, Florida

GRAND PRIZE MICHIGAN PUNCH

Serves: 30 to 40

2 (2-liter) bottles ginger ale, chilled
1 (46-ounce) can unsweetened
  pineapple juice, chilled
1 quart brewed tea, chilled

1 orange, very thinly sliced
¼ cup lemon juice
½ gallon rainbow sherbet
1 (1-liter) bottle seltzer

- In cold punch bowl, combine ginger ale, pineapple juice and tea. Add orange slices and lemon juice, stirring to blend.
- Drop scoops of sherbet into punch; do not stir.
- Pour seltzer over sherbet.
- Serve immediately.

Faye B. Weiner
Delray Beach, Florida

SALADS

AVOCADO RING MOLD

Serves: 8 to 12

2 envelopes unflavored gelatin
½ cup grapefruit juice
1¼ cups boiling water
⅓ cup lime juice
2½ teaspoons salt
Dash of hot pepper sauce

2 large ripe avocados
¾ cup mayonnaise
1½ teaspoons grated onion
1 (2-ounce) jar pimento, drained, or
    ¼ cup sliced ripe olives or pickle
    relish or 1 cucumber, grated

- In small mixing bowl, soften gelatin in grapefruit juice. Add boiling water and stir until gelatin is dissolved.
- Add lime juice, salt and hot pepper sauce; mix well.
- In medium-sized mixing bowl, mash avocados and press through sieve. Stir in mayonnaise.
- Add gelatin liquid to avocado mixture. Stir in onion, pimento, olives, pickle relish or cucumber. Pour into oiled 6-cup mold. Chill until firm.
- Invert on serving plate and serve cold.

Hassie Melnick
Delray Beach, Florida

MEDITERRANEAN BEAN SALAD

Serves: 4

1 (16-ounce) can vegetarian beans in
    tomato sauce, drained
2 green onions, sliced
1 small sweet red or green pepper,
    chopped
1 small cucumber, thinly sliced
1 small zucchini, cut in half length-
    wise and thinly sliced

2 tablespoons olive or vegetable oil
1 tablespoon kosher wine vinegar
1 teaspoon dried basil leaves
¼ teaspoon dried oregano leaves
1 (4-ounce) package mozzarella
    cheese, diced

- In large mixing bowl, combine vegetables, oil, vinegar and herbs. Chill.
- Just before serving, add cheese and toss lightly.
- Serve cold.

Sari F. Rutt
Fort Myers, Florida

GREEN BEAN SALAD

Serves: 4

Dressing

Salt and pepper to taste
1 teaspoon honey

2 tablespoons olive oil
¼ cup cider vinegar

- In small mixing bowl, mix salt, pepper, honey, oil and vinegar; whisk to mix thoroughly.

1 pound fresh green beans, cut in
   1-inch pieces and blanched
2 onions, thinly sliced

2 stalks celery, cut in ¼-inch slices
1 large clove garlic, chopped
1 hard-cooked egg, diced

- In medium-sized mixing bowl, combine beans, onion, celery, garlic and egg.
- Pour dressing over vegetables. Chill for 24 hours.
- Serve cold.

Kimberly Sheintal
Sarasota, Florida

BROCCOLI AND CAULIFLOWER SALAD

Serves: 8

Dressing

1 cup mayonnaise
2 tablespoons vinegar

1 tablespoon sugar
1 teaspoon salt

- In small mixing bowl, blend mayonnaise, vinegar, sugar and salt.

1 medium bunch broccoli, stems and
   florets cut in 1-inch pieces
1 medium head cauliflower, cut in
   1-inch pieces

1 medium-sized onion, chopped

- In large mixing bowl, combine vegetables.
- Pour dressing over vegetables.
- Chill for 3 hours or longer.
- Serve cold.

Marlene Shapiro
Atlanta, Georgia

ITALIAN BROCCOLI VINAIGRETTE

Serves: 3 to 4

Dressing

¾ cup olive oil or partial vegetable oil
¼ cup vinegar
1 tablespoon sugar
1 teaspoon salt
¼ teaspoon pepper

⅛ teaspoon paprika
1 teaspoon minced onion
1 tablespoon minced parsley
3 tablespoons relish or chopped pickle
1 hard-cooked egg, grated

- In small mixing bowl, combine oil, vinegar, sugar, salt, pepper and paprika; beat thoroughly. Add onion, parsley, relish and egg; mix well.

Salad

1 bunch broccoli, ends trimmed and
    stems peeled
Water

1 teaspoon salt
Lettuce leaves
2 hard-cooked eggs, quartered

- In steamer, saucepan or microwave, cook broccoli until tender. Season with salt.
- Pour dressing over hot broccoli. Chill several hours.
- Place broccoli on lettuce-lined serving plate. Garnish with egg quarters.
- Serve cold.

Joan Youdelman
Hollywood, Florida

WALDORF COLESLAW

Serves: 8 to 10

6 cups shredded cabbage
2 cups chopped firm, tart apples
½ cup raisins

¼ cup peanuts or walnuts
Mayonnaise-style salad dressing to
    taste

- In large mixing bowl, combine cabbage, apples, raisins and nuts.
- Stir in enough salad dressing to moisten and mix thoroughly. Chill before serving.
- Serve cold.

Arlene Klinger
Roswell, Georgia

SLAW

Serves: 12

Dressing

1 cup vinegar
1 cup vegetable oil
1 teaspoon salt

¾ cup sugar
1 teaspoon celery seed (optional)

- In small saucepan, combine vinegar, oil, salt, sugar and celery seed. Bring to a boil, then remove from heat.

1 small head green cabbage, shredded
1 small head red cabbage, shredded
1 sweet red pepper, cut in thin strips

1 green pepper, cut in thin strips
1 small onion, cut in thin rings
2 large carrots, cut in thin strips

- In large mixing bowl, combine vegetables and mix thoroughly.
- Pour hot dressing over vegetables and toss lightly. Chill for 1 to 2 days before serving.
- Serve cold.

Janet Weismark
Nashville, Tennessee

CABBAGE SLAW

Serves: 8 to 10

Dressing

1 cup vinegar
1 cup vegetable oil
2 cups sugar

1 tablespoon salt
1 tablespoon celery seed

- In 1-quart saucepan, mix vinegar, oil, sugar, salt and celery seed; bring to a boil.

1 large head cabbage, finely chopped
1 green pepper, finely chopped

1 or 2 onions, minced

- In large mixing bowl, combine cabbage, green pepper and onion.
- Pour dressing over vegetables and mix thoroughly. Chill several hours. Slaw may be stored in refrigerator for up to 3 weeks; flavor is best after 1 week.
- Serve cold.

Bunny Ellin
Atlanta, Georgia

CLAREMONT SALAD

Serves: 10 to 12

Dressing

¾ cup sugar
1 cup white vinegar
⅓ cup water

⅓ cup vegetable oil
Pepper to taste

- In container with tightly-fitting lid, combine sugar, vinegar, water, oil and pepper; shake to blend thoroughly.

1 medium head green cabbage, shredded
2 teaspoons salt
2 green peppers, chopped

2 cucumbers, peeled, seeded and chopped
1 large onion, finely chopped
2 carrots, coarsely shredded

- In large mixing bowl, sprinkle cabbage with salt. Let stand 30 minutes; drain excess liquid.
- Add green pepper, cucumbers, onion and carrots to drained cabbage.
- Pour dressing over vegetables and mix well. Chill.
- Serve cold.

Irma Garment
Boca Raton, Florida

BEET-HORSERADISH MOLD

Serves: 6 to 8

1 (6-ounce) package lemon-flavored gelatin
1½ cups boiling water
1 cup beet liquid

2 tablespoons lemon juice or vinegar
1½ cups grated beets
2 to 3 tablespoons horseradish
Salt and pepper to taste

- In medium-sized mixing bowl, dissolve gelatin in boiling water. Stir in beet liquid and lemon juice.
- Add beets, horseradish and seasonings; mix well.
- Pour into 5-cup mold. Chill until firm.
- Invert on lettuce-lined serving plate.
- Serve cold. Salad is good accompaniment with gefilte fish for Pesach.

Dana Gilbert
St. Petersburg, Florida

CUCUMBER SALAD

Serves: 6

½ cup vinegar
1 cup water

¼ cup sugar or 8 packets sugar
substitute

- In 2-quart container with tightly-fitting lid, combine vinegar, water and sugar; mix well.

2 large cucumbers, lightly pared and
thinly sliced

3 scallions or 1 medium-sized onion,
cut in small pieces

- Add cucumber and onion to dressing; shake well. Chill for 2 hours or longer.
- Serve cold.

Louise R. Weinthal
Hallandale, Florida

LIME AND CUCUMBER MOLD

Serves: 12

2 (3-ounce) packages lime flavored
gelatin
3 cups boiling water
1 (8-ounce) package cream cheese,
softened

2 tablespoons lemon juice
1 large cucumber, peeled, seeded and
sliced
1 (20-ounce) can crushed pineapple,
drained

- In large mixing bowl, dissolve gelatin in boiling water. Add cream cheese and beat with rotary beater until well mixed. Chill until consistency of syrup.
- Stir in lemon juice, cucumber and pineapple.
- Pour into 10-cup mold. Chill until very firm; may be prepared 2 to 3 days in advance.
- Invert on serving plate. Serve cold.

Pauline Coburn
Boca Raton, Florida

CARROT RAISIN SALAD

Serves: 4

3 carrots, grated
½ cup raisins

½ cup chopped walnuts
3 tablespoons mayonnaise

- In medium-sized mixing bowl, combine carrots, raisins and nuts.
- Stir in mayonnaise, using enough to hold mixture together. Chill.
- Serve cold.

Sari F. Rutt
Fort Myers, Florida

SWEET POTATO SALAD

Serves: 12 to 16

3 pounds sweet potatoes, peeled and
cut in ½-inch cubes
Water
Salt
⅔ cup mayonnaise
¾ (16-ounce) carton sour cream
Grated zest of 1 orange

2 tablespoons chopped crystallized
candied ginger
4 stalks celery, sliced
1 cup walnut halves
1 cup raisins
1 (20-ounce) can crushed pineapple,
well drained

- In large saucepan, cook sweet potatoes in salted water for 10 to 15 minutes or just until tender. Drain and cool.
- In small mixing bowl, combine mayonnaise, sour cream, orange zest and ginger; beat until creamy.
- In large mixing bowl, combine cooled potatoes, celery, walnuts, raisins and pineapple.
- Gradually add dressing, tossing lightly to avoid mashing potatoes. Chill several hours. May be stored in refrigerator a few days.
- Serve cold.

Elise Dolgow
Parkland, Florida

POTATO SALAD FRANCAISE

Serves: 25

5 pounds potatoes
Water
1 large onion, grated
3 carrots, grated
Diced celery to taste
1 teaspoon salt

½ teaspoon pepper
1 cup mayonnaise
¼ cup French salad dressing
1 tablespoon prepared mustard
2 tablespoons Indian relish
5 hard-cooked eggs

- In large saucepan, cook unpared potatoes in enough water to cover for about 20 minutes or until tender. Cool until comfortable to handle.
- Remove skins and dice potatoes into large mixing bowl.
- Add onion, carrots, celery, salt and pepper to potatoes.
- In small mixing bowl, combine mayonnaise, salad dressing, mustard and relish. Pour dressing over vegetable mixture and mix well.
- Separate yolks from whites of eggs; add yolks to vegetables and mix thoroughly.
- Cut egg whites in ¼-inch squares; fold into salad. Chill for at least 2 hours.
- Serve cold.

Ruthe Naftal
North Miami Beach, Florida

TOMATO-GARLIC SALAD

Serves: 4 to 6

Dressing

½ cup olive oil
2 tablespoons red wine vinegar
2 cloves garlic, minced

1 tablespoon finely chopped parsley
Salt and freshly ground pepper to taste

- In container with tightly-fitting lid, combine oil, vinegar, garlic, parsley and seasonings; shake until well blended.

2 pints cherry tomatoes, cut in halves   1 medium-sized onion, thinly sliced

- In serving bowl, place tomatoes and onion.
- Pour dressing over vegetables and stir gently. Chill for at least 1 hour before serving.
- Serve cold.

Linda Kahn
Miami, Florida

LAYERED SPINACH SALAD

Serves: 10

1 pound spinach, torn in bite-sized
 pieces
1 small bunch red leaf lettuce,
 shredded
1 (8-ounce) carton sour cream
1 cup mayonnaise
1 (1⅕-ounce) packet creamy Italian or
 ranch style salad dressing mix

2 hard-cooked eggs, sliced
1 (10-ounce) package frozen peas,
 thawed
½ cup chopped green onion
⅔ cup imitation bacon bits

- Combine spinach and lettuce; place half of the greens in glass serving bowl.
- In small mixing bowl, combine sour cream, mayonnaise and salad dressing mix. Spread dressing over greens in bowl.
- Top with layers, in order, of eggs, peas, onion and imitation bacon bits.
- Cover with remaining greens. Spread with remaining dressing. Chill, covered, overnight.
- Serve cold as side dish.

Ruth Klein
Tampa, Florida

COLD VEGETABLE SALAD

Serves: 8 to 10

1 large head cauliflower, cut in bite-
 sized pieces
1 bunch broccoli, cut in bite-sized
 pieces
1 cup chopped celery
½ cup chopped scallions

1 (8-ounce) bottle Italian salad
 dressing
1⅓ cups mayonnaise
¼ cup chili sauce
2 tablespoons lemon juice
2 teaspoons dill weed

- In large mixing bowl, combine vegetables and Italian salad dressing. Chill, covered, overnight. Stir several times.
- Drain liquid from vegetables.
- Add mayonnaise, chili sauce, lemon juice and dill weed to vegetables. Toss until thoroughly mixed. Sprinkle with additional dill, if desired.
- Serve cold.

Rhoda Gould
Parkland, Florida

GARDEN SALAD

Serves: 10

¾ cup wine vinegar
½ cup vegetable or olive oil
1 teaspoon salt
¼ teaspoon pepper
½ teaspoon dried oregano
2 teaspoons sugar
Garlic powder to taste
2 carrots, cut in 2-inch strips

1 (7-ounce) jar green olives
½ pound mushrooms, cut in halves
1 small head cauliflower, cut in
  flowerets and sliced
2 stalks celery, cut in 1-inch pieces
1 (7-ounce) can black olives
1 (4-ounce) jar pimento
1 green pepper, cut in 2-inch strips

- In large skillet, combine vinegar, oil and seasonings.
- Add vegetables and mix lightly.
- Bring mixture to a boil, stirring occasionally; reduce heat and simmer, covered, for at least 15 minutes. Cool.
- Place in plastic container and chill for 24 hours, stirring occasionally.
- Drain some liquid from vegetables and serve cold.

Andrea Glasser
Coral Springs, Florida

SUPER DELICIOUS SALAD

Serves: 8 to 10

Dressing

1¼ cups sugar
1 cup vinegar

½ cup vegetable oil
1 tablespoon water

- In small saucepan, mix sugar, vinegar, oil and water; bring to a boil.

1 (16-ounce) can petit pois peas,
  drained
1 (16-ounce) can French-style green
  beans, drained

4 stalks celery, finely chopped
1 large red onion, sliced
1 green pepper, thinly sliced
1 (3-ounce) jar chopped pimento

- In large mixing bowl, combine vegetables.
- Pour hot dressing over vegetables.
- Chill for 24 hours.
- Drain vegetables and serve cold.

Mimi Gardner
Fort Lauderdale, Florida

CAESAR SALAD

Serves: 4

½ head iceberg lettuce
½ head Romaine lettuce
⅓ cup garlic olive oil
2 tablespoons wine vinegar
½ lemon
1 egg, coddled for 1 minute
Salt to taste

Dash of Worcestershire sauce
Freshly ground pepper
¼ cup plus 2 tablespoons grated
    Parmesan or Romano cheese
1 (2-ounce) can anchovies
1 cup croutons

- Tear lettuce, placing in chilled salad bowl.
- Pour garlic olive oil over lettuce; then pour vinegar over lettuce.
- Squeeze lemon over lettuce and break in egg.
- Season with salt and Worcestershire sauce; grind pepper over salad.
- Sprinkle with cheese and add anchovies. Toss until well mixed.
- Add croutons and toss lightly.
- Serve immediately.

Ann Speroni
North Miami, Florida

FAUX CAESAR SALAD

Serves: 4

Dressing

6 tablespoons olive oil
3 tablespoons wine vinegar
2 tablespoons chopped fresh parsley
Salad seasoning to taste

Ground pepper to taste
Garlic powder to taste
Grated Parmesan cheese to taste

- In small mixing bowl, combine oil, vinegar, seasonings and cheese; mix well.

1 or 2 tomatoes, diced
1 cucumber, peeled, seeded and diced

½ head iceberg lettuce, torn in bite-
    sized pieces

- In serving bowl, place tomatoes, cucumber and lettuce.
- Pour dressing over vegetables.
- Serve without chilling.

Note: Salad may be varied with addition of onion or Swiss cheese.

Fran Meyers
Hollywood, Florida

SINGER'S SALAD

Serves: 6

Dressing

2 tablespoons olive oil
2 tablespoons wine vinegar
¾ teaspoon salt
Dash of pepper

½ teaspoon dried oregano
1 packet sugar substitute
½ teaspoon Worcestershire sauce

- In small mixing bowl, blend oil, vinegar and seasonings.

1 head lettuce, torn in bite-sized pieces
1 (8-ounce) can chickpeas
1 tomato, diced
1 cucumber, peeled, seeded and diced
1 large or 2 small carrots, diced

1 red pepper, diced
1 (3¾-ounce) jar stuffed green olives, drained
1 (6-ounce) jar marinated artichoke hearts, drained

- Prepare lettuce and place in plastic bag; chill until ready to serve salad.
- In large mixing bowl, combine chickpeas, tomato, cucumber, carrots, red pepper, olives and artichoke hearts.
- Pour dressing over vegetables. Chill.
- Just before serving, combine lettuce and vegetables with dressing.
- Serve cold.

Mildred Fenigstein
Coconut Creek, Florida

SEVEN LAYER SALAD

Serves: 8

1 head iceberg lettuce, shredded
½ cup finely chopped celery
½ cup minced onion
1 (8-ounce) can sliced water chestnuts

2 (10-ounce) packages frozen peas
2 cups mayonnaise (not salad dressing)
6 hard-cooked eggs
Imitation bacon bits

- In large salad bowl, place layers, in order, of lettuce, celery, onion, water chestnuts and peas.
- Spread mayonnaise over peas. Cover salad with aluminum foil and chill overnight.
- Sprinkle eggs and bacon bits over salad.
- Serve cold.

Barbara Leeds
Hollywood, Florida

LAYERED LETTUCE

Serves: 6 to 8

½ head iceberg lettuce, torn in bite-sized pieces
½ cup chopped celery
1 green pepper, chopped
1 (10-ounce) package frozen peas, thawed
½ medium-sized red onion, minced

1 cup mayonnaise
¼ cup vegetable oil
2 tablespoons sugar
¼ cup grated Parmesan cheese
1 (4-ounce) package grated Cheddar cheese
Croutons for garnish (optional)

- In 13x9x2-inch baking dish, place layers, in order, of lettuce, celery, green pepper, peas and onion.
- In small mixing bowl, combine mayonnaise, oil, sugar and Parmesan cheese. Carefully spread dressing on onion layer of salad.
- Sprinkle Cheddar cheese over dressing.
- Cover salad with plastic wrap and chill for 24 hours.
- Serve cold, untossed and garnished with croutons.

Sari F. Rutt
Fort Myers, Florida

TACO SALAD

Serves: 5 to 6

1 head iceberg lettuce, torn in bite-sized pieces
2 or 3 tomatoes, diced
1 (16-ounce) can ranch style beans, drained
1 purple onion, thinly sliced or diced

1 (8-ounce) package grated Cheddar cheese
1 (8-ounce) bottle French salad dressing
2 (6-ounce) packages corn chips, crumbled

- In large serving bowl, combine lettuce, tomatoes, beans, onion and cheese.
- Pour dressing over vegetables; toss to mix. Chill.
- Just before serving, stir in corn chips. Serve cold.

Bonnie Beerman
Atlanta, Georgia

ORANGE SALAD

Serves: 6 to 8

Croutons

½ cup walnut pieces
1 tablespoon butter, melted

¼ teaspoon salt

- In small skillet, combine walnuts, butter and salt. Stir-fry over medium-high heat until walnuts are coated and toasted. Set aside to cool.

Dressing

1 cup vegetable oil
¼ cup orange juice
3 tablespoons lemon juice
1 tablespoon vinegar

⅓ cup sugar
1 teaspoon salt
1 teaspoon paprika
1 teaspoon grated onion

- In container with tightly-fitting lid, combine all ingredients and shake until well blended.

1 head iceberg lettuce, torn in bite-
   sized pieces
½ bunch Romaine lettuce (optional),
   torn in bite-sized pieces

2 cups fresh orange sections
1 mild purple onion, sliced in rings

- In large serving bowl, place lettuce, orange sections, onion rings and walnut croutons.
- Pour dressing over mixture and toss lightly.
- Serve without chilling.

Terrie Temkin
Hollywood, Florida

CALIFORNIA SALAD

Serves: 4

Dressing

½ cup vegetable oil
⅓ cup wine vinegar
1 clove garlic, crushed
2 tablespoons firmly-packed brown
sugar

2 tablespoons chopped chives
1 tablespoon curry powder
1 teaspoon soy sauce

- In container with tightly-fitting lid, combine all ingredients and shake until sugar is dissolved and dressing well blended.

1 bunch red leaf lettuce
1 cup torn spinach
1 (11-ounce) can mandarin oranges,
chilled and drained

1 cup seedless grapes
½ cup toasted slivered almonds
1 avocado, sliced

- In medium-sized serving bowl, combine lettuce, spinach, oranges, grapes and almonds.
- Pour dressing over vegetable mixture. Top with avocado slices.
- Serve without chilling.

Rhoda Gould
Parkland, Florida

RICE CURRY SALAD

Serves: 6

2 cups cooked rice
1 small onion, grated
2 tomatoes, chopped
1 (16-ounce) can sliced peaches,
chopped

2 tablespoons chutney
½ cup chopped nuts
1 teaspoon curry powder
½ cup mayonnaise

- In medium-sized bowl, combine rice, onion, tomatoes, peaches, chutney and nuts.
- Sprinkle mixture with curry powder and stir in mayonnaise. Mix until thoroughly blended.
- Serve without chilling.

Louise Heymann
Greensboro, North Carolina

SUMMER PASTA SALAD

Serves: 8

1 (8-ounce) package spinach fettucine
Boiling water
¾ cup Italian or Caesar salad dressing
1 (4-ounce) can black olives, drained, pitted
2 (6-ounce) jars marinated artichokes, undrained and quartered

1 (2-ounce) jar chopped pimento, drained
1 red onion, thinly sliced
3 or 4 stalks heart of palm, cut in ½-inch slices
1 pint cherry tomatoes
Parmesan cheese to taste

- In large saucepan, cook noodles in boiling water for 4 minutes; drain.
- Place noodles in large bowl; add half of salad dressing and toss to mix.
- Add vegetables, remaining dressing and cheese; toss to mix thoroughly.
- Chill. May be prepared several hours in advance.
- Serve cold.

Elaine Gruenhut
Atlanta, Georgia

RED ROSE SALAD

Serves: 4

2 tablespoons pickle relish
2 tablespoons thousand island or Russian salad dressing or to taste
2 (6½-ounce) cans white tuna
1 hard-cooked egg, grated
2 stalks celery, diced
1 carrot, grated
1 (4-ounce) package shredded Cheddar cheese

½ pound spinach
½ head Romaine lettuce
4 large firm tomatoes
1 large cucumber, unpeeled, scored and sliced
1 large green pepper, cut in rings
1 (16-ounce) can ceci peas
¼ pound alfalfa sprouts

- In medium-sized mixing bowl, combine pickle relish, salad dressing, tuna, egg, celery, carrot and cheese.
- Arrange individual plates with generous layer of spinach and lettuce leaves.
- Place tomato in center of each plate. Cut ¾ depth of tomato to form 8 wedges, leaving tomato joined at base. Fill with ¼ of tuna salad.
- Place cucumber slices, green pepper rings, teaspoonfuls of peas and small bunches of sprouts around tomato, alternating vegetables for attractive arrangement. Chill before serving.
- Serve cold with melba toast, toast, or crackers.

Betty Siegel
Delray Beach, Florida

TABBOULEH SALAD

Serves: 8

½ cup cracked wheat (bulgar)
½ cup water
2 cups diced firm tomatoes
1 cup diced peeled cucumber
1 head lettuce, chopped
1½ cups finely chopped parsley

1 cup sliced green onion
½ cup fresh mint or ¼ cup dried mint
⅓ cup olive oil
½ cup fresh lemon juice
Salt and pepper to taste

- In small mixing bowl, combine wheat and water; let stand for 30 minutes.
- Drain all excess liquid from wheat; spread wheat on paper towels to dry.
- In large salad bowl, combine wheat, vegetables and mint. Add oil, lemon juice, salt and pepper and toss gently until thoroughly mixed.
- Serve without chilling.

Sylvia Falk
Coconut Creek, Florida

CHICKEN TABBOULEH

Serves: 6

2 cups cracked wheat (bulgar)
4 cups water
2¼ teaspoons salt, divided
1 cup minced green onion
1 cup minced fresh parsley

2 cups finely chopped fresh tomatoes
2½ cups chopped cooked chicken
2 teaspoons dried mint
½ cup lemon juice
½ cup olive oil

- In 2-quart saucepan, place wheat, water and ¼ teaspoon salt; bring to a boil and cook for 15 minutes. Let stand for 15 minutes for wheat to absorb water. Drain excess water, pressing wheat lightly.
- In large mixing bowl, combine wheat, onion, parsley, tomatoes, chicken and mint.
- Add lemon juice and oil and toss lightly; season with 2 teaspoons salt. Chill several hours. Wheat and/or salad made be prepared a day in advance.
- Serve cold in lettuce cups. Garnish with cucumber slices and parsley sprigs if desired.

Kala B. Norton
Coral Gables, Florida

EASY CHICKEN OR TURKEY SALAD

Serves: 6

1 large stalk celery, cut in 1-inch
pieces
2 cups cooked chicken or turkey

¼ cup mayonnaise
1 teaspoon pepper
½ teaspoon fresh or dried dill, minced

- Using metal blade of food processor, chop celery. Set celery aside.
- Process chicken or turkey until texture of canned tuna; do not purée.
- In small mixing bowl, combine chicken or turkey, celery, mayonnaise, pepper and dill, adding additional mayonnaise to moisten if necessary and adjusting seasoning to taste. No salt is required. Chill.
- Serve cold.

Ruth Rothfarb
Roswell, Georgia

BASIC VEGETARIAN SALAD

Serves: 8

Dressing

1 cup vegetable oil
⅓ cup vinegar
2 tablespoons water
1 teaspoon garlic powder or 1 clove
garlic, minced

½ teaspoon dried oregano
½ teaspoon dried basil
Fresh herbs to taste

- Combine all ingredients in container with tight-fitting lid; shake to mix thoroughly. Chill for several hours.

½ head Romaine lettuce, torn in bite-
sized pieces
½ head red leaf lettuce, torn in bite-
sized pieces
1 tomato, thinly sliced
¼ green pepper, thinly sliced
½ cup cooked chickpeas
1 cup sprouts
1 small zucchini, thinly sliced

1 cup mushrooms, thinly sliced
½ cucumber, thinly sliced
½ avocado, thinly sliced
1 hard-cooked egg, grated
¼ cup sesame seeds
¼ cup sunflower seeds
2 tablespoons wheat germ
½ cup shredded cheese

- In large serving bowl, combine vegetables, egg, seeds, wheat germ and cheese.
- Pour dressing over salad and toss to mix thoroughly.
- Serve without chilling.

Carol Wendkos
Atlanta, Georgia

PICKLED GARDEN ANTIPASTO

Serves: 6 to 8

½ head cauliflower, cut in flowerets
2 carrots, cut in 2-inch strips
2 stalks celery, cut in 1-inch pieces
1 green pepper, cut in 2-inch strips
1 (2-ounce) jar pimento, drained and cut in strips
1 (7-ounce) jar stuffed green olives, drained

¼ cup water
¾ cup wine vinegar
½ cup olive or vegetable oil or combination
2 tablespoons sugar
1 teaspoon salt
¼ teaspoon pepper
½ teaspoon dried oregano

- In large saucepan, combine all ingredients. Bring to a boil, stirring occasionally. Reduce heat and simmer, covered, for 5 minutes. Cool.
- Chill mixture at least 24 hours.
- Serve cold and well drained.

Arlene Gelber
Boca Raton, Florida

KOSHER DILL PICKLES

Yield: 24

3 tablespoons kosher salt
1 cup boiling water
2 tablespoons mixed pickling spices
2 cloves garlic, split

3 sprigs dill weed
1 slice rye bread
2 quarts cold water
24 small kirby cucumbers

- In small mixing bowl, dissolve salt in boiling water.
- Add spices, garlic, dill weed and rye bread.
- Combine seasoning mixture with cold water.
- Place cucumbers in 1-gallon jar. Pour seasoned cold water over pickles. Let stand in lighted area for several days.

Ruth Jawetz
Deerfield Beach, Florida

FRENCH DRESSING

Yield: 1 cup

¼ cup lemon juice or vinegar
¾ cup vegetable oil
¾ teaspoon salt
Pinch of pepper
Dash of paprika

¼ teaspoon sugar
½ teaspoon caraway seeds
1 teaspoon prepared mustard
1 clove garlic, crushed, or 1 teaspoon
  minced onion

- In container with tightly-fitting lid, combine all ingredients and shake until well blended.

Evelyn Bussin
Delray Beach, Florida

GREEN GODDESS

Yield: 4 cups

2 cups mayonnaise
3 scallions, cut in chunks
3 anchovies
3 cloves garlic, crushed
1 large stalk celery, sliced

1 green pepper, seeded and cut in
  chunks
½ cup parsley sprigs
1 tablespoon wine vinegar
1 teaspoon Dijon mustard

- Combine all ingredients in electric blender container. Blend until vegetables are finely chopped and mixture is creamy.
- Store in refrigerator.
- Serve cold over greens or combination salad.

Arlene Gelber
Boca Raton, Florida

CRANBERRY RELISH

Serves: 8 to 10

2 (16-ounce) cans whole cranberry
sauce

2 navel oranges, unpeeled and diced
1 cup broken walnuts

- In medium-sized mixing bowl, combine cranberry sauce, oranges and walnuts. Chill for several hours. Relish may be prepared 2 to 3 days in advance and stored in refrigerator or frozen.
- Serve cold as accompaniment with chicken or turkey main course.

Zena Druss
Lauderhill, Florida

PINEAPPLE-CRANBERRY RELISH

Serves: 10 to 12

1 (16-ounce) can whole cranberry
  sauce
1 (20-ounce) can crushed pineapple,
  drained

½ cup seedless raisins
½ cup orange marmalade
½ cup finely chopped celery

- In medium-sized mixing bowl, combine all ingredients and mix thoroughly. Store, covered, in refrigerator.
- Serve cold.

Fannie M. Scharf
West Palm Beach, Florida

HOMEMADE CRANBERRY RELISH

Serves: 12 to 14

4 cups (16-ounces) cranberries
1 cup chopped pecans
2 oranges, unpeeled

1½ cups sugar
1 (20-ounce) can crushed pineapple

- Using food grinder, grind cranberries, pecans and oranges into medium-sized mixing bowl.
- Stir in sugar and pineapple, mixing thoroughly. Chill for several hours.
- Serve cold.

Jill Kind
Boca Raton, Florida

CRANBERRY LIME OR LEMON VINEGAR

Yield: 5 cups

¾ cup fresh or frozen cranberries,
  rinsed and dried
1 lime or lemon

4 cups white wine vinegar, rice
  vinegar or cider vinegar

- Cut 2 tablespoons cranberries into halves. Place all cranberries in 5-cup sterilized bottle.
- Add peel of 1 lime or lemon.
- In 1½-quart saucepan, heat vinegar until simmering; remove from heat and let cool.
- Pour vinegar into bottle with cranberries. Seal with tight-fitting cap.
- Remove cranberries after 1 week; peel may also be removed.
- Vinegar may be stored at room temperature for several months.

Sylvia Natowitz Pudaloff
Lauderhill, Florida

ORANGE-CREAM FRUIT SALAD

Serves: 10

1 (20-ounce) can pineapple tidbits, drained
1 (16-ounce) can peach slices, drained
1 (11-ounce) can mandarin oranges, drained
3 medium bananas, sliced
2 medium apples, cored and chopped

1 (3¾-ounce) package instant vanilla pudding mix
1½ cups milk
½ (6-ounce) can frozen orange juice concentrate, thawed and undiluted
¾ cup sour cream

- In large serving bowl, combine fruit.
- In small mixing bowl, combine pudding mix, milk and orange juice. Beat with rotary beater for 1 to 2 minutes or until well blended. Add sour cream and beat thoroughly.
- Fold pudding mixture into fruit. Chill, covered, for several hours.
- Serve cold, garnished with additional mandarin oranges, if desired.

Barbara Zucker
Charleston, South Carolina

WINE GELATIN MOLD

Serves: 10 to 12

2 (6-ounce) packages black cherry flavored gelatin
2 cups boiling water

2 (16-ounce) cans Bing cherries, drained with juice reserved
1 (750 ml) bottle blackberry wine

- In large mixing bowl, dissolve gelatin in boiling water.
- Combine wine with enough cherry juice to measure 5 cups; add to dissolved gelatin
- Pour into 8-cup mold. Chill until partially firm, then add cherries.
- Chill until firm. Unmold on lettuce-lined serving plate.

Mary Ellen Peyton
Miami, Florida

FRUIT COMPOTE

Serves: 16

2 (6-ounce) packages dried mixed fruit
Boiling water
2 (16-ounce) cans whole cranberry
  sauce

1 (29-ounce) can pears, drained
1 (29-ounce) can peaches, drained
1 (29-ounce) can apricots, drained

- Place dried fruit in heatproof bowl and cover with boiling water. Allow fruit to soften, covered, overnight.
- In large saucepan, combine mixed fruit with cranberry sauce, pears, peaches and apricots. Simmer until thoroughly heated.
- Serve hot.

Note: Other fruits such as pineapple chunks can be added.

Edythe Sadowsky
Wesley Chapel, Florida

CHIFFON GELATIN MOLD

Serves: 8

1 (⅓-ounce) package sugar-free lemon
  or peach flavored gelatin
1 cup boiling water
1 (8-ounce) carton low-fat lemon or
  peach yogurt

1 (8-ounce) carton frozen non-dairy
  whipped topping, thawed
¼ cup sliced canned fruit, drained
  (optional)
¼ cup chopped walnuts (optional)

- In medium-sized mixing bowl, dissolve gelatin in boiling water. Chill until consistency of syrup.
- Using electric mixer on low speed, fold in yogurt and whipped topping, beating until well blended.
- Add fruit and walnuts. Pour mixture into 5-cup mold and chill until firm.
- Serve cold.

Dorothy K. Sacks
Miramar, Florida

SOUPS

BLACK BEAN AND ONION SOUP

Serves: 6

6 to 8 thick slices black bread
(Russian or pumpernickel)
Milk
2 large Spanish onions, sliced
1 carrot, diced
1 cup diced celery
3 cloves garlic, minced
2 tablespoons vegetable oil
6 cups fresh or canned vegetable stock

1 large bay leaf
Salt and pepper to taste
Dried thyme, basil, parsley and
oregano to taste
1 cup dry red wine
1 (4-ounce) package Fontina, mozzarella, white Cheddar or Swiss
cheese, shredded

- Remove crust from bread and tear into pieces. Soak overnight in milk.
- Squeeze bread to remove milk. Purée in blender or food processor.
- In large stockpot, cook onion, carrot, celery and garlic in oil for 4 to 5 minutes.
- Add vegetable stock, herbs and seasonings. Bring to a boil, then simmer for 30 minutes.
- Add wine and simmer for 10 minutes. Remove bay leaf.
- Stir in bread and simmer for 5 minutes.
- Add cheese and continue to cook until cheese is melted or pour soup into individual soup crocks, cover with cheese and place in preheated oven until cheese is melted.
- Serve hot.

Irma Garment
Boca Raton, Florida

PASTA FAGOLI

Serves: 4

½ medium-sized onion, diced
2 cloves garlic, minced
2 tablespoons olive oil
1 (8-ounce) can tomato purée
1 (16-ounce) can crushed tomatoes

¼ teaspoon dried oregano
¼ teaspoon dried basil
1 (16-ounce) can cannelloni beans,
undrained
1 cup cooked ditillini pasta

- In large saucepan, cook onion and garlic in oil until onion is tender.
- Add purée, tomatoes, oregano and basil. Simmer for 20 minutes.
- Stir in beans and pasta. Simmer for 5 minutes.
- Season with salt and pepper.

Paula Wolfson
Boca Raton, Florida

CABBAGE BORSCHT

Serves: 8 to 10

1 pound flanken plus soup bones
1 large onion, diced
2 stalks celery, sliced
1 head cabbage, grated
6 cups cold water
1 (29-ounce) can tomatoes or 3
  pounds fresh tomatoes, peeled and
  quartered

1 (10½-ounce) can condensed tomato
  soup, undiluted
Juice of 2 lemons
Sugar or sugar substitute to taste
½ cup raisins (optional)

- In large stockpot, combine flanken, bones, onion, celery, cabbage and water. Bring to a boil and cook for 15 minutes.
- Add tomatoes, tomato soup, lemon juice, sugar and raisins. Simmer until meat and cabbage are tender.
- Remove flanken from soup, slice and serve with hot soup.

Frances Rutstein
Delray Beach, Florida

CABBAGE SOUP

Serves: 12

2 pounds beef chuck roast or brisket
Water
1 head cabbage, cut in chunks
2 tomatoes, chopped
1 large onion, sliced

1 cup firmly-packed brown sugar
½ cup lemon juice or sour salt
  solution
Salt to taste

- Place beef in 8-quart stockpot, cover with water and bring to a boil. Skim foam from surface of liquid.
- Add vegetables, brown sugar, lemon juice and salt. Simmer, partially covered, for about 2½ hours.
- Serve hot. Soup freezes well.

Kimberly Sheintal
Sarasota, Florida

CUCUMBER SOUP

Serves: 10

3 large cucumbers, peeled, seeded and
  cubed
3 large potatoes, peeled and cubed
2 quarts water

1 bunch parsley, stems removed
1 tablespoon salt
¼ teaspoon pepper

- In 4-quart stockpot, combine cucumbers, potatoes and water. Cook, covered, over medium heat until vegetables are tender.
- Add parsley and bring to a boil. Cool slightly.
- Using electric blender, purée vegetable-liquid mixture. Season with salt and pepper. Chill.
- Serve cold. May be prepared in advance and frozen.

Felice Greenstein
Coral Springs, Florida

SPRING GREEN SOUP

Serves: 8 to 10

18 medium-sized green onions
2 large cloves garlic, crushed
2 medium-sized leeks, sliced
¼ cup butter or margarine
6 cups vegetable broth
2 medium potatoes, peeled and cubed

2 carrots, cut in ¼-inch slices
1 pound spinach, cut in crosswise
  strips
½ teaspoon salt or to taste
½ teaspoon freshly ground pepper or
  to taste

- Slice onions, including some of green tops.
- In 4-quart stockpot, cook onion, garlic and leeks in butter, stirring occasionally, until vegetables are transparent.
- Stir in broth, potatoes and carrots. Bring to a boil, then simmer, covered, for 10 minutes or until vegetables are tender.
- Add spinach, salt and pepper. Simmer for 5 to 10 minutes.
- Serve hot.

Esther Brody
Atlanta, Georgia

CHICKEN SOUP
AND TWICE-COOKED CHICKEN

Serves: 24

Soup

2 (6- to 7-pound) chickens, cut up
   eighthed
2 medium-sized onions, sliced
2 large carrots, diced
2 stalks celery, diced
2 cloves garlic, minced

3 tablespoons soup greens seasoning
½ teaspoon salt
5 peppercorns
½ teaspoon chicken bouillon granules
6 quarts water

- Place all ingredients in 10-quart stockpot. Bring to a boil, then simmer, covered, for 3 hours.
- Carefully strain soup through colander into large container to reserve broth. Separate chicken from vegetables; set both aside. Cool at room temperature; store in refrigerator if soup will not be used until following day.
- Skim fat from surface of broth. Purée onions, carrots, celery and garlic; return to broth in stockpot.
- Bring to a boil. Pour into tureen for serving.

Chicken

Cooked chicken (from soup
   preparation)
2 (8-ounce) packages dried apricots

1 (8-ounce) package dried prunes
4 cups orange juice
2 cups water

- Preheat oven to 300°.
- Place chicken in roasting or baking pan. Cover chicken with dried fruit, orange juice and water.
- Bake, covered (if using aluminum foil, place shiny side up), for 45 minutes.
- Remove cover, baste, and bake, uncovered, for 15 minutes.
- Serve hot with sauce from pan.

Loisbeth Emanuel
Miami, Florida

GRANDMA EVA'S VEGETABLE SOUP

Serves: 8

3 quarts water
1 (3½-pound) broiler-fryer chicken or
    soup bones or flanken
½ cup dried small lima beans
¾ cup dried split peas
½ cup medium barley, uncooked
1 large or 2 medium carrots

1 onion
3 stalks celery, diced
½ (10-ounce) package frozen mixed
    vegetables
Sprigs of dill
Salt to taste
Pepper to taste (optional)

- In 4-quart stockpot, bring water to a boil. Add chicken, soup bones or flanken. Bring to a boil, skimming foam from surface.
- Add beans, peas, barley, carrots, onion and celery. Simmer for about 1 hour or until beans and meat are tender.
- Stir in frozen vegetables and simmer for about 20 minutes.
- Tie dill sprigs together with white thread and add to soup. Remove carrots and onion, purée and return to soup. Simmer for about 10 minutes.
- Season with salt and pepper.
- Serve hot.

Esther H. Rubin
West Palm Beach, Florida

CARROT SOUP

Serves: 4

4 to 6 carrots, sliced in circles
2½ cups chicken broth, divided
Salt and pepper to taste
½ teaspoon curry powder

⅛ teaspoon hot pepper sauce
Imitation sour cream for garnish
Dill weed for garnish

- In 1-quart saucepan, cook carrots in ½ cup chicken broth until carrots are soft.
- Add remaining broth. Purée carrot-broth mixture in electric blender or food processor. If necessary, thin with additional broth or water. Return to saucepan.
- Add seasonings and simmer for 5 minutes.
- Serve either hot or cold. Garnish individual servings with 1 tablespoon imitation sour cream and sprinkle with dill weed.

Carolyn Ring
West Palm Beach, Florida

LEEK SOUP

Serves: 6 to 8

6 leeks
½ cup butter, divided
3 quarts boiling water
3 medium potatoes, peeled and cubed

2 bay leaves
1 teaspoon salt
1 teaspoon white pepper

- Cut leeks between green and white portions. Chop green part and sauté in ¼ cup butter in 6-quart stockpot until soft.
- Add boiling water, potatoes, bay leaves, salt and pepper to leeks. Simmer, uncovered, for 30 minutes. Cool slightly. Remove bay leaves.
- Using electric blender, purée vegetable-liquid mixture or blend by hand until smooth.
- Chop white part of leeks and sauté in remaining butter in small skillet. Add to soup and mix thoroughly.
- Serve hot.

Felice Greenstein
Coral Springs, Florida

MINESTRONE

Serves: 6 to 8

1 pound top round beef steak, cubed
6 cups hot water
¾ cup frozen chopped onion
¼ teaspoon pepper
½ teaspoon dried basil
1 (10-ounce) package frozen peas and carrots

1 (16-ounce) can tomatoes
½ cup orzo or other small pasta
1 (16-ounce) can white beans, drained
2 medium zucchini, sliced
1 cup shredded cabbage

- Place beef in 5-quart microwave-safe casserole. Add water, onion and seasonings. Cook, covered, on high for 30 minutes or until meat is tender.
- Add peas and carrots and tomatoes. Cook, covered, on high for 10 minutes.
- Stir in pasta, beans, zucchini and cabbage. Cook, covered, on high for 10 minutes, stirring occasionally. Allow 5 minutes standing time, covered.
- Serve hot with salad and garlic bread for complete meal. May be reheated by the bowl.

Peggy Ageloff
Jacksonville, Florida

MUSHROOM BISQUE

Serves: 2

½ pound mushrooms, minced
1 small onion, minced
4 tablespoons butter or margarine, divided
3 tablespoons all-purpose flour

1 cup half and half or cream substitute
1 cup water
Salt and pepper to taste
1 tablespoon sherry (optional)

- In small skillet, sauté mushrooms and onion in 1 tablespoon butter for 15 minutes.
- Melt remaining butter in 2-quart saucepan. Add flour and cook over low heat, stirring frequently, until well blended but not browned.
- Add half and half and water; simmer, stirring frequently, until thickened.
- Add mushrooms and onion to white sauce and season with salt and pepper. Simmer for about 5 minutes.
- Add sherry just before serving. Serve hot. Soup may be frozen.

Esther Brody
Atlanta, Georgia

MUSHROOM-BARLEY SOUP

Serves: 4 to 6

½ cup uncooked barley
4 cups water or vegetable or chicken stock
1 large bay leaf
2 carrots, sliced
1 small parsnip, sliced
½ cup chopped onion

1½ teaspoons chopped garlic
1 tablespoon vegetable oil
½ pound mushrooms, sliced
½ teaspoon dried thyme
1 tablespoon tamari soy sauce
White pepper to taste
½ cup chopped parsley

- In large stockpot, combine barley, water and bay leaf. Simmer for about 1 hour or until barley is tender.
- Add carrots and parsnip; simmer for 15 minutes.
- In skillet, cook onion and garlic in oil until onion is soft.
- Add onion-garlic mixture, mushrooms, thyme, soy sauce and white pepper to barley mixture; bring to a boil. Remove bay leaf.
- Sprinkle soup with parsley and ladle into preheated individual bowls. Serve hot. Soup may be reheated but will thicken slightly.

Cecelia Lieberman
Wesley Chapel, Florida

SPLIT PEA SOUP WITH FLANKEN

Serves: 8 to 10

2 to 3 pounds flanken
2 to 3 quarts water
1 (16-ounce) package split peas
2 onions, grated

4 to 6 sprigs dill
2 or 3 cloves garlic, crushed
Salt and pepper to taste

- In 8-quart stockpot, place flanken and add water to cover. Simmer for 1 hour. Cool, then skim excess fat from stock surface.
- Add vegetables and seasonings. Simmer for 1 hour or until meat is tender.
- Serve hot.

Evelyn Blackman
Miami, Florida

CREAMY PUMPKIN SOUP

Serves: 2

1 small onion, minced
½ green pepper, chopped
1 teaspoon vegetable oil
½ (16-ounce) can pumpkin (not pumpkin pie filling)
1 (14½-ounce) can chicken broth

1 teaspoon ground cumin
2 tablespoons chopped cilantro (fresh coriander) plus 2 whole leaves for garnish or parsley
¼ cup imitation sour cream
Crushed red pepper flakes

- In medium-sized saucepan, cook onion and green pepper in oil over high heat for about 2 minutes or until onion is translucent.
- Add pumpkin and chicken broth, stirring with wire whisk until smooth. Bring to a boil and cook for 2 minutes, stirring constantly. Stir in cumin and cilantro.
- Pour soup into individual serving bowls. Place 1 tablespoon imitation sour cream in center of each serving and swirl with knife. Sprinkle with red pepper and garnish with cilantro leaf.
- Serve hot.

Miriam Pomeranc
Altamonte Springs, Florida

SPRING GARDEN VEGETABLE SOUP

Serves: 10 to 12

2 leeks, cut in ½-inch slices including
    some green portion
2 medium carrots, cut in ¼-inch slices
1 cup fresh or frozen peas
2 stalks celery, cut in ¼-inch slices
¼ cup margarine

½ pound mushrooms, sliced
5 cups beef broth
1 tablespoon chopped fresh basil or
    ½ teaspoon dried basil or to taste
Salt and pepper to taste

- In 4-quart stockpot, sauté leeks, carrots, peas and celery in margarine for 20 minutes, stirring occasionally.
- Add mushrooms and sauté for 5 minutes.
- Stir in broth and seasonings. Bring to a boil.
- Serve hot. Soup may be frozen.

Esther Brody
Atlanta, Georgia

FANNIE'S TURKEY SOUP

Serves: 6

Turkey bones
Water
½ cup dried split peas
1 cup barley, uncooked

½ cup dried lima beans
3 or 4 carrots, diced
2 medium onions, chopped
Pepper to taste

- Place turkey bones in large stockpot with water to cover. Bring to a boil.
- Stir in peas, barley and beans; boil for about 25 minutes or until tender.
- Add carrots and continue cooking until carrots are tender.
- Add onion and cook for about 5 minutes or until onion is tender.
- Season with pepper.
- Serve hot.

Sari F. Rutt
Fort Myers, Florida

GAZPACHO

Serves: 8

1 large cucumber, peeled and cut in
chunks
1 large onion, cut in chunks
1 large green or red sweet pepper, cut
in chunks
⅓ cup wine vinegar
⅓ cup sunflower or olive oil
½ to 1 teaspoon hot pepper sauce or to
taste

1 teaspoon seasoned salt
1 teaspoon dried oregano, crushed
1 teaspoon dried sweet basil, crushed
1 (46-ounce) can unsalted tomato
juice or combination of ½ tomato
juice and ½ fresh chopped tomatoes

- Place cucumber, onion and pepper in blender container; blend until vegetables are puréed.
- In large mixing bowl, combine puréed vegetables and vinegar, oil, seasonings and tomato juice.
- Chill until very cold. May be frozen.
- Serve cold.

Gloria R. Solop
Boca Raton, Florida

TOMATO CORN SOUP

Serves: 4

¼ cup chopped onion
2 tablespoons vegetable oil
2 tablespoons all-purpose flour
2 cups tomato juice

1 (16-ounce) can cream-style corn
2 cups low-fat milk
Pepper to taste
Parsley for garnish

- In 2-quart saucepan, cook onion in oil over low heat until onion is transparent.
- Stir in flour and cook, stirring often, until slightly thickened.
- Pour mixture into blender; add tomato juice and corn and blend until smooth.
- Pour tomato mixture into saucepan and add milk. Simmer, stirring constantly; do not boil. Season with pepper.
- Serve hot with parsley garnish.

Note: Puréed fresh tomatoes may be substituted for juice. Drained canned corn plus 1 cup milk and 1 to 2 teaspoons flour may be substituted for cream-style corn.

Nadine King
Memphis, Tennessee

CASCADILLA

Serves: 4 to 6

1 cucumber, seeded and chopped
1 green pepper, seeded and chopped
4 or 5 mushrooms, thinly sliced
1 scallion, chopped
1 clove garlic, pressed
4 cups tomato juice

1 cup yogurt and/or sour cream
1 teaspoon honey
½ teaspoon dill weed
Salt and pepper to taste
Watercress sprigs for garnish

- In large mixing bowl, combine vegetables, juice, yogurt, honey and seasonings. Mix well. Chill.
- Serve with croutons and garnish individual servings with watercress.

Carolyn Ring
West Palm Beach, Florida

VEGETARIAN LENTIL SOUP

Serves: 8

2 quarts water
2 tablespoons chicken-flavored
  bouillon granules
1 onion, cut in chunks
2 or 3 carrots, sliced
1 parsnip, sliced
1 sweet red pepper, cut in chunks

2 stalks celery, sliced
1 cup dried lentils
1 cup chopped mushrooms (optional)
Black pepper to taste
Dash of cayenne pepper (optional)
Dash of salt (optional)
½ pound okra, sliced

- In 8-quart stockpot, combine water, bouillon, onion, carrots, parsnip, red pepper, celery, lentils, mushrooms and seasonings. Bring to a boil, then simmer, covered, for 1 hour.
- Add okra about 10 minutes before serving, cover and let steam.
- Serve hot.

Sue Rosenbluth
Largo, Florida

MEAT

EASY PRIME RIB ROAST

Prime rib roast
Pepper
Garlic salt

Onion salt
Worcestershire sauce
Mustard

- Preheat oven to 450°.
- Line roasting pan with aluminum foil. Place roasting rack in pan.
- Season roast with pepper, garlic salt and onion salt. Rub Worcestershire sauce, then mustard evenly on all sides of roast. Place roast in standing position on rack.
- Bake for about 15 to 20 minutes, reduce oven temperature to 350° and bake for about 20 minutes per pound for medium-done roast.
- Let stand a few moments before carving and serving.

Elaine Gruenhut
Atlanta, Georgia

TENDER MEDALLIONS
IN MUSTARD-COGNAC SAUCE

Serves: 6

1 beef bouillon cube
1 cup boiling water
¾ cup margarine
1 teaspoon salt
Freshly ground pepper to taste
¼ cup cognac
2 tablespoons Dijon mustard
1 tablespoon moutard de meaux
5 teaspoons white Dijon mustard with scallions or tarragon

1 tablespoon mustard with green chili and garlic or Bavarian mustard with seeds
5 teaspoons chili sauce
¼ cup plus 1½ teaspoons steak sauce
2 pounds beef fillets, cut in ⅜-inch slices

- Dissolve bouillon in boiling water; set aside.
- In large sauté pan or skillet over medium heat, melt margarine with salt and pepper. Add cognac, ignite and shake until flame is extinguished.
- Stir mustards into cognac liquid and mix well. Blend in chili sauce. Add steak sauce and mix well. Blend in 2 tablespoons bouillon.
- Add beef to sauce; cook over high heat for about 1 minute on each side of slices or until desired doneness.
- Serve immediately with sauce.

Note: Other mustards may be substituted.

Terrie Temkin
Hollywood, Florida

BEEF BURGUNDY

Serves: 6

2 pounds beef, cubed
3 tablespoons all-purpose flour
3 tablespoons vegetable oil
⅓ cup chopped onion
1 tablespoon chopped parsley
1 clove garlic, minced

1 bay leaf
¼ teaspoon salt
Dash of pepper
¾ cup Burgundy
¾ cup water
½ pound mushrooms

- Dredge beef cubes in flour. Brown in vegetable oil in skillet over medium heat. Remove beef from skillet.
- Combine onion, parsley, garlic, bay leaf, salt and pepper in skillet. Stir in Burgundy, water and mushrooms. Bring mixture to a boil. Add meat and simmer, covered, for 1 hour.
- Remove bay leaf.
- Serve hot over noodles or rice.

Carol A. Glazer
Cape Coral, Florida

STUFFED FLANK STEAK

Serves: 4 to 6

1½ to 2½ pounds flank steak
Salt and pepper to taste
2 tablespoons chopped onion
2 tablespoons chopped green pepper
⅓ cup margarine (parve)

1 tablespoon tomato paste
½ teaspoon red horseradish
¼ teaspoon sugar
½ cup water
2 cups herb seasoned stuffing mix

- Preheat oven to 500°.
- Score one side of flank steak in diamond pattern. Rub steak with salt and pepper.
- In skillet, sauté onion and green pepper in margarine until vegetables are tender. Stir in tomato paste, horseradish, sugar, water and stuffing mix.
- Spoon stuffing down center of unscored side of flank steak but not quite to each end. Fold ends over stuffing, then bring long edges together and overlap, securing with skewers. Place in shallow baking pan.
- Roast for 15 minutes, reduce oven temperature to 350° and bake for 40 to 50 minutes longer.
- Cut in crosswise slices and arrange on serving platter. Serve hot.

Frani Imbruno
Sarasota, Florida

CLAREMONT BEEF TENDERLOIN SAUTÉ

Serves: 6

1 Spanish onion, sliced
1 pound mushrooms, sliced
1 clove garlic, crushed
¼ cup margarine
2½ pounds beef tenderloin, cubed
1 teaspoon salt
Pepper to taste

1 teaspoon paprika
2 teaspoons seasoned flavor enhancer
¼ cup cooking sherry
1 cup beef bouillon
1 tablespoon bottled brown bouquet
sauce

- In large skillet, sauté onions, mushrooms and garlic in margarine until golden brown.
- Add beef and dry seasonings to vegetables; sauté over medium heat until meat is browned.
- Stir in sherry, bouillon and sauce; simmer for about 10 minutes.
- Serve hot. Sauté may be prepared in advance and frozen.

Mildred Libman
Tamarac, Florida

CHINESE BEEF

Serves: 4 to 6

2 pounds flank steak, partially frozen
¼ teaspoon ground ginger
1 clove garlic, crushed
Dash of pepper
2 tablespoons vegetable oil
¼ cup soy sauce
½ teaspoon sugar

2 tomatoes, cut in wedges
2 green peppers, cut in strips
1 tablespoon cornstarch
¼ cup water
1 (16-ounce) can bean sprouts,
drained

- Slice steak into thin strips. Season with ginger, garlic and pepper.
- In large skillet or wok, stir-fry beef in hot oil until no longer red. Add soy sauce and sugar; simmer, covered, for 5 minutes.
- Add tomatoes and green peppers to steak; bring to a boil and maintain boil for 5 minutes.
- In container with tight fitting lid, combine cornstarch and water; shake until blended. Add to steak and vegetables and cook for about 5 minutes or until sauce is thickened. Add bean sprouts and mix.
- Serve hot with rice.

Arlene Gelber
South Palm Beach, Florida

CHINESE SWEET/SOUR BEEF AND TOMATOES

Serves: 6 to 8

4 tablespoons cornstarch, divided
1 teaspoon salt (optional)
3 tablespoons soy sauce, divided
3 cups cooked beef, thinly sliced and
  cut in bite-sized pieces
¼ cup vegetable oil
3 large sweet onions, cut in thin strips
1 pound green peppers, cut in thin
  strips
3 large tomatoes, cut in very thin
  wedges

1 (8-ounce) can water chestnuts,
  thinly sliced (optional)
1 (8-ounce) can bamboo shoots
  (optional)
¼ cup sugar
1⅓ cups water
2 tablespoons vinegar
4 cups hot cooked rice
Chinese noodles

- In small mixing bowl, combine 1 tablespoon cornstarch, salt and 2 tablespoons soy sauce. Pour mixture over meat.
- In large skillet or wok, cook meat in oil for 5 minutes.
- Add onions and green peppers to beef; steam until onions are transparent and peppers are soft. Add tomatoes, water chestnuts and bamboo shoots.
- In small mixing bowl, combine 3 tablespoons cornstarch, 1 tablespoon soy sauce, sugar, water and vinegar; stir into beef and vegetable mixture. Cook, stirring constantly, until sauce is thickened.
- Serve hot with rice and chow mein noodles. Dish may be prepared to point of adding tomatoes, then frozen. Thaw and reheat before adding tomatoes and remaining ingredients.

Linda Kahn
Miami, Florida

BEEF SHORT RIBS

Serves: 4 to 6

3 pounds short ribs, cut in pieces
1 envelope onion soup mix
1 cup water
1 (8-ounce) can tomato sauce

1 tablespoon Worcestershire sauce
2 bay leaves
2 tablespoons all-purpose flour
  (optional)

- Coat ribs with soup mix and place in 3-quart casserole. Stir in water, tomato and Worcestershire sauces and bay leaves.
- Cook, covered tightly with lid or plastic wrap, on high (100%) for 10 to 12 minutes or until liquids are boiling. Stir.
- Cook, covered, on medium (50%) for 55 to 60 minutes or until meat is fork tender. Allow 15 minutes standing time.
- Serve warm. Remove bay leaves from gravy; gravy may be thickened with 2 tablespoons all-purpose flour.

Ann Speroni
North Miami, Florida

BARBECUE SHORT RIBS

Serves: 4 to 6

3 pounds beef short ribs
1 large onion, chopped
2 tablespoons vegetable oil
2 tablespoons sugar
2 teaspoons salt
¼ cup vinegar

1 cup catsup
½ cup water
3 tablespoons Worcestershire sauce
1 teaspoon prepared brown mustard
½ cup sliced celery

- In large skillet, brown short ribs with onion in oil.
- Add sugar, salt, vinegar, catsup, water, Worcestershire sauce, mustard and celery to ribs.
- Simmer, covered, for 1½ to 2 hours or until meat is tender.
- Serve hot.

Note: 1 pound chuck steak, cubed, may be substituted for the short ribs. Ribs may be baked at 350°.

Arlene Gelber
South Palm Beach, Florida

BEEF AND BROCCOLI

Serves: 4 to 6

1 bunch broccoli, sliced
1 pound flank steak, thinly sliced
  across grain
3 tablespoons soy sauce
1 tablespoon dry sherry
2 tablespoons cornstarch
1 clove garlic, minced

2 teaspoons grated ginger root
3 tablespoons peanut oil
1 large onion, thinly sliced
¼ cup beef broth
1 (16-ounce) package fettucine,
  cooked and drained
Bean sprouts (optional)

- In 1½-quart saucepan, cook broccoli in water to cover until crisp-tender.
- Marinate steak in mixture of soy sauce, sherry, cornstarch, garlic and ginger. Stir-fry in hot oil in large skillet or wok until meat is no longer red; remove from skillet.
- Stir-fry onions in skillet. Add meat, then stir in broth.
- Spoon meat mixture over fettucine on serving plate. Layer bean sprouts over meat and top with hot broccoli.
- Serve with additional soy sauce, if desired.

Note: Chicken may be substituted for beef.

Arlene Klinger
Roswell, Georgia

PEPPER STEAK ORIENTAL

Serves: 6

1½ pounds round or lean shoulder
  beef steak, cut to 2-inch thickness
¾ teaspoon unseasoned instant meat
  tenderizer
3 tablespoons vegetable oil
2 large green peppers, cut in 1-inch
  squares
3 scallions with tops, thinly sliced
1½ cups diagonally sliced celery

1½ cups water
1 tablespoon cornstarch
⅓ cup molasses
3 tablespoons soy sauce
1 teaspoon garlic powder
1½ teaspoons ground ginger
2 teaspoons lemon juice
4 cups hot cooked rice
Chinese noodles

- Cut beef in paper-thin slices and sprinkle with tenderizer according to package directions.
- In large skillet or wok, heat oil over high heat and cook beef until no longer red. Add peppers, scallions and celery; cook for 3 to 5 minutes, stirring frequently.
- In small mixing bowl, blend water and cornstarch. Blend in molasses, soy sauce, garlic powder, ginger and lemon juice. Add to beef mixture, stirring constantly until slightly thickened and boiling.
- Serve over rice and sprinkle with Chinese noodles. Dish may be prepared in advance and rewarmed in microwave oven.

Note: Water chestnuts, bean sprouts, snow peas or chopped onion may be substituted or added to the ingredients.

Shirley Stracher
North Miami Beach, Florida

CARROT AND SWEET POTATO TZIMMES

Serves: 12

1 large onion, minced
2 to 3 pounds boneless beef chuck
2 or 3 marrow bones
1 teaspoon salt
1 teaspoon paprika
¼ cup all-purpose flour

2 pounds carrots, sliced
2 pounds sweet potatoes or yams,
  sliced
½ cup firmly-packed brown sugar
Boiling water

- Preheat oven to 375°.
- In large mixing bowl, combine onion, beef, bones, salt, paprika and flour. Pour into 5-quart casserole and place in oven to sear beef.
- Add carrots, sweet potatoes and brown sugar to beef mixture. Add boiling water until casserole is ⅔ full.
- Bake, covered, for 2 hours, checking after 1 hour to adjust seasonings and add more water if necessary. Total baking time may range from 2 to 4 hours; add dumplings 1 hour before serving time.

Dumplings

2 large potatoes, grated
1 medium-sized onion, grated
1 egg

½ cup matzo meal
½ teaspoon baking powder
Salt and pepper

- In medium-sized mixing bowl, combine potatoes, onion, egg, meal, baking powder, salt and pepper; mixture should be consistency of thick pancake batter.
- Drop batter by large spoonfuls on top of bubbling tzimmes; spoon cooking liquid over dumplings.
- Bake, covered, for 1 hour.
- Serve hot. Tzimmes may be prepared in advance to point of adding dumplings or may be frozen. To use for Passover, eliminate baking powder and substitute potato starch for flour.

Anita Kessler
Boca Raton, Florida

BRISKET WITH GRAVY

Serves: 8 to 10

2 onions, coarsely chopped
8 pounds whole brisket
2 cloves garlic, crushed
Freshly ground pepper to taste
1 tablespoon Worcestershire sauce
2 envelopes onion soup mix

1 (12-ounce) bottle chili sauce
1 (12-ounce) can beer
8 carrots
3 slices corn-rye bread, torn in small pieces

- Preheat oven to 350°.
- In roasting pan with tight fitting cover, arrange onions evenly in bottom of pan. Rub brisket with garlic and place on onions.
- In order, sprinkle or pour pepper, Worcestershire sauce, soup mix, chili sauce and beer over brisket. Place carrots around and bread pieces under edges of brisket so liquid covers bread.
- Bake, covered, for 45 minutes. Reduce oven temperature to 275° and braise for 2 hours and 15 minutes or until tender, checking once to be sure bread is covered with pan juices.
- Cool brisket. Slice and arrange with carrots on ovenproof platter, covered with aluminum foil.
- Place bread, half of onions and 2 cups pan juices in food processor bowl or blender; process or blend until smooth. Return mixture to pan and mix with balance of pan juices. Reheat.
- Pour some gravy over brisket on platter; serve remainder from gravy boat.

Anne L. Hoffman
Fort Lauderdale, Florida

SAUCY BRISKET

Serves: 6

4 to 5 pound brisket
½ cup catsup
½ cup barbecue sauce
½ cup firmly-packed brown sugar

½ cup cider vinegar
½ cup duck sauce
1 envelope onion soup mix
3 or 4 bay leaves

- Preheat oven to 350°.
- In large skillet, sear brisket to seal in juices. Place in 3-quart roasting pan.
- In medium-sized mixing bowl, combine catsup, barbecue sauce, brown sugar, vinegar, duck sauce and onion soup mix. Spread sauce over brisket and place bay leaves around it.
- Bake, covered, for about 2 hours or until brisket is tender.
- Cool. Cut in thin slices. Before serving, remove bay leaves from sauce; spoon sauce over slices and reheat.

Ruth Mizrahi
North Miami Beach, Florida

GLAZED CORNED BEEF

Serves: 6 to 8

3 pound corned beef
Water
1 cup dark orange marmalade

¼ cup Dijon mustard
¼ cup firmly-packed brown sugar

- Place beef in large saucepan with water to cover. Bring to a boil, then simmer, covered, for 3 hours or until very tender.
- Preheat oven to 350°.
- In small mixing bowl, combine marmalade, mustard and brown sugar.
- Remove beef from cooking liquid, drain and place in foil-lined baking dish. Pour glaze over beef.
- Bake for 30 minutes or until glaze is crisp and browned.
- Serve beef hot.

Dale Flam
North Miami Beach, Florida

BELGIAN BRISKET OF BEEF

Serves: 8

5 pound beef brisket
2 teaspoons salt
¼ teaspoon pepper
2 onions, sliced

4 stalks celery, sliced
1 cup chili sauce
¼ cup water
1 (12-ounce) can beer

- Preheat oven to 325°
- Place brisket in roasting pan. Season with salt and pepper. Place onion, celery and chili sauce on brisket. Add water to pan.
- Roast, uncovered, for 2 hours and 30 minutes.
- Pour beer over brisket and roast, covered, for 1 hour.
- Serve hot.

Elayne L. Fischer
Boynton Beach, Florida

CORNED BEEF ALA BOURBON

Serves: 12 to 14

7 to 8 pound corned beef
Water
⅞ cup bourbon, divided
2 carrots
2 stalks celery
Onion
4 bay leaves

4 peppercorns
¼ cup orange juice
¾ cup firmly-packed brown sugar
1 teaspoon dry mustard
Pineapple slices (optional)
Maraschino cherries (optional)

- In stockpot, cook beef in water to cover for 1 hour and 30 minutes. Drain liquid.
- Add ½ cup bourbon with enough water to cover corned beef. Add vegetables, bay leaves and peppercorns. Cook for about 1 hour and 30 minutes or until beef is tender. Remove beef from pan. Reserve 3 tablespoons stock for sauce.
- Preheat oven to 375°.
- Place beef in 13x9x2-inch baking pan. Score fat for appearance.
- In small saucepan, combine orange juice, brown sugar, reserved stock, mustard and 6 tablespoons bourbon; simmer until sugar is dissolved.
- Arrange pineapple and cherries on beef. Pour syrup over beef.
- Bake for about 30 minutes, basting with syrup every 10 minutes until well glazed.
- Serve hot or at room temperature.

Arlene Gelber
South Palm Beach, Florida

SWEET AND SOUR BRISKET

Serves: 10

6 pound single beef brisket (first cut)
2 medium-sized onions, sliced
1 large clove garlic, minced
¾ cup firmly-packed brown sugar
½ cup white vinegar

1 cup catsup
1 cup water
1 tablespoon salt
Freshly ground pepper

- In large heavy skillet or Dutch oven, sear brisket on all sides to brown and seal juices.
- Add onions and garlic; cook until lightly browned.
- In small mixing bowl, combine brown sugar, vinegar, catsup, water, salt and pepper. Add to brisket. Simmer, covered, for 2½ to 3 hours or until brisket is tender. Cool before slicing.
- Serve hot.

Lenore Engle Band
Boca Raton, Florida

GINGERSNAP MEAT LOAF

Serves: 4 to 6

2 eggs
¼ cup water
1½ pounds ground beef
½ cup crushed corn flakes
Salt and pepper to taste
4 teaspoons vegetable shortening

1 medium-sized onion, diced
1 (8-ounce) can tomato sauce
1 cup water
5 gingersnaps, broken in pieces
1 rounded teaspoon sugar

- Preheat oven to 425°.
- In large mixing bowl, beat eggs lightly with water. Add ground beef, corn flakes, salt and pepper; mix thoroughly.
- Shape mixture into loaf and place in roasting pan. Place shortening and onions around loaf.
- Bake for about 15 minutes; do not allow onions to burn.
- In small saucepan, combine tomato sauce, water, gingersnaps and sugar. Bring to a boil, then simmer for 5 minutes.
- Pour sauce over browned loaf, mixing sauce with onions.
- Reduce oven temperature to 350°.
- Bake, covered, for 1 hour, basting occasionally with sauce. Add small amount of water to sauce if too thick.
- Serve hot with sauce, skimming any fat from surface.

Elaine Gruenhut
Atlanta, Georgia

ZESTY MEAT LOAF

Serves: 4 to 6

1½ pounds ground beef
1 medium-sized onion, chopped
½ cup seasoned breadcrumbs
½ teaspoon salt
1 egg

3 tablespoons catsup
1 tablespoon horseradish
2 teaspoons Dijon mustard
Catsup

- Preheat oven to 350°.
- In large mixing bowl, combine beef, onion, breadcrumbs, salt, egg, 3 tablespoons catsup, horseradish and mustard; blend well by hand.
- Firmly press mixture into 9x5x3-inch loaf pan. Spread additional catsup over loaf.
- Bake for 1 hour and 15 minutes.
- Serve warm. Meat loaf may be frozen.

Ann Speroni
North Miami, Florida

SWEET AND SOUR MEATBALLS

Yield: 48

Sauce

2 small onions, diced
4 (8-ounce) cans tomato sauce
5⅝ cups water

¾ cup firmly-packed brown sugar
1½ tablespoons lemon juice
Salt and pepper to taste

- Combine all ingredients in large saucepan. Simmer for 15 minutes.

Meatballs

2 pounds ground beef
¼ cup plus 2 tablespoons catsup
⅔ cup finely crushed cornflakes
2 eggs

Paprika to taste
5 gingersnaps
1 (8-ounce) can pineapple chunks,
   well drained

- In medium-sized mixing bowl, combine ground beef, catsup, cornflake crumbs, eggs and paprika. Mix well and shape into 1-inch balls.
- Simmer meatballs in sauce for 1½ to 1¾ hours.
- Stir in gingersnaps and pineapple chunks and cook for additional 15 minutes.
- Serve as entrée over rice or appetizer. May be prepared in advance and frozen.

Beverly Toll
Lauderhill, Florida

CHILI CON CARNE

Serves: 4 to 6

1 pound ground beef
1 medium-sized onion, minced
1 green pepper, diced
2 tablespoons vegetable oil
1 teaspoon salt (optional)
½ teaspoon pepper
1 teaspoon paprika
¼ teaspoon garlic powder

¼ teaspoon chili powder
⅛ teaspoon cayenne or dried red
   pepper
1 (10½-ounce) can tomato soup,
   undiluted
1 (16-ounce) can kidney beans
1 (8-ounce) can tomato sauce

- In large skillet or electric skillet at 350°, brown beef, onion and green pepper in oil, stirring frequently.
- Add remaining ingredients to beef. Simmer, covered, for about 20 minutes, stirring occasionally.
- Serve hot over rice.

Note: Ground turkey may be substituted for beef.

Iris Levin
Wellington, Florida

QUICK MEXICAN DELIGHT

Serves: 4 to 6

1 pound ground beef
Chili seasoning mix to taste
1 (16-ounce) can tomatoes, drained
   and chopped
1 (16-ounce) can whole kernel corn,
   undrained

1 (8½-ounce) package corn bread mix
1 egg
½ cup non-dairy creamer

- Preheat oven to 400°.
- In large skillet, brown beef. Drain excess fat.
- Add chili seasoning mix, tomatoes and corn to beef; bring to a boil.
- Spoon mixture into 2-quart casserole.
- In small mixing bowl, combine corn bread mix, egg and creamer, stirring just until moistened. Spoon batter over meat mixture.
- Bake, uncovered, for 20 minutes.
- Serve hot.

Joanne Kooden
Savannah, Georgia

CHICKEN OR MEAT MARINADE

Yield: 2½ cups

2 tablespoons soy sauce
4 tablespoons kosher salt
5 tablespoons sugar
4 teaspoons monosodium glutamate
(optional)

1 tablespoon garlic powder
3 cloves garlic, minced
2 cups boiling water

- In large mixing bowl, combine all ingredients and mix thoroughly.
- Marinate chicken pieces or meat in mixture for at least 1 hour or longer if possible, keeping meat submerged in liquid.
- Drain chicken or meat and grill or barbecue.

Florie Schwartzberg
Coconut Creek, Florida

STUFFED CABBAGE

Serves: 10

1 large head cabbage, cored
2 pounds ground turkey or veal or
combination
2 cups cooked rice
3 tablespoons barbecue seasoning
1 (15-ounce) can tomato sauce or
2 cups tomato juice

½ cup raisins
2 large carrots
2 tablespoons firmly-packed brown
sugar
Barbecue sauce

- Place cabbage on paper towel or plate; cook in microwave oven on high (100%) for 6 minutes. Separate leaves.
- In large mixing bowl, combine meat, rice and barbecue seasoning. Place tablespoon of mixture in each cabbage leaf, roll to enclose and secure with wooden pick. Place in 2-quart microwave-safe casserole.
- In bowl, combine tomato sauce, raisins, carrots, brown sugar and barbecue sauce to taste; pour over cabbage rolls.
- Cook, covered with plastic wrap, on high (100%) for 6 minutes. Cook on medium high (60%) for 15 minutes or until cabbage is tender and meat is cooked.
- Serve hot with sauce, reminding diners to remove wooden picks.

Note: Stuffed cabbage, covered with glass lid or aluminum foil, may be baked in conventional oven at 350° for 45 minutes.

Louise R. Weinthal
Hallandale, Florida

UNSTUFFED CABBAGE

Serves: 8 to 10

1 medium head cabbage, sliced
3 tablespoons vegetable oil
2 large onions, sliced
1 tablespoon paprika
2 large carrots, sliced
2 medium Idaho potatoes, unpeeled,
cut in ¼-inch slices

1 (10-ounce) package frozen French-
cut green beans, thawed
2 to 3 pounds chopped beef or veal
1½ (16-ounce) cans sauerkraut, rinsed
and drained
1 (32-ounce) jar marinara sauce
1 (15-ounce) can tomato sauce

- In 2-quart saucepan, boil cabbage with water to cover for 5 minutes; drain.
- Preheat oven to 375°.
- Pour oil into large roasting pan. Spread onion in bottom of roaster and sprinkle with paprika.
- In order, layer half of cabbage, carrots, potatoes, green beans, meat, sauerkraut. Combine marinara and tomato sauces; pour half over vegetables and meat. Repeat layers.
- Bake, covered with aluminum foil, for 2 hours.
- Serve hot.

Bunny Tillem
Deerfield Beach, Florida

UNSTUFFED STUFFED CABBAGE

Serves: 4

3 onions, divided
½ cup instant rice, cooked
1 egg
1 pound ground beef or veal
Salt and pepper to taste

Garlic powder to taste
1 cup plus 2 tablespoons sugar, divided
2 (8-ounce) cans tomato sauce
1 large head cabbage, sliced
Sour salt to taste

- Grate 1 onion into large mixing bowl. Add rice, egg, meat, salt, pepper, garlic powder and 2 tablespoons sugar; mix well and shape into meatballs. Slice 2 onions.
- In large saucepan or Dutch oven prepared with non-stick vegetable spray, in order layer half of tomato sauce, cabbage, onion slices and meatballs; repeat layers.
- Cook, covered, over medium low heat for 1 hour. Add 1 cup sugar and several shakes sour salt; stir and cook for 5 minutes. Adjust seasoning and continue cooking for 25 minutes or until cabbage is tender and meat is done.
- Serve hot.

Allyn M. Kanowsky
North Lauderdale, Florida

SAUCY STUFFED CABBAGE

Serves: 6 to 8

1 large head cabbage
Boiling water
2 pounds ground beef chuck
¼ cup regular rice, uncooked
1 egg
1 onion, grated

1 carrot, grated
¼ teaspoon salt
Pinch of pepper
3 (8-ounce) cans tomato sauce
¼ cup lemon juice
½ cup firmly-packed brown sugar

- In Dutch oven, boil cabbage leaves in water for 15 minutes. Drain.
- In medium-sized mixing bowl, combine beef, rice, egg, onion, carrot, salt and pepper. Shape into small balls and place in cabbage leaves, rolling to enclose and securing with a wooden pick. Cut up extra cabbage leaves.
- In Dutch oven, combine tomato sauce, lemon juice and brown sugar. Place cabbage rolls and extra cabbage in sauce.
- Simmer, tightly covered, for 1 hour and 30 minutes.
- Serve hot. Cabbage rolls may be stored in refrigerator for 3 to 4 days.

Note: Cabbage may also be softened by placing in freezer overnight; leaves will separate easily and be pliable.

Jean Robbins
Tampa, Florida

CABBAGE ROLLS

Serves: 6 to 8

1 large head cabbage, cored
2 pounds ground meat
¾ cup long grain rice, uncooked
2 teaspoons salt
1 teaspoon pepper

6 medium-sized onions, grated
1 (29-ounce) can tomato purée, divided
½ cup water
Salt and pepper to taste

- Freeze cabbage several hours. Thaw, then separate leaves.
- In large mixing bowl, combine meat, rice, salt, pepper, onions, ½ cup purée and water; mix lightly. Place tablespoonful of mixture in each cabbage leaf, roll to enclose and secure with wooden pick. Place in large saucepan or Dutch oven.
- Cut up remaining cabbage and add to pan. Pour remaining purée over cabbage rolls. Simmer for about 1 hour and 30 minutes.
- Serve hot.

Note: Meat bones placed in bottom of saucepan add flavor and help thicken the sauce. Onion pieces that do not grate easily may also be added with the extra cabbage.

Harriet Kotler
Tamarac, Florida

MEAT OR CHICKEN KREPLACH

Yield: 50

1 small onion, diced
1 stalk celery, minced
Margarine
2¼ cups cooked beef roast or steak,
    turkey or chicken
5 eggs, divided
Salt and pepper to taste

2¼ cups sifted all-purpose flour
1 teaspoon salt
2 tablespoons water
Boiling water
Salt
Chicken fat or vegetable oil

- In small skillet, sauté onion and celery in margarine until vegetables are tender. Remove from heat.
- Grind meat. Lightly beat 2 eggs. Add both to vegetables; mix well. Season with salt and pepper.
- In medium-sized mixing bowl, mix flour and salt; make a well in the dry ingredients.
- Beat egg and add with water to dry ingredients. Mix to form a dough, shape into a ball and divide in 2 portions.
- On lightly-floured surface, roll half of dough to thickness of pie pastry. Cut into 2-inch squares. Place 1 teaspoon of meat filling on each square; press opposing corners together at center.
- Drop into stockpot of boiling salted water and cook for 30 minutes. Repeat with remaining dough and filling.
- Drain cooked kreplach in colander, place in large bowl, add small amount chicken fat or oil and shake gently.
- Serve warm.

Mary Resk, Sara Black
West Palm Beach, Florida

VEAL WITH OLIVES

Serves: 4

1½ pounds veal cutlets
Salt and pepper to taste
¼ cup margarine or vegetable oil

⅓ cup Marsala wine
10 green olives

- Pound veal cutlets until very thin. Wipe to remove surface moisture. Sprinkle with salt and pepper.
- In large skillet, sauté cutlets in margarine, lightly browning on both sides.
- Add wine and olives. Cut veal in narrow strips. Cook for 1 minute; total cooking time for veal should be within 5 minutes.
- Serve immediately.

Sandy Pecker
Orlando, Florida

SMOKED VEAL ROAST

Serves: 4

½ cup soy sauce
¼ cup honey
½ cup sherry

1 clove garlic, crushed
1 teaspoon ginger
4 to 5 pound rolled veal shoulder roast

- In small mixing bowl, combine soy sauce, honey, sherry, garlic and ginger.
- Marinate roast in soy sauce mixture overnight, basting or turning roast occasionally.
- In grill basin, place charcoal briquettes to one side and catch pan for drippings on opposite side. When briquettes are hot, place roast directly on cooking grate. Cook for 2 to 2½ hours, turning every 30 minutes; do not allow to burn.
- Let stand for 10 to 15 minutes before slicing.
- Serve warm.

Bunnie Taratoot
Dunwoody, Georgia

OSSO BUCCO

Serves: 8

1 cup sliced onion
1 cup chopped celery
1 cup chopped carrots
½ cup vegetable oil, divided
3 strips lemon peel
2 cloves garlic, chopped
8 pieces veal shanks
½ cup all-purpose flour
1 cup white wine

1½ cups canned tomatoes
1 cup beef broth
1 bay leaf
1 teaspoon pepper
Salt to taste
1 teaspoon grated lemon peel
¼ teaspoon chopped garlic
2 tablespoons chopped parsley

- Preheat oven to 350°.
- In small skillet, cook onions, celery and carrots in ¼ cup oil until onions are translucent. Add lemon peel strips and garlic; set aside.
- Dredge shanks in flour. In large ovenproof pan with lid, lightly brown meat in ¼ cup oil, turn without displacing marrow in shank and lightly brown second side.
- Add wine, tomatoes, broth, bay leaf, pepper and salt. Cover and bring to a simmer, then transfer to oven.
- Bake for 2 hours, adding small amounts of broth or water if necessary. When meat is done, reduce any remaining liquid by bringing to a boil. Remove bay leaf.
- In small mixing bowl, combine grated peel, ¼ teaspoon garlic and parsley. Sprinkle on shanks and serve with orzo or rice pilaf.

Erika Brodsky
Boca Raton, Florida

ROAST BONELESS VEAL

Serves: 4

1 teaspoon dried rosemary
1 teaspoon dried tarragon
1 teaspoon garlic powder
1 teaspoon dried sage
1 teaspoon dried oregano

1 tablespoon vegetable oil
3 pounds boneless veal roast
⅓ cup vegetable oil
½ cup white wine

- In small mixing bowl, combine herbs and oil. Rub mixture on inside and outside of roast. Marinate for 24 hours.
- Preheat oven to 325°.
- Roll and tie roast and place in 13x9x2-inch baking pan.
- Bake for 1 hour and 30 minutes, basting every 20 minutes with oil. Drain excess oil, then baste with wine for remaining roasting time.
- Let stand 10 to 15 minutes before slicing.
- Serve warm.

Evelyn Rotz
Coconut Creek, Florida

VEAL BRISKET DINNER

Serves: 4 to 6

3 to 4 pound veal brisket (not breast)
2 cloves garlic
1 (4-ounce) jar mushrooms, drained
1 envelope onion soup mix
½ cup catsup

½ cup water
1 (10-ounce) package frozen baby carrots
4 to 6 potatoes, cut up

- Preheat oven to 325°.
- Place brisket in large aluminum foil baking pan. Rub with garlic and sprinkle with mushrooms.
- In small mixing bowl, combine soup mix, catsup and water; mix well and pour over brisket. Arrange carrots and potatoes around brisket.
- Bake, tightly covered with aluminum foil, for about 2 hours and 30 minutes.
- Let stand for 10 to 15 minutes; slice across grain.
- Serve warm with carrots and potatoes and may be reheated the next day. Brisket may be frozen.

Florence Frankle
Pembroke Pines, Florida

VEAL SCALLOPINI

Serves: 4 to 6

1½ pounds veal steak, cut ½-inch thick
1 teaspoon salt
1 teaspoon paprika
½ cup vegetable oil
¼ cup lemon juice
1 clove garlic, crushed
1 teaspoon prepared mustard
¼ teaspoon nutmeg
½ teaspoon sugar

½ cup all-purpose flour
¼ cup vegetable shortening
1 medium-sized onion, thinly sliced
1 green pepper, cut in strips
1 (10½-ounce) can chicken broth
¼ pound mushrooms, sliced
1 tablespoon margarine
6 pimento-stuffed olives, sliced
2 tablespoons sherry (optional)

- Cut veal into serving pieces. Place in shallow baking dish.
- In small mixing bowl, combine salt, paprika, oil, lemon juice, garlic, mustard, nutmeg and sugar; beat well. Pour marinade over veal, turning pieces to coat evenly. Let stand 15 minutes.
- Lift veal from sauce and dip into flour. In large skillet, brown veal in shortening.
- Add onion and green pepper to veal. Combine chicken broth with remaining marinade and pour over veal. Simmer, covered, for about 20 minutes.
- In small skillet, sauté mushrooms in margarine; add with olives to veal, stirring and spooning sauce over veal and vegetables. Cook about 5 minutes. Stir in sherry.
- Serve immediately.

Sylvia Greenberger
Hollywood, Florida

GESCHNAETZELS

Serves: 4

1 medium-sized onion, chopped
3 tablespoons margarine
1½ pounds veal, sliced or diced
8 large mushrooms

Fresh chopped parsley to taste
Salt and pepper to taste
All-purpose flour
½ cup white wine

- In large skillet, sauté onions in margarine until translucent.
- Add meat to onions and stir-fry over high heat. Add mushrooms, parsley, seasoning and small amount of flour, reducing heat if necessary to avoid burning. Stir in wine.
- Serve hot with Roesti (Sauté Potatoes).

Margrit Schechtman
Sarasota, Florida

VEAL TZIMMES

Serves: 6 to 8

3 to 3½ pounds diced veal
Water
1 pound carrots, sliced
2 medium-sized onions, sliced
2 tablespoons firmly-packed brown sugar

½ cup light corn syrup
Salt and pepper to taste
3 cups biscuit baking mix
1 cup water

- Place veal in large ovenproof pot and add water to cover. Bring to a boil, removing fat from surface.
- Add carrots, onions, brown sugar, syrup, salt and pepper to veal and liquid. Simmer for 1 to 1½ hours.
- Preheat oven to 300°.
- In small mixing bowl, combine baking mix with water to form soft dough.
- Drop spoonfuls of dough into boiling broth; cook, uncovered, over low heat for 10 minutes. Turn dumplings or baste with broth.
- Bake, covered, for 45 minutes; bake, uncovered, for 15 minutes, adding hot water if necessary.
- Serve hot.

Shirley Sutter
West Palm Beach, Florida

HERBED LAMB ROAST DIJON

Serves: 12

Leg of lamb, with or without bone
Few cloves garlic, sliced
⅔ (5-ounce) jar Dijon mustard
Chopped parsley

Dried thyme
Dried oregano
Dried basil
½ cup dry red wine

- Preheat oven to 550°.
- Cut slits in lamb and insert garlic slices. Spread mustard over entire roast and apply thick coating of herbs. Place in roasting pan.
- Bake for 30 minutes or until herbs form crust.
- Reduce oven temperature to 350°. Pour wine over roast. Bake for about 20 minutes per pound, basting regularly.
- Let stand 15 minutes before slicing.
- Serve warm with rice sprinkled with minced fresh parsley.

Sylvia Pudaloff
Lauderhill, Florida

LAMB CHOPS WITH VEGETABLE SAUCE

Serves: 8

½ cup all-purpose flour
1 teaspoon salt
¼ teaspoon pepper
8 shoulder lamb chops
⅔ cup diced celery

⅔ cup sliced carrots
⅔ cup chopped chives
3 tablespoons margarine
2 (16-ounce) cans stewed tomatoes

- On waxed paper, combine flour, salt and pepper. Lightly dredge chops in seasoned flour.
- In large skillet, sauté celery, carrots and chives in margarine for 5 minutes; remove vegetables. Brown chops in same skillet.
- Add sautéed vegetables and tomatoes to chops. Simmer for 45 minutes or until meat is tender.
- Serve hot with rice, noodles or mashed potatoes.

Note: To bake, layer chops, sautéed vegetables and tomatoes in roasting pan; cover and bake at 350°.

Diana Saunders
Memphis, Tennessee

GREEK LAMB STEW

Serves: 4

1 large onion, chopped
1 large clove garlic, crushed
1 tablespoon chopped fresh basil
2 pounds lean lamb, cubed
3 tablespoons olive oil
Salt and pepper to taste

1 (28-ounce) can tomatoes, crushed
½ cup dry red wine
1 cup cut fresh green beans
3 red potatoes, peeled and cubed
1 cinnamon stick
¼ pound mushrooms, sliced

- In Dutch oven, sauté onion, garlic, basil and lamb in oil until onion is tender. Season with salt and pepper. Continue to sauté until lamb is lightly browned.
- Add tomatoes and wine to lamb and vegetables; cook for 10 minutes.
- Stir in beans, potatoes, cinnamon stick and mushrooms. Simmer, covered, for 1 to 1½ hours or until lamb is tender. Remove cinnamon stick.
- Serve hot.

Gloria Chekanow
Miami, Florida

SHISH KEBAB MARINADE

Yield: 3½ cups

1½ cups vegetable oil
¾ cup soy sauce
¼ cup Worcestershire sauce
2 tablespoons dry mustard
⅓ cup lemon juice

2½ teaspoons salt
1½ tablespoons parsley
1 tablespoon pepper
½ cup wine vinegar
3 cloves garlic, crushed

- Place all ingredients in blender container; blend until smooth.
- Place tender meat cubes on skewers; place green and red peppers, cherry tomatoes, white parboiled onions and mushrooms on separate skewers. Pour marinade over meat and vegetables and chill for 12 hours or overnight before grilling.

Arlene Gelber
South Palm Beach, Florida

POULTRY

BAKED CHICKEN

Serves: 3 to 4

1 envelope onion soup mix
1¼ cups boiling water

4 medium carrots, thinly sliced
1 (3-pound) broiler-fryer, cut up

- Preheat oven to 425°.
- Sprinkle soup mix in 13x9x2-inch baking pan. Stir in boiling water.
- Place carrots evenly on soup mixture; top with chicken pieces.
- Bake, uncovered, basting occasionally, for about 1 hour or until chicken is golden brown and tender. More boiling water may be added if needed.
- Serve hot.

Frieda K. Rauch
North Miami Beach, Florida

CRUNCHY ALMOND CHICKEN

Serves: 4 to 6

1 cup slivered blanched almonds
Dry mustard to taste
Salt and pepper to taste
½ teaspoon paprika
1 clove garlic, sliced

1 slice ginger root
1 (2½ to 3-pound) broiler-fryer, cut up
⅓ cup melted margarine

- Preheat oven to 375°.
- In food processor bowl, combine almonds, seasonings, garlic and ginger root; use steel knives and process to make fine crumbs.
- Dip chicken pieces in margarine, roll in almond crumbs, pressing to coat thickly, and place in 13x9x2-inch baking pan.
- Bake for 30 to 40 minutes.
- Serve hot.

Sally Chancey
Boca Raton, Florida

CANTON OVEN CHICKEN

Serves: 4

1 (3-pound) broiler-fryer, cut up and skin removed
Pepper to taste
1 cup regular rice, uncooked

½ (16 or 20-ounce) package frozen Oriental vegetables, thawed
1 (14½-ounce) can chicken broth
3 tablespoons soy sauce, divided

- Preheat oven to 375°.
- Season chicken with pepper.
- Combine rice, vegetables, broth and 1 tablespoon soy sauce in 12x8x2-inch baking dish; mix well.
- Arrange chicken pieces on rice mixture.
- Bake, tightly covered with aluminum foil, for 55 minutes. Brush chicken with 2 tablespoons soy sauce, cover loosely, and bake 5 minutes or until chicken is tender and most of liquid is absorbed.
- Serve hot with vegetables and rice.

Ceil Lieberman
Wesley Chapel, Florida

CHICKEN MARENGO

Serves: 4 to 6

2 (2½-pound) broiler-fryers, cut up
2 tablespoons margarine
1 (29-ounce) can whole tomatoes, undrained
2 or 3 cloves garlic, minced

Salt and pepper to taste
¼ teaspoon dried tarragon
1 (4-ounce) can mushrooms, undrained
1 envelope onion-mushroom soup mix

- In large skillet, brown chicken in margarine. Remove chicken.
- Combine tomatoes, garlic, seasonings, mushrooms and soup mix in skillet; add chicken.
- Simmer, covered, stirring occasionally, for 45 minutes or until chicken is tender.
- Serve hot over broad or medium noodles.

Arlene Gelber
Boca Raton, Florida

CHICKEN LA BODEGA

Serves: 3 to 4

1 (2½ to 3-pound) broiler-fryer
1 teaspoon salt
1 teaspoon paprika
⅓ cup olive oil
2 tablespoons margarine
1 cup regular rice, uncooked
¼ teaspoon saffron

1 cup white wine
1 cup chicken broth
2 bay leaves
½ cup black olives
1 (10-ounce) package frozen peas, cooked

- Season chicken with salt and paprika.
- In large skillet over low heat, brown chicken in olive oil.
- In separate skillet, sauté rice in margarine with saffron, stirring frequently, for about 10 minutes or until rice is golden brown.
- Add wine and broth to rice. Simmer, covered, for 15 minutes.
- Preheat oven to 350°.
- Place bay leaves in 13x9x2-inch baking pan. Add rice, chicken and olives.
- Bake for 40 minutes.
- Add peas and heat thoroughly.
- Serve hot, reminding diners of bay leaves.

Bella Seidman
Pembroke Pines, Florida

CHICKEN WITH PEACH SLICES

Serves: 6 to 8

1 (16-ounce) can cling peach slices
2 tablespoons lemon juice
1 teaspoon soy sauce

2 (2½ to 3-pound) broiler-fryers, quartered or cut up

- Preheat oven to 400°.
- Drain peaches, reserving syrup. Add lemon juice and soy sauce to syrup.
- Arrange chicken in single layer in shallow baking dish. Brush half of syrup over chicken.
- Bake for 1 hour, basting chicken with syrup every 15 minutes. Place peach slices around chicken, baste with pan juices and bake for 5 to 10 minutes or until peaches are thoroughly heated.
- Serve hot.

Ann Speroni
North Miami, Florida

HAWAIIAN CHICKEN

Serves: 3 to 4

1 (2½ to 3-pound) broiler-fryer, cut up
1 (16-ounce) can sliced pineapple, drained with juice reserved
2 tablespoons cornstarch
¼ cup soy sauce

1 cup chicken broth
¾ cup vinegar
Ground ginger
1 green pepper, cut in chunks
3 carrots, sliced

- Arrange chicken pieces in 13x9x2-inch baking pan or dish.
- Preheat oven to 350°.
- In medium-sized saucepan, combine pineapple juice, cornstarch, soy sauce, chicken broth, vinegar and ginger. Bring to a boil, stirring constantly; boil for 2 minutes. Pour sauce over chicken.
- Bake, uncovered, for 30 minutes.
- Add pineapple slices, green pepper and carrot slices to chicken. Bake, uncovered, for 30 minutes.
- Serve hot over white rice.

Kate Stone
West Palm Beach, Florida

ALOHA CHICKEN

Serves: 2 to 3

½ cup soy sauce
1 tablespoon Worcestershire sauce
½ cup dry white wine
1 clove garlic, minced

2 tablespoons firmly-packed brown sugar
1 (2½-pound) broiler-fryer, cut up

- In small mixing bowl, combine soy sauce, Worcestershire sauce, wine, garlic and brown sugar; blend thoroughly.
- Place chicken in shallow round microwave-safe dish. Pour marinade over chicken. Chill for 2 hours, turning occasionally.
- Arrange chicken with thicker pieces at edge of dish and smaller pieces in the center.
- Cook, covered loosely with waxed paper, on high (100%) for 22 to 24 minutes. Allow 4 minutes standing time before serving.
- Serve hot.

Norma Pilzer
Lauderhill, Florida

HEARTY WESTERN CHICKEN DELIGHT

Serves: 4 to 5

1 (3½-pound) broiler-fryer, cut up
2 cloves garlic, crushed
Salt and pepper to taste
⅛ teaspoon dried thyme
3 onions, quartered
3 red potatoes, quartered

4 carrots, quartered
1 medium zucchini, cut in ½-inch slices
1 (16-ounce) can green beans
1 (10½-ounce) can tomato soup, undiluted

- Preheat oven to 350°.
- Place chicken in 4-quart casserole. Add garlic and season with salt, pepper and thyme. Arrange onions, potatoes and carrots around chicken; place zucchini on top of chicken and other vegetables.
- Pour ¾ of liquid from green beans over chicken and vegetables. Add beans. Spoon tomato soup over all ingredients.
- Bake, covered, for 1 hour and 45 minutes.
- Serve hot.

Cookie Berman
Tamarac, Florida

PIGNOLI CHICKEN

Serves: 3 to 4

1 onion, chopped
3 cloves garlic, minced
Olive oil
1 (2½ to 3-pound) broiler-fryer, cut up
Salt and pepper to taste

Paprika to taste
¼ pound mushrooms, sliced
1 teaspoon crushed red pepper
1 teaspoon dried rosemary
2 tablespoons pignoli nuts

- In large skillet, brown onions and garlic in oil.
- Season chicken with salt, pepper and paprika; add to onions. Over high heat, brown chicken on both sides. Remove chicken.
- Combine mushrooms, red pepper, rosemary and nuts in skillet, stirring until well mixed. Add chicken to mushroom mixture.
- Cook, covered, for 30 to 40 minutes or until chicken is tender.
- Serve hot with rice pilaf. Prepared chicken may be prepared in advance and reheated or frozen.

June Klein
Marietta, Georgia

INEBRIATED CHICKEN

Serves: 8

2 (2½ to 3-pound) broiler-fryers, quartered
1 pound mushrooms, sliced

1 envelope spaghetti sauce mix
1 (1-liter) bottle white wine

- Preheat oven to 325°.
- Place chicken in roasting pan lined with aluminum foil. Sprinkle mushrooms on chicken, then sprinkle sauce mix over mushrooms. Pour wine over all ingredients.
- Bake, covered with aluminum foil, for 45 minutes.
- Remove foil, baste with pan juices, increase oven temperature to 350° and bake 15 minutes or until chicken is browned.
- Serve hot with rice.

Esther W. Lasker
Sarasota, Florida

MEDITERRANEAN CHICKEN

Serves: 2

6 slices beef fry
3 large onions, chopped
3 cloves garlic, minced
2 green peppers, cut in chunks
½ pound mushrooms, sliced
Salt and freshly ground pepper to taste
1 (4-ounce) can black olives, sliced

1 tablespoon capers
1 (1½-pound) broiler-fryer, cut up
1 tablespoon paprika
¼ cup olive oil
½ cup white wine
½ cup chicken broth

- In large skillet, combine beef fry, onion, garlic, green peppers and mushrooms; cook until vegetables are soft.
- Remove beef fry; transfer vegetables to dish and add salt, pepper, olives and capers.
- Season chicken with salt, pepper and paprika. Brown in oil in skillet. Add wine, broth and vegetables.
- Simmer, covered, for 45 minutes.
- Serve hot.

Terrie Temkin
Hollywood, Florida

SWEET AND SPICY CHICKEN

Serves: 6 to 8

2 (2½ to 3-pound) broiler-fryers,
  cut up
Salt and pepper to taste
2 cups orange juice
Ground ginger

1 (6-ounce) jar fruit preserves or
  marmalade
1 (10-ounce) package frozen mixed
  vegetables, thawed

- Preheat oven to 300°.
- Place chicken in large shallow baking dish. Season to taste. Add orange juice and generous sprinkle of ginger.
- Bake for 20 minutes. Turn chicken pieces and bake for 20 minutes.
- Add fruit preserves and vegetables. Increase oven temperature to 450° and bake for 15 to 20 minutes.
- Serve on warmed plates with rice.

Eileen Cahn
Dunwoody, Georgia

CHICKEN WITH POTATOES

Serves: 4

2 tablespoons olive oil
1 onion, minced
2 cloves garlic, minced
1 (2½ to 3-pound) broiler-fryer, cut in
  8 pieces and skin removed
1 (8-ounce) can tomato sauce
1 (4-ounce) can mushroom pieces,
  drained

3 tablespoons stuffed green olives
3 tablespoons light or dark raisins
1 teaspoon capers
4 potatoes, halved
½ cup cooking wine (optional)

- Pour oil into Dutch oven. Add onion and garlic. Arrange chicken pieces, bone side down, over onion and garlic. Add tomato sauce, mushrooms, olives, raisins and capers.
- Cook over medium heat, covered, for 5 minutes, then add potatoes. Cook, stirring occasionally and keeping potatoes at bottom of pan, for 20 to 25 minutes or until chicken and potatoes are tender. Add wine and cook for 5 minutes.
- Serve hot with French bread for dunking and pan sauce.

Trudy Levitt
Altamonte Springs, Florida

VINTAGE CHICKEN

Serves: 4 to 5

2 tablespoons all-purpose flour
1 teaspoon garlic salt
¼ teaspoon paprika
½ teaspoon dried rosemary
4 or 5 large pieces chicken

½ cup margarine, divided
¼ cup Chablis wine
¼ cup sliced green onions
1 cup sliced fresh mushrooms

- On waxed paper, combine flour and seasonings. Dredge chicken pieces in seasoned flour.
- In large heavy skillet, fry chicken in 6 tablespoons margarine until browned on both sides.
- Add wine to chicken. Simmer, covered, for 15 to 20 minutes.
- In small skillet, sauté onions and mushrooms in 2 tablespoons margarine until vegetables are soft. Add to chicken. Simmer, covered, for 15 to 20 minutes.
- Serve hot.

Ruth Mizrahi
North Miami Beach, Florida

PLUM SAUCE CHICKEN

Serves: 4 to 6

1 clove garlic, minced
2 slices ginger root, minced
¼ cup pineapple juice
2 tablespoons vinegar
2 tablespoons sugar
¾ cup plum sauce

1 (2½ to 3-pound) broiler-fryer, cut in small pieces
2 tablespoons vegetable oil
2 tablespoons soy sauce
½ cup pineapple chunks

- In small mixing bowl, combine garlic, ginger, juice, vinegar, sugar and plum sauce.
- Place chicken in shallow baking dish; pour marinade over chicken. Marinate overnight in refrigerator.
- Remove chicken from marinade and use paper towel to remove excess moisture. In wok or large skillet, cook chicken in oil until browned on all sides.
- Add marinade, soy sauce and pineapple to chicken. Simmer until chicken is tender and done.
- Serve hot with rice.

Gertrude Dreyfus
Hallandale, Florida

CHICKEN BREAST IN HOISIN SAUCE

Serves: 5 to 6

2 pounds chicken breasts, boned and cut in small pieces
1 tablespoon cornstarch
1 tablespoon soy sauce
6 or more water chestnuts, sliced
2 medium-sized green peppers, cut in thin strips

¼ pound fresh or canned mushrooms, sliced
¼ cup vegetable oil, divided
2 tablespoons hoisin sauce
¼ to ½ cup roasted cashews

- In large mixing bowl, sprinkle chicken with cornstarch and toss to coat lightly. Add soy sauce, toss to coat chicken evenly, and let stand 10 to 15 minutes.
- In 12-inch skillet or wok, stir-fry chestnuts, green peppers and mushrooms in 3 tablespoons oil; cook for about 5 minutes or until vegetables are tender but not soft. Remove from skillet.
- Add 1 tablespoon oil to skillet. Stir-fry chicken for 3 to 5 minutes or until firm and white. Add hoisin sauce and cashews; mix well. Add vegetables.
- Serve hot over rice.

Marcia Kosofsky
Pompano, Florida

CHICKEN YAKITURI

Serves: 4

1½ pounds boneless chicken breasts, skin removed and cut in 1-inch cubes
1 medium-sized red pepper, cut in 1-inch squares
1 medium-sized green pepper, cut in 1-inch squares

1 (15-ounce) jar baby corn, drained
⅓ cup teriyaki sauce
⅓ cup honey
1 clove garlic, crushed
¼ teaspoon ground ginger

- Preheat broiler or grill.
- Arrange chicken and vegetables on 8 skewers.
- In small mixing bowl, combine teriyaki sauce, honey, garlic and ginger. Brush sauce on chicken and vegetables.
- Broil or grill with skewers about 6 inches from heat, basting and turning occasionally, for 12 to 15 minutes or until chicken is tender.
- Serve hot with rice.

Roberta Shafer
Boca Raton, Florida

ZESTY CHICKEN

Serves: 4

1 large green pepper, cut in bite-sized
pieces
1 large red pepper, cut in bite-sized
pieces
1 large yellow pepper, cut in bite-sized
pieces
Boiling water
1 large yellow onion, cut in bite-sized
pieces
½ pound mushrooms

2 tablespoons olive oil
1½ teaspoons extra spicy salt-free
seasoning
1 teaspoon ground ginger
½ teaspoon garlic powder
1 pound boneless chicken breasts, skin
removed
2 tablespoons white wine
Worcestershire sauce

- In 2-quart saucepan, parboil peppers for 1 minute; drain and use paper towel to remove excess moisture.
- In 12-inch skillet, cook peppers, onions and mushrooms in oil until tender but not soft. Stir in seasonings, then chicken. Cook until chicken is tender, adding Worcestershire sauce about 1 minute before chicken is done.
- Serve hot over rice. Chicken and vegetables may be frozen.

Note: Veal, turkey or fish may be substituted for chicken.

Sonny Lipschultz
Largo, Florida

CHICKEN JERUSALEM

Serves: 4

2 chicken breasts, skin removed and
split
½ pound mushrooms, quartered
1 (6-ounce) jar marinated artichoke
hearts, drained
2 cloves garlic, minced

½ teaspoon dried oregano
Freshly ground black pepper to taste
2 cups canned or fresh tomatoes,
chopped
½ cup sherry

- Preheat oven to 350°.
- In 2-quart casserole, place chicken, mushrooms and artichoke hearts.
- In small mixing bowl, combine garlic, oregano, pepper and tomatoes; pour over chicken.
- Bake for 45 minutes to 1 hour or until chicken is tender, adding sherry for last 10 minutes cooking time.
- Serve hot.

Carolyn Ring
West Palm Beach, Florida

ORIENTAL CHICKEN

Serves: 6

4 chicken breasts, skin removed, boned and cut in 1-inch strips
4 tablespoons vegetable oil or margarine, divided
1 small green or red pepper or combination, cut in ½-inch strips
½ cup firmly-packed brown sugar
¼ cup vinegar
1½ teaspoons soy sauce

2 tablespoons ginger preserves or equivalent fresh grated ginger root or ground ginger
1 (8-ounce) can pineapple chunks, drained with juice reserved
2 tablespoons cornstarch
1 (11-ounce) can mandarin oranges, drained
Salt and pepper to taste

- In wok or 10-inch skillet over medium heat, stir-fry chicken in 2 tablespoons oil for 4 to 5 minutes or until opaque; remove chicken.
- Add 2 tablespoons oil to wok; stir-fry pepper strips until tender but not soft.
- In small mixing bowl, combine brown sugar, vinegar, soy sauce and ginger; add to pepper strips and cook for 2 minutes.
- Combine pineapple juice and cornstarch, blending until smooth. Stir into peppers and sauce and cook until bubbling.
- Add chicken strips, pineapple and oranges; cook for 1 minute.
- Serve immediately over rice. Dish may be prepared in advance and reheated or frozen.

Gertrude B. Jaffee
Boca Raton, Florida

SWEET AND SOUR CHICKEN

Serves: 6 to 8

2 eggs or equivalent egg substitute
¾ cup water
1 cup all-purpose flour
4 chicken breasts, boned, skin removed and cut in 1-inch pieces
Salt and pepper to taste
Vegetable oil

1 (8-ounce) jar apricot sweet and sour sauce
1 (8-ounce) can pineapple chunks, drained
1 (8-ounce) can water chestnuts, drained

- In small mixing bowl, combine egg, water and flour, beating until smooth.
- Season chicken with salt and pepper. Dip pieces in batter.
- In electric skillet or wok, deep fry chicken until golden brown, remove and drain on paper towel.
- Remove oil from skillet. Heat sweet and sour sauce in skillet. Add pineapple and water chestnuts and cook until hot. Stir in chicken.
- Serve immediately with rice. Chicken may be prepared in advance; reheat under broiler to crisp before adding to sauce.

Allyn M. Kanowsky
North Lauderdale, Florida

SWEET AND SOUR CHICKEN

Serves: 6

3 chicken breasts, boned, skin removed and partially frozen
1 (16-ounce) can pineapple, drained with juice reserved
3 tablespoons soy sauce
1 teaspoon garlic powder or 2 cloves garlic, minced

2 carrots, sliced
1 medium-sized green pepper, cut in chunks
1 cup instant rice

- Cut chicken into thin slices. Place in 3-quart microwave-safe casserole. Add pineapple juice, soy sauce and garlic. Cook on high (100%) for 15 minutes.
- Add pineapple, carrots and green pepper to chicken. Cook on high for 4 to 5 minutes or until carrots are tender.
- Remove chicken-vegetable mixture from casserole. Pour rice in bottom of casserole and spoon chicken-vegetable mixture over rice. Cook on high for about 6 minutes or until rice is cooked.
- Serve hot.

Louise R. Weinthal
Hallandale, Florida

THAI CHICKEN WITH PEANUT SAUCE

Serves: 4

3 tablespoons creamy or crunchy peanut butter
2 tablespoons soy sauce
2 tablespoons water
2 teaspoons firmly-packed light brown sugar
2 teaspoons sesame oil
1 canned flat anchovy
½ teaspoon ground red pepper

1 pound boneless chicken breasts, skin removed and cut in strips
1 tablespoon peanut oil
1 clove garlic, chopped
1 teaspoon ground ginger
4 green onions, sliced
1 medium-sized red pepper, cut in strips

- In blender container, combine peanut butter, soy sauce, water, brown sugar, sesame oil, anchovy and ground red pepper; blend thoroughly.
- In wok or 12-inch skillet over high heat, stir-fry chicken in oil for about 4 minutes or until browned.
- Add garlic, ginger, onions and red pepper strips to chicken; stir-fry over medium heat for 3 minutes.
- Stir in peanut butter mixture and cook for 1 minute, stirring to coat chicken.
- Serve hot over rice.

Frani Imbruno
Sarasota, Florida

QUICK GOURMET CHICKEN

Serves: 8

4 chicken breasts, skin removed, boned and split
1 (4½-ounce) jar sliced mushrooms, drained with liquid reserved
1 (10¾-ounce) can cream of mushroom or chicken soup, undiluted

¼ to ½ cup white wine
1 cup bread stuffing mix
¼ to ½ cup margarine, melted

- Preheat oven to 350°.
- Place chicken in 13x9x2-inch baking dish prepared with non-stick vegetable spray. Sprinkle mushrooms over chicken.
- In medium-sized mixing bowl, combine soup, wine and mushroom liquid; pour over chicken. Sprinkle stuffing mix over chicken. Pour margarine over stuffing mix.
- Bake for 50 to 60 minutes.
- Serve hot.

Norma Heit
Boca Raton, Florida

CHICKEN BREAST
WITH HONEY-WINE SAUCE

Serves: 4

1 cup dry white wine
½ cup soy sauce
¼ teaspoon garlic powder
4 chicken breasts, skin removed,
  boned and cut in chunks

¼ cup all-purpose flour
1 teaspoon salt
¼ teaspoon pepper
¼ cup vegetable oil
¼ cup honey

- In medium-sized mixing bowl, combine wine, soy sauce and garlic powder. Add chicken. Marinate for 1 hour.
- Remove chicken from marinade, reserving liquid.
- On waxed paper, combine flour, salt and pepper. Dredge chicken in seasoned flour.
- In large skillet over medium heat, fry chicken in oil, turning after 10 minutes to evenly brown both sides.
- Add honey to reserved marinade and pour over chicken. Simmer, covered, for about 20 minutes or until chicken is tender.
- Serve hot, spooning sauce over chicken.

Shirley Steier
North Miami Beach, Florida

DON'T PASS-ME-OVER-CHICKEN

Serves: 5 to 6

4 chicken breasts, skin removed,
  boned and cut in 2-inch pieces
1 large sweet onion, chopped
Vegetable oil
2 eggs

1 cup matzo meal
Salt and pepper to taste
1 tablespoon minced garlic
2 tablespoons chopped parsley
Matzo meal

- Place chicken in blender container; blend at high speed until chicken is pulverized.
- In small skillet, cook onion in oil until lightly browned.
- In large mixing bowl, combine chicken, onion, eggs, 1 cup matzo meal and seasonings. Mix with hands until thoroughly blended. Moisten hands and shape mixture into patties. Lightly coat patties with matzo meal.
- In 12-inch skillet, fry patties in oil until browned on both sides.
- Serve hot with duck sauce, honey or other sauces. Patties may be frozen.

Cathy Morris Alterman
Marietta, Georgia

BARBECUE CHICKEN

Serves: 4

4 chicken breasts
Seasoned salt to taste
Garlic powder to taste

Cajun seasoning to taste
1 (16-ounce) bottle French dressing
1 cup regular rice, uncooked

- Season chicken with seasoned salt, garlic powder and Cajun seasoning; place in 13x9x2-inch baking dish. Pour dressing over chicken. Chill for several hours or overnight.
- Preheat oven to 250°.
- Bake, uncovered, turning chicken every 15 minutes, for 1 hour. Cover tightly and bake for 1 hour, turning chicken every 15 minutes.
- Prepare rice according to package instructions. Spread cooked rice in 8x8x2-inch baking dish. After chicken has cooked for 1 hour and 30 minutes, pour most of gravy over rice and mix well. Bake dish of rice, uncovered, with chicken for 30 minutes.
- Serve hot. Chicken may be prepared in advance and frozen; thaw and reheat, covered, at 300° for about 30 minutes.

Harriet Schaffer
Memphis, Tennessee

CHOLODETZ

Serves: 6

6 chicken thighs
2 large onions, thinly sliced
2 carrots, thinly sliced
2 stalks celery, sliced
3 or 4 large cloves garlic, thinly sliced
2 bay leaves

Salt and pepper to taste
Peppercorns to taste
1 teaspoon vinegar
2 cups water (approximate)
1 envelope unflavored gelatin
2 hard-cooked eggs, sliced

- In stockpot, combine chicken, onions, carrots, celery, garlic, bay leaves, salt, pepper, peppercorns and vinegar with just enough water to cover. Simmer, covered, until chicken is tender. Pour through colander, reserving stock in bowl. Cool.
- Discarding skin and bones, chop chicken.
- Soften gelatin in ¼ cup cooled stock in saucepan; dissolve over low heat, then add to remaining stock.
- In 8x8x2-inch baking dish, place carrots and eggs. Add small amount of stock. When firm, arrange chicken on gelatin layer; pour remaining stock over chicken. Chill until firm.
- Cut into squares to serve.

Hilda Seligmann
Longboat Key, Florida

CHICKEN IN RED WINE

Serves: 4

4 chicken leg-thigh quarters
1 tablespoon salt, divided
1 teaspoon paprika
¼ teaspoon dried thyme
1 bay leaf

¾ cup dry red wine
1 cup water
½ cup tomato juice
Chopped parsley
¼ teaspoon pepper

- Separate chicken thighs and legs, if desired. Combine 2 teaspoons salt and paprika; rub into chicken pieces. Place on broiling pan.
- Broil chicken until browned on both sides.
- Preheat oven to 400°.
- In 13x9x2-inch baking dish, arrange chicken pieces and add thyme, bay leaf, wine and water.
- Bake, covered, for 1 hour or until chicken is tender. Transfer chicken to heat-proof serving dish. Remove bay leaf from pan juices.
- In small saucepan, combine juices from baking dish, tomato juice, parsley, pepper and 1 teaspoon salt. Heat until flavors are blended. Pour sauce over chicken. Garnish with parsley.
- Serve immediately.

Felice Greenstein
Coral Springs, Florida

CHICKEN POT PIE

Serves: 4

2 unbaked 9-inch pastry shells
5 tablespoons margarine
5 tablespoons all-purpose flour
2½ cups chicken broth

1½ to 2 cups cooked cubed chicken or turkey
1 (10-ounce) package frozen Japanese vegetables

- Preheat oven to 350°.
- Place 1 pastry shell in 10-inch pie plate.
- In 1-quart saucepan, melt margarine. Stir in flour and cook until thickened. Blend in chicken broth and cook until consistency of gravy.
- In order, layer ½ thickened broth, chicken, vegetables and ½ thickened broth in pastry shell. Cover with second pastry shell, pressing at edges to seal. Cut slit in top to vent steam. Place on baking sheet.
- Bake, uncovered, for 1 hour or until crust is golden brown.
- Serve immediately.

Nancy Marin
Palm City, Florida

HOT CHICKEN SALAD

Serves: 6

2½ tablespoons margarine
2½ tablespoons all-purpose flour
1¼ cups chicken broth
1 (3 to 4-pound) chicken, cooked, boned and cut in chunks
2 hard-cooked eggs, chopped

1 cup diced celery
⅓ cup chopped green pepper
1 tablespoon minced onion
1 tablespoon lemon juice
½ cup mayonnaise
1 cup crushed potato chips

- Preheat oven to 400°.
- In 1-quart saucepan, melt margarine. Stir in flour and cook until thickened. Blend in broth and cook until consistency of gravy.
- In large mixing bowl, combine thickened broth, chicken, eggs, celery, green pepper, onion, lemon juice and mayonnaise; mix lightly.
- Spread mixture in lightly-greased 8x8x4-inch casserole. Sprinkle chips over mixture.
- Bake for about 20 minutes or until thoroughly heated and lightly browned.
- Serve hot. Salad may be assembled to point of adding chips, then chilled until baked; allow extra baking time. Salad may be baked and then frozen.

Note: 3 (6¼-ounce) cans tuna may be substituted for chicken.

Cecelia H. Fink
Sarasota, Florida

CHICKEN CHOW MEIN

Serves: 3

3 tablespoons chicken fat or vegetable oil
3 cups diagonally sliced celery
2 cups diced onion
1½ cups chicken broth or water
2 cups diced cooked chicken

1 (16-ounce) can bean sprouts, drained
3 tablespoons soy sauce, divided
2 tablespoons cornstarch
2 tablespoons sugar

- In 12-inch skillet, combine fat, celery, onion and broth; simmer until vegetables are tender.
- Add chicken, sprouts and 1 tablespoon soy sauce to vegetables. Cook, covered, for 15 minutes.
- In small saucepan, combine 2 tablespoons soy sauce, cornstarch and sugar. Cook, stirring frequently, for 15 minutes. Add thickened sauce to chicken-vegetable mixture.
- Serve hot.

Rhoda Hertz
Boca Raton, Florida

CHICKEN AND SAUSAGE JAMBALAYA

Serves: 6

¼ cup chopped green pepper
¼ cup chopped onion
¼ cup chopped celery
2 cloves garlic, crushed
3 tablespoons olive oil, divided
1½ cups converted rice, uncooked
3 cups water
1 bay leaf
¼ teaspoon ground thyme
2 tablespoons chicken bouillon
  granules

1 pound chicken breast, cut in bite-
  sized pieces
½ teaspoon garlic powder
2 (16-ounce) cans peeled tomatoes,
  drained and chopped
½ teaspoon mild hot sauce or to taste
1 pound turkey kielbasa sausage, cut
  in bite-sized pieces

- In 5-quart stockpot over low heat, cook green pepper, onion, celery and garlic in 2½ tablespoons oil for about 8 minutes or until vegetables are tender.
- Add rice to vegetables; cook for about 1 minute or until rice is translucent. Add water, bay leaf, thyme and bouillon; bring to a boil. Simmer, covered, for about 15 minutes or until rice is fluffy and all moisture is absorbed.
- In small skillet prepared with non-stick vegetable spray, cook chicken with garlic powder for about 10 minutes or until chicken is tender.
- Remove bay leaf from rice mixture; add tomatoes, hot sauce, sausage and chicken. Cook, covered, over medium heat for 10 to 15 minutes or until sausage is thoroughly heated, stirring occasionally.
- Serve hot, offering Jamaican tomato-pepper sauce.

Merri Robinson
Raleigh, North Carolina

GRILLED TURKEY BREAST

Serves: 4

¼ cup vegetable oil
Juice of 1 lemon
¾ teaspoon salt
¼ teaspoon pepper
½ teaspoon paprika

½ teaspoon dried oregano
¼ teaspoon garlic powder or 1 clove
  garlic, crushed
½ turkey breast, boned

- In small saucepan, combine oil, lemon and seasonings; simmer until flavors are blended. Cool.
- Pour marinade over turkey and let stand for at least 2 hours.
- In covered gas or charcoal grill, roast turkey over indirect heat for 1 hour and 15 minutes, checking for doneness after 1 hour.
- Let stand 10 to 15 minutes before slicing.
- Serve hot, warm or cold.

Marlene Tropper
Tamarac, Florida

ORANGE GLAZED TURKEY BREAST

Serves: 4 to 6

1 large onion, thinly sliced
3 stalks celery, thinly sliced
2 carrots, thinly sliced
1 (4 to 6-pound) turkey breast
1 (6-ounce) can frozen orange juice
  concentrate, undiluted

Lemon pepper to taste
Garlic powder to taste
Paprika to taste

- Preheat oven to 375°.
- Place vegetables in bottom of roasting pan. Set rack over vegetables and place turkey on rack.
- Pour orange juice over turkey. Season with lemon pepper, garlic powder and paprika or other preferred herbs.
- Bake, covered with aluminum foil tent, for 1 hour; remove foil and bake for 30 minutes, basting with pan juices.
- Let stand 10 to 15 minutes before slicing.
- Serve hot or warm with vegetables.

Mary Ellen Peyton
Miami, Florida

TURKEY STIR-FRY WITH NOODLES

Serves: 4

1 clove garlic, minced
¼ cup plus 1 tablespoon cornstarch, divided
¼ cup plus 1 tablespoon teriyaki sauce, divided
½ pound turkey breast cutlet, cut in ½-inch strips
2 teaspoons catsup

1 cup water
3 ounces fine egg noodles
2 tablespoons vegetable oil, divided
2 medium zucchini, halved lengthwise and cut diagonally in 1-inch slices
1 medium-sized onion, cut in chunks
10 cherry tomatoes, halved (optional)

- In small mixing bowl, combine garlic, 1 tablespoon cornstarch and 1 tablespoon teriyaki sauce. Stir in turkey strips. Let stand 30 minutes.
- In small mixing bowl, combine ¼ cup cornstarch, ¼ cup teriyaki sauce, catsup and water; set aside.
- Prepare noodles according to package directions.
- In wok or large skillet over high heat, stir-fry turkey in 1 tablespoon oil for about 2 minutes or until turkey is no longer pink. Remove or push to side.
- Add 1 tablespoon oil, zucchini and onion to wok; stir-fry for 4 minutes or until vegetables are tender. Stir in teriyaki-catsup mixture. Bring to a boil and cook until thickened. Add tomatoes and stir.
- Serve hot over noodles. Turkey can be cooked and set aside with uncooked vegetables until ready to cook just before serving.

Note: 1 chicken breast, skin removed and boned, may be substituted for turkey.

Evelyn Garb
Sarasota, Florida

TURKEY SPINACH LOAF

Serves: 4

1½ to 1¾ pounds ground turkey
1 egg
1 (10-ounce) package frozen chopped
spinach, thawed and well drained
1 (4-ounce) can chopped mushrooms

½ medium-sized green pepper, chopped
2½ tablespoons onion flakes
½ teaspoon pepper
1 tomato, chopped

- Preheat oven to 350°.
- In large mixing bowl, combine turkey, egg, spinach, mushrooms, green pepper, onion and pepper; mix thoroughly. Shape into a loaf and place in 9x5x3-inch loaf pan or 12x7x2-inch baking pan. Sprinkle tomato over loaf.
- Bake for 45 to 50 minutes.
- Serve hot or cold. Loaf may be assembled in advance.

Marilyn Kaye
Boca Raton, Florida

TURKEY FINALE

Serves: 6

1 green pepper, chopped
2 medium-sized onions, chopped
½ pound mushrooms, sliced
Vegetable oil
1 (8-ounce) can tomato sauce
1 (16-ounce) can stewed tomatoes,
mashed

½ teaspoon garlic powder
1 teaspoon salt-free seasoning
¼ teaspoon pepper
¼ teaspoon ground oregano
3 to 4 cups cubed cooked turkey or
chicken

- In large skillet, cook green pepper, onions and mushrooms in small amount of oil until vegetables are tender but not soft.
- Add tomato sauce and tomatoes to vegetables. Stir in seasonings. Bring to a boil, then simmer, covered, for 10 minutes.
- Add turkey and heat thoroughly.
- Serve hot over rice or noodles. Turkey and vegetables may be frozen.

Marti Bernard
Delray Beach, Florida

TURKEY CHILI

Serves: 8

2 pounds ground turkey
6 cups water
2 medium-sized onions, minced
1 (15-ounce) can tomato sauce
½ teaspoon ground allspice
½ teaspoon ground red pepper
1 teaspoon ground cumin
¼ cup chili powder
½ ounce unsweetened baking
  chocolate

4 cloves garlic, minced
2 tablespoons red wine vinegar
2 large bay leaves
2 teaspoons Worcestershire sauce
1 teaspoon ground cinnamon
1 (29-ounce) can kidney beans
  (optional)

- In 4-quart saucepot, crumble turkey. Add water. Bring to a boil, stirring frequently to separate turkey, then simmer, uncovered, for 30 minutes.
- Stir remaining ingredients (except beans) into turkey and broth. Bring to a boil, then simmer, uncovered, for 2½ hours, checking during final hour on liquid; when preferred consistency, add beans, cover and complete cooking time. Remove bay leaves.
- Serve plain or over thin spaghetti, garnished with chopped onion.

Beverly Pechenik
North Miami Beach, Florida

SAUCY TURKEY CHILI

Serves: 4

1 pound ground turkey
1 tablespoon vegetable oil
½ cup chopped onion
1 clove garlic, chopped
½ cup chopped celery
1 (10¾-ounce) can tomato soup,
  undiluted
1 (16-ounce) can tomatoes

1 (16-ounce) can kidney beans,
  drained
½ cup tomato paste
2 teaspoons chili powder
1 bay leaf
Salt and freshly ground pepper to taste
½ teaspoon hot pepper sauce
  (optional)

- In large skillet or saucepan over medium-high heat, brown turkey in oil, crumbling it as it cooks. Add onion, garlic and celery; cook for about 4 minutes.
- Add soup, tomatoes, beans, tomato paste and seasonings. Simmer, partially covered, for 20 to 25 minutes, stirring often to prevent sticking. Remove bay leaf.
- Serve hot with crackers or rice.

Flo Don
Sarasota, Florida

SURPRISE TURKEY CHILI

Serves: 6

1 cup chopped onion
5 cloves garlic, minced
6 tablespoons olive oil, divided
2 sweet red peppers, diced
2 to 4 jalapeño peppers, seeded and
   minced (optional)
2 to 3 tablespoons chili powder
1 tablespoon ground cinnamon
1½ teaspoons ground cumin

1 teaspoon ground coriander
6 cups cubed skinless turkey breast
1 (15-ounce) can tomato purée
1 (6-ounce) can black olives, drained
   and sliced
1 cup beer or chicken broth
¼ cup grated unsweetened chocolate
Chopped avocado for garnish

- In large saucepan or Dutch oven over medium-high heat, cook onion and garlic in 3 tablespoons oil for 2 to 3 minutes, stirring frequently. Add peppers and cook for 10 minutes, stirring frequently. Stir in seasonings, reduce heat and simmer while preparing turkey.

- In 12-inch skillet, stir-fry turkey in 3 tablespoons oil until turkey is white. Remove with slotted spoon and add to vegetables.

- Add tomato sauce, olives and broth to turkey mixture. Stir in chocolate. Simmer for 15 to 20 minutes, stirring occasionally.

- Serve with avocado.

Note: 6 chicken breasts may be substituted for turkey.

Frani Imbruno
Sarasota, Florida

ROAST DUCK A L'ORANGE

Serves: 3 to 4

1 duck, halved
Salt and pepper to taste
2 medium-sized onions, sliced
2 unpeeled apples, cut in wedges
1 (6-ounce) can frozen orange juice
concentrate, thawed and undiluted

1 (16-ounce) can pineapple chunks
2 oranges, peeled and sliced
Grand Marnier

- Season duck with salt and pepper. Broil, piercing skin with fork to release fat, until all excess fat is removed.
- Preheat oven to 350°.
- In roasting pan, place onions and apples in bottom. Arrange duck on onions and apples. Pour orange juice and spoon pineapple and orange slices over duck.
- Bake for 1 hour and 20 minutes.
- To serve, add Grand Marnier and ignite.

Doreen Fasberg
Lake Worth, Florida

GRILLED CORNISH HENS WITH GINGER

Serves: 4

½ cup dry sherry
2 tablespoons grated ginger root
2 tablespoons soy sauce
2 tablespoons sesame oil
½ teaspoon pepper

1 teaspoon sugar
2 large Cornish hens, halved
3 tablespoons hoisin sauce
1 teaspoon ground coriander

- In container with tight-fitting lid, combine sherry, ginger, soy sauce, oil, pepper and sugar; shake to blend.
- Place hen halves in single layer in shallow baking dish. Pour marinade over hens. Chill, covered with plastic wrap, for 2 hours or longer.
- Reserve marinade. Place hens on hot grill, skin side down. Grill for 10 to 12 minutes. Add hoisin sauce and coriander to marinade. Turn hens and brush with marinade; grill for 10 to 23 minutes or until hens are golden brown and juices run clear.
- Serve hot.

Fran Gould
Boca Raton, Florida

CORNISH HENS WITH PEACHES

Serves: 6

1½ cups dried peaches
Hot water
3 Cornish hens, cut in halves
Salt and pepper to taste
2 teaspoons ground cinnamon, divided
6 tablespoons vegetable oil, divided
2 cups chopped Spanish onions

⅛ teaspoon ground cloves
1½ cups canned plum tomatoes,
    drained with juice reserved, and
    chopped
1 cup chicken stock, divided
½ cup firmly-packed brown sugar

- In medium-sized mixing bowl, soak peaches in hot water to cover for about 2 hours. Drain.
- Season hens with salt, pepper and ½ teaspoon cinnamon. In large skillet, brown hens in 3 tablespoons oil.
- In 2-quart saucepan, cook onion in 3 tablespoons oil over low heat for 5 minutes or until onions are transparent. Add 1½ teaspoons cinnamon and cloves; cook for 2 more minutes, stirring occasionally. Add about ¼ cup reserved tomato juice.
- Using food processor, purée ½ peaches; coarsely chop remainder.
- Add puréed peaches, tomatoes and ½ cup chicken stock to onion mixture. Simmer, uncovered, for 5 minutes.
- Preheat oven to 350°.
- Purée 1 cup onion mixture; return to pan. Add chopped peaches, brown sugar, ½ cup chicken stock and enough liquid to make medium-thick sauce.
- In large casserole, layer ½ of sauce, hens and remaining sauce.
- Bake for about 35 minutes or until hens are tender.
- Serve hot.

Betty Sarlin
Sarasota, Florida

FISH

FRESH FISH CAKES

Serves: 4

½ pound scrod (codfish), sliced
1 medium potato, quartered
1 carrot, sliced
1 onion, quartered
½ teaspoon salt

¼ teaspoon pepper
Water
1 egg
½ cup breadcrumbs, divided
Vegetable oil

- In large saucepan, place scrod, vegetables and seasonings with water to cover. Cook until carrots are tender.
- Drain fish and vegetables. Discard fish skin and bones and onion.
- In medium-sized mixing bowl, mash fish, carrots and potatoes together. Stir in egg and ¼ cup breadcrumbs. Shape mixture into 2-inch balls. Roll in remaining breadcrumbs.
- In large skillet, fry fish cakes in oil. Cakes may also be baked in toaster oven until browned.
- Serve hot. Assembled cakes may be frozen before frying or baking.

Isabelle Katzen
Delray Beach, Florida

BAKED SALMON

Serves: 4

2 pounds salmon fillets or steaks
Mayonnaise
4 to 5 tablespoons lemon juice
3 to 4 tablespoons white wine

Onion powder to taste
Grated Parmesan cheese
Paprika
1 to 2 teaspoons dill weed

- Preheat oven to 350°.
- Coat both sides fillets with mayonnaise. Place in 12x9x2-inch baking dish prepared with non-stick vegetable spray. Add lemon juice and wine. In order, sprinkle fillets with onion powder, cheese, paprika and dill weed.
- Bake, covered with aluminum foil, for 25 minutes. Remove foil and broil briefly to brown; cheese should puff.
- Serve hot.

Bunnie Taratoot
Dunwoody, Georgia

SALMON CROQUETTES

Serves: 2

1 egg or equivalent egg substitute
1 small onion, diced
1 carrot, diced
1 small potato, diced
1 (7½-ounce) can pink or red salmon, drained

¼ cup milk
¼ cup breadcrumbs or matzo meal
¼ teaspoon salt or salt substitute
Dash of freshly ground pepper
¼ cup vegetable oil

- Place egg and vegetables in food processor bowl; process using on/off until blended; avoid liquefying ingredients.
- In medium-sized mixing bowl, combine egg-vegetable mixture, salmon, milk, breadcrumbs and seasonings.
- Drop large spoonfuls of salmon mixture into hot oil in 12-inch skillet over medium high heat; fry until browned on both sides, being careful when turning croquettes as mixture is lightly textured.
- Serve hot. Cold croquettes may be used in sandwiches or frozen. To reheat cook in microwave on high (100%) for 3 minutes.

Ida G. Block
Pembroke Pines, Florida

SALMON-TUNA LOAF

Serves: 12

1 (15-ounce) can pink salmon, drained and boned
2 (6¼-ounce) cans tuna, drained
3 carrots
3 onions
3 eggs, beaten

1 (16-ounce) can peas, drained
1 (4-ounce) can sliced mushrooms, drained
1 teaspoon baking powder
½ cup vegetable oil

- Preheat oven to 350°.
- In large mixing bowl, combine salmon and tuna, blending thoroughly.
- Using food processor, grate carrots and onions; add to fish. Beat eggs and add to fish.
- Stir peas and mushrooms into fish mixture. Add baking powder and oil; mix well.
- Spread mixture in greased 13x9x3-inch baking pan.
- Bake for 1 hour or until golden brown.
- Cut in squares and serve hot.

Laura Rosenberg
Delray Beach, Florida

SALMON SOUFFLÉ

Serves: 8

Sauce

1 (8-ounce) carton sour cream
½ cup peeled, seeded and finely
  chopped cucumber

½ teaspoon salt
1 teaspoon dill weed
1 teaspoon minced onion

- In small mixing bowl, combine all ingredients and mix thoroughly. Chill for 1 to 2 hours before serving with soufflé.

Filling

4 shallots, chopped
2 tablespoons butter
8 mushrooms, chopped
1 (16-ounce) can red salmon, dark
  skin removed and boned

1 tablespoon dill weed
2 (3-ounce) packages cream cheese,
  softened
Salt and pepper

- In large skillet, cook shallots in butter until tender. Add mushrooms; cook for about 3 minutes and most of mushroom juices have evaporated.
- Add salmon and dill to vegetables; heat thoroughly. Stir in cream cheese and season with salt and pepper.
- Filling may be prepared in advance and frozen; thaw and reheat at 350° for about 10 minutes.

Soufflé Roll

¼ cup butter
½ teaspoon salt
⅛ teaspoon pepper

½ cup all-purpose flour
2 cups milk
5 eggs, separated

- In saucepan, melt butter; blend in salt, pepper and flour. Gradually stir in milk. Bring to a boil, stirring constantly; cook for 1 minute.
- In small mixing bowl, lightly beat egg yolks. Beat small amount of hot sauce into yolks, then add yolks to sauce and cook over medium heat for 1 minute, stirring constantly. Do not boil. Cool to room temperature, stirring occasionally.
- Grease 15x10x1-inch jellyroll pan, line with parchment paper, grease again and dust lightly with flour.
- Preheat oven to 450°.
- In medium-sized mixing bowl, beat egg whites until stiff but not dry. Fold into cooled sauce. Spread mixture in prepared pan.

- Bake on center rack for 12 to 15 minutes or until puffed and browned.
- Invert on towel. Spread with filling and roll up, using towel to guide edge. Slide onto serving platter or board with seam side down.
- Serve slices of soufflé with cucumber sauce on side.

Marian Pressman
Tamarac, Florida

SALMON LOAF

Serves: 8

2 small onions, chopped
1 green pepper, chopped
¼ cup margarine, divided
1 (16-ounce) can red salmon, skin removed, boned and flaked
1 (10-ounce) package frozen peas and carrots, partially thawed

¾ (8-ounce) carton sour cream or yogurt
1 cup milk
1 cup cornflake crumbs
4 eggs, beaten

- Preheat oven to 350°.
- In small skillet, sauté onion and pepper in 2 tablespoons margarine until soft.
- In large mixing bowl, combine salmon, peas and carrots, sour cream, milk, crumbs (1 tablespoon reserved), eggs and sautéed vegetables; mix thoroughly.
- Melt 1 tablespoon margarine in 11x9x2-inch baking dish. Spread salmon mixture in dish, sprinkle with remaining crumbs and dot with 1 tablespoon margarine.
- Bake for 45 to 60 minutes or until firm and browned.
- Cut in squares and serve hot.

Eleanor F. Victor
Delray Beach, Florida

TUNA OR SALMON STUFFED POTATO

Serves: 3

3 large baking potatoes, baked
1 egg, beaten
1 tablespoon butter
1 (6¼-ounce) can tuna or (7½-ounce) can salmon, drained
Milk
Paprika

6 slices American cheese
1 tablespoon all-purpose flour
1 tablespoon melted butter
1 cup milk
⅓ cup catsup
1 teaspoon onion juice

- After baking potatoes at preferred temperature, set oven at 375°.
- Cut potatoes in half lengthwise or trim top ¼ from potatoes. Scoop out potato pulp.
- In medium-sized mixing bowl, mash pulp with egg and butter. Stir in tuna or salmon, adding small amount of milk if necessary for creamy consistency.
- Spoon filling into potato shells. Sprinkle with paprika and top with cheese slices.
- Bake for a few minutes to melt cheese and brown potatoes.
- In saucepan over medium heat, combine flour and melted butter. Add milk, stirring constantly. Add catsup and onion juice and mix well.
- Serve hot potatoes with hot tomato sauce.

Bert G. Zalles
Miami Beach, Florida

GRILLED TUNA STEAKS

Serves: 4

¼ cup soy sauce
¼ cup Worcestershire sauce
Juice of 1 lime
Juice of 1 lemon

1 tablespoon honey
2 tablespoons Dijon mustard
2 cloves garlic, pressed
2 pounds fresh tuna steaks

- In small mixing bowl, combine soy sauce, Worcestershire sauce, lime and lemon juices, honey, mustard and garlic.
- Place tuna steaks in plastic bag and add marinade, turning to thoroughly coat steaks. Marinate for at least 30 minutes.
- Heat gas grill at high setting; prepare grill surface with non-stick vegetable spray.
- Grill steaks for 4 minutes on each side, brushing generously with marinade.
- Serve hot.

Note: Swordfish, salmon or any firm fish steaks may be substituted for tuna.

Louise Pohl Horowitz
Parkland, Florida

TUNA SKILLET SURPRISE

Serves: 4 to 6

1⅓ cups regular rice, uncooked
1½ cups water
1 (16-ounce) package frozen mixed
  vegetables
1 (15-ounce) can tomato sauce
1 (6-ounce) can tomato paste

½ medium-sized onion, chopped
3 tablespoons catsup
Garlic salt to taste
1 (12-ounce) can tuna, drained and
  flaked
Fried onion rings to garnish

- Prepare rice according to package directions; set aside.
- In 12-inch skillet, combine water and vegetables; cook until vegetables are tender and 90% of water is evaporated. Add tomato sauce and paste, onion, catsup and garlic salt; mix well. Stir in hot rice. Fold in tuna. Cook over low heat until all ingredients are hot. Spoon into serving dish and garnish with fried onions.
- Serve hot. Casserole may be prepared in advance and reheated.

Joy A. Chanin
Marietta, Georgia

TUNA CASSEROLE

Serves: 3 to 4

3½ cups small elbow macaroni,
  uncooked
1 (10¾-ounce) can cream of
  mushroom or cream of celery soup,
  undiluted
½ cup milk
1 (6¼-ounce) can tuna, drained and
  flaked

1 cup sliced celery
½ cup diced onion
¼ cup diced green pepper
½ cup diced pimentos
½ cup mayonnaise
½ cup slivered almonds

- Prepare macaroni according to package directions; drain and set aside.
- In 1-quart saucepan, blend soup and milk; heat thoroughly.
- In large mixing bowl, combine tuna, celery, onion, pepper, pimentos and mayonnaise; mix well. Stir in macaroni. Spread mixture in ungreased 3-quart casserole.
- Pour soup over tuna-macaroni mixture and toss lightly to mix. Sprinkle with almonds. Let stand 1 hour.
- Preheat oven to 425°. Bake for 20 to 30 minutes.
- Serve hot.

Rae Wasserstein Kress
North Miami Beach, Florida

GRANDMA EMMA'S TUNA CASSEROLE

Serves: 6

1 (8-ounce) package shell pasta
¼ cup margarine
1 (8-ounce) package shredded Cheddar cheese

2 (6¼-ounce) cans water-packed white tuna, flaked
2 (8-ounce) cans tomato sauce
Salt and pepper to taste

- Prepare pasta according to package directions. Drain and return to saucepan.
- Preheat oven to 350°.
- Add margarine, cheese, tuna, tomato sauce and seasonings to macaroni; mix thoroughly. Spread mixture in 1¾-quart casserole.
- Bake for 30 minutes. Casserole may be assembled in advance and stored in refrigerator; bake chilled casserole for 45 minutes.
- Serve hot.

Pepi Dunay
Boca Raton, Florida

TUNA MACARONI CASSEROLE

Serves: 6

1 (8-ounce) package elbow macaroni, uncooked
1 (8-ounce) jar pasteurized process cheese spread
1 (8-ounce) carton sour cream

1 (10¾-ounce) can cream of mushroom soup, undiluted
1 (6¼-ounce) can tuna, drained and flaked
¾ cup milk

- Prepare macaroni according to package directions; drain and return to saucepan.
- Preheat oven to 350°.
- Add cheese to hot macaroni and mix well. Stir in sour cream, soup, tuna and milk; blend thoroughly. Spread mixture in greased 12x8x2-inch baking dish.
- Bake for 1 hour.
- Serve hot. Casserole may be frozen.

Blanche Rubenstein
Delray Beach, Florida

MARINATED FISH

Serves: 12

4 to 6 pounds trout, pike or pickerel,
cut in 2-inch pieces
Salt
3 onions, sliced
2 carrots, sliced
1 tablespoon pickling spice

Water
2½ cups cider vinegar
1 cup sugar
1 envelope unflavored gelatin
½ cup water
1 lemon, sliced

- Salt fish and chill overnight.
- Clean fish. In stockpot, place fish heads, onions, carrots and spices with enough water to cover. Simmer for 20 minutes.
- Add vinegar and sugar to stock and simmer for 15 minutes.
- Add fish to stock and simmer for 15 minutes, adding water if necessary.
- Lift fish from stock and place in serving dish with tight-fitting cover; reserve stock.
- In large mixing bowl, soften gelatin in ½ cup water. Strain stock and mix with gelatin. Pour over fish. Chill for at least 48 hours.
- Serve chilled, garnished with lemon and carrot slices. May be stored in refrigerator for 2 to 3 weeks. Do not freeze.

Laura Robbins
Bay Harbor Island, Florida

CREAMY FISH SALAD

Serves: 6

2 pounds scrod, cod or halibut
Water
¼ cup vinegar
½ cup chili sauce
½ cup mayonnaise

½ (8-ounce) carton sour cream
2 hard-cooked eggs, chopped
2 stalks celery, chopped
Parsley sprigs for garnish

- In 2-quart saucepan, place fish with water to cover plus vinegar. Simmer for 5 minutes. Drain, cool and flake fish.
- In medium-sized mixing bowl, combine chili sauce, mayonnaise and sour cream. Fold in eggs, celery and fish. Spoon into serving bowl and chill.
- Serve cold, garnished with parsley.

Kay Freedman
Boca Raton, Florida

STUFFED RED SNAPPER WITH LEMON RICE

Serves: 2 to 3

3 cups cooked rice
2 large lemons, peeled, seeded and
  sectioned
Dash of salt
Dash of pepper
1 (8-ounce) carton sour cream
½ cup chopped parsley

1 cup chopped onion
1 (2½-pound) whole red snapper,
  cleaned
½ teaspoon vegetable oil
Lemon slices for garnish
Parsley sprigs for garnish

- Preheat oven to 375°.
- In large mixing bowl, combine rice, lemon, seasonings, sour cream, parsley and onion; mix lightly. Spoon mixture into cavity of fish.
- Brush outside of fish with oil; place on baking sheet lined with greased aluminum foil. Cover fins and tail with foil.
- Bake for 20 minutes or until fish is cooked.
- Serve hot, garnished with sliced lemons and parsley sprigs.

Carolyn Kerner Stein
North Miami, Florida

GRILLED SWORDFISH

Serves: 4

¼ cup white wine
Worcestershire sauce to taste
¼ cup olive oil
Juice of 1 lime

2 pounds swordfish steaks
Garlic powder to taste
Pinch of dill weed
Lemon wedges

- In small mixing bowl, combine wine, Worcestershire sauce, oil and lime juice.
- Place steaks in shallow pan; pour marinade over steaks and let stand for 30 minutes to 1 hour. Lift steaks from marinade.
- Sprinkle both sides of steaks with garlic powder and dill weed; place on hot grill and brush with marinade. Grill on each side until fish flakes.
- Serve hot with lemon wedges.

Sue Rosenbluth
Largo, Florida

MARINATED GRILLED FISH

Serves: 4

½ cup teriyaki sauce
1 small green pepper, minced
1 medium-sized yellow onion, minced
1 small clove garlic, minced

2 pounds red snapper or any white fish
  fillets
Non-stick vegetable spray

- In small mixing bowl, combine teriyaki sauce, pepper, onion and garlic. Marinate fillets for at least 1 hour.
- Spray shiny side of aluminum foil sheet with non-stick vegetable spray and place on hot grill. Lift fillets from marinade and arrange on foil.
- Grill, with hood closed, for 15 minutes; turn and grill until fish flakes.
- Heat marinade and serve over hot fish.

Loisbeth Emanuel
Miami, Florida

AUNT SYLVIA'S GEFILTE FISH

Serves: 24

3 medium-sized onions, sliced
4 carrots, sliced
6½ cups water, divided
3 tablespoons salt, divided
⅛ teaspoon pepper
Fresh parsley sprigs
5 pounds white fish, bones and heads
  reserved

3 pounds pike, bones and heads
  reserved
5 stalks celery
1 large onion
5 eggs
¼ cup sugar or to taste
1½ cups matzo meal

- In 10-quart stockpot, combine sliced onions, carrots, 6 cups water, 1½ tablespoons salt, pepper, parsley and fish heads and bones. Simmer while preparing fish balls.
- In food processor bowl, combine celery, large onion and eggs; process with metal blade until well ground.
- Remove skin from fish and cut into small chunks. Combine with vegetable-egg mixture, sugar, ½ cup water and matzo meal; season with salt and pepper. Process for 20 seconds on and off until well ground and thick.
- Shape into oval balls and drop into stock. Bring to a boil, then simmer, covered, for 2 hours. Cool, then store covered in refrigerator.

Carol Sue Press
Hollywood, Florida

THE BEST BAKED GEFILTE FISH

Serves: 10 to 12

5 large onions, chopped
Vegetable oil
4 pounds ground boneless whitefish
and pike with small amount of trout
5 eggs
½ cup matzo meal

2¼ cups ice water
4 teaspoons salt
2 teaspoons pepper
¼ cup sugar
5 large carrots, grated

- In large skillet, cook onions in oil until soft but not browned.
- In large electric mixer bowl, mix fish with eggs, adding 1 at a time and beating well after each addition. Add meal, ice water, salt, pepper, sugar and onions. Beat for 20 minutes; mixture will increase in volume. If using hand electric mixer, beat mixture in several portions. Stir in carrots.
- Preheat oven to 350°.
- Spread mixture in greased 10-inch tube pan and place on baking sheet.
- Bake for 1 hour, cover with tent of aluminum foil and bake for 1½ hours.
- Cool, then remove from pan. Fish may be prepared 1 to 2 days in advance and stored in refrigerator.

Adrianne Weissman
Palm Beach Gardens, Florida

AUNTIE CELIA'S FISH

Serves: 4

¼ cup chili sauce
¼ cup mayonnaise
2 tablespoons sugar or equivalent
substitute

2 tablespoons lemon juice
1½ pounds cod, perch or orange
roughy fillets

- Preheat oven to 350°.
- In small mixing bowl, combine chili sauce, mayonnaise, sugar and lemon juice.
- Roll fish fillets and place in 8x8x2-inch baking pan. Pour sauce over fillets.
- Bake for 30 minutes.
- Serve hot over white or brown rice.

Rosanne Lutz
Dunwoody, Georgia

SZECHUAN FISH

Serves: 2

2 fish fillets
Cornstarch
Vegetable oil
2 tablespoons soy sauce
2 tablespoons sherry

2 teaspoons sugar or honey
½ to 1 teaspoon hot chili paste
¼ cup water
1 medium-sized onion, sliced
½ green pepper, thinly sliced

- Lightly dust fillets with cornstarch. In large non-stick skillet over medium heat, fry fillets in oil, turning to lightly brown on both sides.
- In small mixing bowl, combine soy sauce, sherry, sugar, chili paste and water; set aside.
- Remove fish from skillet and drain on paper towel.
- Stir-fry onion and green pepper in 2 tablespoons oil until vegetables are soft. Return fish to skillet. Spoon sauce over fish. Cook over medium heat until all ingredients are hot.
- Serve hot over white rice.

Peppe Dragoni
Seminole, Florida

GOURMET BAKED FISH

Serves: 4

1½ pounds fish fillets
2 tablespoons safflower or olive oil, divided
1½ teaspoons lemon juice
½ teaspoon seasoning
⅓ large onion, chopped

⅓ cup chopped celery
1 (15-ounce) can tomato sauce
2 cloves garlic, crushed
⅓ cup white wine
10 fresh mushrooms, halved
6 slices American cheese

- Preheat oven to 300°.
- Place fillets in 12x8x2-inch baking dish with 1 tablespoon oil. Sprinkle with lemon juice and seasoning.
- Bake for 15 minutes or until almost done.
- In small skillet, cook onion in 1 tablespoon oil until soft. In order, add celery, tomato sauce, garlic, wine and mushrooms, cooking over medium heat.
- Pour sauce over fillets; bake for 5 minutes. Arrange cheese slices on fillets; bake for 5 minutes or until cheese is melted.
- Serve hot.

Margaret Newman Stearn
Miami Beach, Florida

CREOLE FISH

Serves: 6 to 8

1 onion, sliced
¼ cup plus 2 tablespoons butter or
  margarine
3 cups chopped green pepper
3 cups chopped celery
1 teaspoon minced garlic
2 cups chopped tomatoes

¼ cup chopped parsley
2 teaspoons drained capers
Hot pepper sauce to taste
2 pounds fish fillets, cut in serving
  pieces
Salt and pepper to taste

- In 3-quart saucepan, sauté onion in butter until translucent. Add green peppers, celery and garlic; sauté for 2 to 3 minutes.
- Stir in tomatoes, parsley, capers and hot pepper sauce. Cook over medium heat, covered, for 15 minutes, then cook uncovered for 5 minutes.
- Preheat oven to 450°.
- Arrange fillets in buttered 12x8x2-inch baking dish. Season with salt and pepper and pour sauce over fillets.
- Bake for 15 to 20 minutes.
- Serve hot with sauce over rice.

Erika Brodsky
Boca Raton, Florida

KEY WEST FISH

Serves: 4

4 fish fillets
2 tablespoons lime juice
Pepper to taste
1 tablespoon garlic butter

2 tomatoes, diced
1 green pepper, diced
1 onion, sliced

- Place fillets in single layer in baking dish. Sprinkle with lime juice and season with pepper. Marinate, covered, for several hours or overnight, storing in refrigerator.
- Preheat oven to 350°.
- Lift fillets from marinade but do not rinse. Place in greased 9x9x2-inch baking dish. Dot with garlic butter. Spoon vegetables over fillets.
- Bake, covered, for 1 hour.
- Serve hot.

Mary Ellen Peyton
Miami, Florida

BAKED FISH ROULADES WITH VEGETABLES

Serves: 4 to 6

5 potatoes, peeled
1 green pepper, seeded
1 red pepper, seeded
1 large onion, quartered and cut in
 ½-inch slices
Salt and pepper to taste
Paprika to taste

2 tablespoons butter or margarine
1 (16-ounce) package frozen fish
 fillets, thawed
1 tablespoon lemon juice
½ cup mayonnaise
1 tablespoon prepared mustard
2 teaspoons all-purpose flour

- Preheat oven to 400°.
- In 12x8x2-inch baking dish, combine potatoes, green and red peppers and onions. Sprinkle with seasonings and dot with butter.
- Bake for 30 minutes, stirring once or twice.
- Sprinkle fillets with lemon juice.
- In small mixing bowl, combine mayonnaise, mustard and flour. Spread ½ of mixture on 1 side of fillets. Roll fillets and place in vegetables. Spoon remaining sauce over fillets. Sprinkle with paprika.
- Bake for 15 to 20 minutes or until fillets flake easily.
- Serve hot.

Frances K. Goldberg
Hollywood, Florida

FISH ROLL-UPS

Serves: 3 to 4

1 teaspoon vegetable oil
¼ cup diced onion
1 (10-ounce) package frozen spinach,
    thawed and drained
¼ teaspoon pepper
2 tablespoons lemon juice, divided

½ cup shredded mozzarella cheese
1 (12-ounce) package frozen fish
    fillets, thawed, or ¾ pound fresh
    fillets
1 tablespoon margarine or butter,
    melted

- In 8x8x2-inch microwave-safe baking dish, combine oil and onion; cook on high (100%) for 2 minutes.
- Add spinach, pepper, 1 tablespoon lemon juice and cheese to onions; mix well.
- Place 1 to 2 tablespoons spinach filling in center of each fillet. Roll up, using wooden pick to secure. Remove extra filling from baking dish and wipe clean. Place rolls, pick side down, in baking dish; spoon extra filling around rolls.
- Mix margarine and 1 tablespoon lemon juice together; pour over fish and filling.
- Cook, covered loosely with heavy duty plastic wrap, on high (100%) for 5 to 8 minutes or until fish flakes easily.
- Serve hot.

Cookie Berman
Tamarac, Florida

BREADS

GOLDEN RAISIN CHALLAH

Yield: 2 loaves

1 package dry yeast
½ cup warm (105° to 115°) water
½ cup milk, coffee whitener or water
¼ cup unsalted butter or margarine
¼ cup sugar
1 teaspoon salt

3 eggs, divided
3½ to 4 cups unbleached flour
1 cup golden raisins
Melted butter
Sesame seeds (optional)
2 teaspoons water

- In medium-sized mixing bowl, dissolve yeast in warm water; set aside.
- In saucepan, heat milk until hot. Remove from heat. Stir in butter, sugar and salt. Let cool slightly.
- Add eggs to milk liquid and beat well. Add egg mixture to dissolved yeast.
- Place about 3 cups flour in large mixing bowl or food processor bowl; add yeast mixture and mix until smooth. Add additional flour until dough forms a ball. Remove from bowl.
- On lightly-floured surface, add raisins to dough, kneading until smooth. Add additional flour if dough is sticky. Place dough in lightly-buttered bowl, turning to coat.
- Let rise, covered with dampened cloth, until doubled in bulk.
- Punch down and divide dough in half; divide each half into 3 pieces. Roll each into 12-inch strip. Braid 3 strips, pinch end and place on greased baking sheet. Repeat with remaining dough strips.
- Brush braids with melted butter and sprinkle with sesame seeds. Let rise until doubled in bulk.
- Preheat oven to 350°.
- Bake for 15 minutes. Beat remaining egg with 2 teaspoons water; brush glaze on partially baked braids. Continue baking for 15 minutes or until golden and hollow-sounding when lightly tapped.
- Serve warm.

Nancy Gillen Doyle
North Miami Beach, Florida

SHABBAT CHALLAH

Yield: 2 loaves

6 cups bread flour	1½ cups warm water
1 package dry yeast	3 tablespoons vegetable oil
3 tablespoons sugar	1 egg yolk
2 teaspoons salt	1 teaspoon water
3 eggs	Sesame or poppy seeds

- Using electric mixer or food processor, place flour, yeast, sugar, salt, 3 eggs and 1½ cups warm water in bowl. Beat with dough hook or process with blade until dough is well mixed. If too sticky, add ¼ cup flour at a time, mixing or processing until dough separates from sides of bowl.
- On floured surface, knead dough until smooth and elastic. Place in large well-oiled bowl and cover with dry cloth. Let rise for about 1½ hours or until doubled in bulk, punch down and let rise again until doubled in bulk. If using microwave oven, cover bowl with dampened cloth and top with dry cloth; microwave on high for 25 seconds, turn dough over and microwave on high for 25 seconds. Let rise for about 40 minutes until doubled in bulk, punch down, microwave on high for 25 seconds and let rise again until doubled in bulk.
- Divide dough in 2 portions for large loaves or 3 portions for medium loaves. Divide each portion into pieces for braiding; roll each piece into strand 1- to 1½-inches around. Braid loaves and place on greased baking sheet. Let rise for about 30 minutes or until doubled in bulk.
- Preheat oven to 400°.
- Combine egg yolk and 1 teaspoon water; brush on braids and sprinkle with seeds.
- Bake for 20 to 25 minutes or until loaf sounds hollow when lightly tapped.

Marion Zeiger
Chapel Hill, North Carolina

WHOLE WHEAT CHALLAH

Yield: 3 loaves

¾ cup plus 2 teaspoons sugar, divided
2 packages dry yeast
¼ cup warm (105° to 115°) water
1 teaspoon salt
½ cup vegetable oil

2 cups warm water
3 eggs, beaten
4 cups whole wheat flour
3 to 4 cups all-purpose flour
Sesame or poppy seeds (optional)

- In small mixing bowl, place 2 teaspoons sugar in ¼ cup warm water; add yeast. Set aside.
- In 4-quart mixing bowl, combine ¾ cup sugar, salt and oil. Stir in 2 cups warm water. Reserving 2 tablespoons of beaten eggs, add remaining eggs to liquids. Add yeast liquid.
- Gradually add flours, 2 cups at a time, beating after each addition.
- Place stiff dough on well-floured surface and knead for 5 to 7 minutes or until dough is smooth; add additional flour when dough becomes sticky.
- Place ball of dough in lightly-oiled bowl. Let rise, covered with plastic wrap, in a warm place for about 45 minutes or until doubled in bulk.
- Punch down, place on floured surface and slap several times to release air.
- Divide dough into 3 pieces; form each into 3 strands. Pinch ends of strands together and braid. Place each braid in 9x5x3-inch loaf pan prepared with non-stick vegetable spray.
- Let rise for 45 minutes. Brush lightly with reserved beaten egg and sprinkle with seeds.
- Preheat oven to 325°.
- Bake for 15 minutes, increase oven temperature to 350° and bake for another 15 minutes. Loaves may be frozen if tightly wrapped.

Nancy Cantor
Plantation, Florida

KASHA BREAD

Yield: 2 loaves

1 cup ground kasha or groats
2½ cups boiling water
2 tablespoons butter or margarine
1 tablespoon salt
3 tablespoons sugar or honey
1 tablespoon molasses
¾ cup milk

2 packages dry yeast
¼ cup warm (105° to 115°) water
4 cups all-purpose flour
2 cups whole wheat flour
1 medium-sized onion, diced
1 tablespoon butter, melted

- In 2-quart saucepan, cook kasha in boiling water for 10 minutes or until liquid is absorbed. Remove from heat.
- Add butter, salt, sugar, molasses and milk to kasha and mix well.
- Dissolve yeast in warm water; add to cooled kasha mixture.
- In large mixing bowl, combine flours; add kasha mixture and knead for about 10 minutes.
- Place dough in greased bowl and let rise, covered, in warm place until doubled in bulk.
- Sauté onion in butter in small skillet until onion is transparent.
- Punch down dough, knead a few times and shape to form 2 loaves, incorporating onion. Place in greased 9x5x3-inch loaf pans. Let rise, covered, until doubled in bulk.
- Preheat oven to 350°.
- Bake for about 35 minutes or until done.
- Serve warm or cold.

Evelyn Garb
Sarasota, Florida

CRUSTY CASSEROLE BREAD

Yield: 1 loaf

2 cups milk
¼ cup butter or margarine
2 tablespoons sugar
2 teaspoons salt
2 packages dry yeast

½ cup warm (105° to 115°) water
6 cups all-purpose flour
2 tablespoons melted butter
2 tablespoons grated Parmesan cheese

- In small saucepan, heat milk until bubbles form around edge of pan; remove from heat. Stir in ¼ cup butter, sugar and salt, mixing until butter is melted. Cool to lukewarm.
- In large mixing bowl, dissolve yeast in warm water. Add cooled milk mixture.
- Using hand electric mixer, add 3 cups flour, beating at medium speed for 2 minutes or until batter is smooth. Scrape sides of bowl and beaters. Gradually add remaining flour, mixing by hand for about 2 minutes or until dough is smooth and stiff. Place dough in greased 2-quart round casserole.
- Let rise in warm place for 1 hour or until dough rises above rim of casserole.
- Preheat oven to 375°. Brush loaf with melted butter and sprinkle with cheese.
- Bake for 45 to 50 minutes or until loaf sounds hollow when rapped lightly. Remove from casserole and cool on wire rack.
- Serve slightly warm.

Note: To make herb bread, combine ½ teaspoon dried sage, ½ teaspoon ground nutmeg, 1 tablespoon caraway seed, 1 tablespoon anise and 2 tablespoons Parmesan cheese; add with last half of flour.

Bernice Goodman
Longboat Key, Florida

MIDDLE EASTERN POCKET BREAD

Pita

Yield: 14

2¼ cups warm (105° to 115°) water, divided
1 tablespoon dry yeast
1 teaspoon sugar
1 teaspoon olive oil
1 teaspoon salt
1 cup bread flour
4½ cups all-purpose flour

- In large mixing bowl, dissolve yeast in ¼ cup warm water with sugar. Let stand 10 minutes.
- Add remaining warm water, olive oil and salt; beat well.
- Using dough hook of electric mixer, beat in bread flour for 2 to 3 minutes. Gradually add all-purpose flour, kneading in enough to form elastic, nonsticking dough.
- Form dough into roll about 14 inches long. Cut into 14 slices, placing each 2 to 3 inches apart on lightly-floured surface. Cover with dry cloth, then with well-dampened cloth. Let slices rise for about 1 hour or until doubled in bulk.
- On lightly-floured surface, roll each dough piece into 6-inch circle; place 2 inches apart on baking sheet. Cover with dry cloth, then with dampened cloth. Let rise for 30 minutes; dough should be slightly less than doubled in bulk.
- Preheat oven to 475°.
- If gas-fueled oven, place 1 baking sheet on oven floor and bake for 4½ minutes. Dough will "balloon". Transfer baking sheet to top shelf of oven and place another baking sheet on oven floor; bake for 4½ minutes. Remove top baking sheet from oven, move lower sheet to top shelf and place third baking sheet on oven floor, continuing to remove, move and place sheets at 4½ minute intervals until all bread has been baked.
- If electric oven, follow same method but place baking sheets first on lowest oven shelf, not oven floor.
- As bread is removed from oven, stack rounds and wrap in dry towel, then in dampened towel, adding to stack and rewrapping. Allow all rounds to cool thoroughly. Loaves will deflate but pockets will remain. Store in plastic bags or freeze.
- Serve pita rewarmed.

Patti Hershorin
Sarasota, Florida

WHOLE WHEAT BREAD

Yield: 1 loaf

4 cups whole wheat flour
1¼ teaspoons baking soda
1 teaspoon salt
2 tablespoons melted honey

1 (8-ounce) carton plain yogurt
⅓ cup milk
Sunflower or sesame seeds

- Preheat oven to 375°.
- In large mixing bowl, combine flour, baking soda and salt.
- Stir in honey, yogurt and milk. Mix well.
- Spoon batter into greased 9x5x3-inch loaf pan. Sprinkle with seeds.
- Bake for 1 hour. Cool in pan 10 minutes, invert and cool on wire rack.
- Serve warm or cold.

Denise Shub
Marietta, Georgia

MOM BUNS

Yield: 12 to 15

2 cups all-purpose flour
2 teaspoons baking powder
1 tablespoon sugar
½ teaspoon salt
½ cup butter
1 egg

½ cup whipping cream
¼ cup melted butter
Sugar
Ground cinnamon
Chopped nuts
Raisins

- Preheat oven to 350°.
- In large mixing bowl, sift flour, baking powder, sugar and salt together. Crumble ½ cup butter into dry ingredients.
- In small mixing bowl, beat egg with whipping cream; add to dry ingredients and mix well.
- Divide dough into 3 portions. On lightly-floured surface, roll each to rectangular shape. Spread with melted butter and sprinkle with sugar, cinnamon, nuts and raisins. Roll, jellyroll fashion, then cut into 2-inch slices. Place on baking sheet.
- Bake for about 20 minutes or until lightly browned. Cool, then roll in confectioner's sugar.
- Serve cold or rewarmed.

Marian Pressman
Tamarac, Florida

POPPYSEED TEA RING

Serves: 16

6 tablespoons butter or margarine
⅔ cup water
2 packages dry yeast
½ teaspoon salt
4 cups all-purpose flour
⅓ cup plus 2 tablespoons sugar,
  divided

1 egg
1 teaspoon vanilla
2 (2¾-ounce) jars poppyseed
Orange juice
1 tablespoon grated orange peel

- In small saucepan, heat butter and water until very warm.
- Using electric mixer, combine yeast, salt, 1 cup flour, ⅓ cup sugar and butter liquid; beat on low speed until blended.
- Add egg, vanilla and 1 cup flour; beat for 2 minutes. Stir in 1 cup flour.
- On well-floured surface, knead dough for about 10 minutes or until smooth, working in remaining flour and shaping dough into a ball. Grease dough ball and let rise, covered, in a warm place for 1 hour.
- On lightly-floured surface, roll dough to 22x12-inch rectangle.
- In small bowl, combine poppyseed with enough orange juice to form spreading consistency; add sugar and orange peel. Spread mixture over dough.
- Starting at long side, roll, jellyroll fashion. Cut roll lengthwise in half; keeping cut sides up, twist two lengths and place on greased baking sheet. Shape into a ring, tucking ends under to seal.
- Let rise, covered, for 30 minutes or until doubled in bulk.
- Preheat oven to 350°.
- Bake for 30 minutes or until golden brown.

Glaze

Confectioner's sugar

1 tablespoon water

- In small mixing bowl, combine sugar and water. Brush glaze over hot tea ring.
- Serve warm.

Ceil Burack
Delray Beach, Florida

YEAST COFFEE CAKE

Serves: 12

1 package dry yeast
¾ cup lukewarm (105° to 115°) milk
1 cup sugar, divided
3 eggs, separated
1 cup melted butter or margarine

3 cups all-purpose flour
Pinch of salt
1 teaspoon ground cinnamon
Raisins
Ground cinnamon and sugar blend

- In large mixing bowl, dissolve yeast in warm milk. Stir in ½ cup sugar, 3 egg yolks, butter, flour and salt; blend until mixture leaves sides of pan and forms a soft ball.
- Chill, covered, overnight.
- Let dough stand at room temperature for 30 minutes to 1 hour.
- Preheat oven to 350°.
- Beat egg whites until stiff. Add remaining sugar and cinnamon to egg whites and beat well.
- On lightly-floured surface, roll half of dough to form 14x12-inch rectangle. Spread with half of egg white mixture, sprinkle with raisins and roll up, jellyroll fashion. Place in half of greased fluted 10-inch tube pan. Repeat with remaining dough and ingredients.
- Let rise, covered, in a warm place until dough reaches top of baking pan. Brush with egg white and sprinkle with blend of cinnamon and sugar.
- Bake for 1 hour. Cool in pan.

Ruth Yaeger
Boca Raton, Florida

RAISED DOUGH COFFEE CAKE

Serves: 12

2 packages dry yeast
½ cup warm (105° to 115°) milk
½ cup sour cream
1¼ cups sugar, divided
1 cup unsalted margarine, softened
3 eggs, separated

2 teaspoons vanilla
4 cups sifted all-purpose flour
2 teaspoons ground cinnamon
1 cup chopped walnuts
1 cup raisins

- In small mixing bowl, dissolve yeast in warm milk. Stir in sour cream.
- In large mixing bowl, cream ¼ cup sugar and margarine until smooth. Add egg yolks, 1 at a time, beating after each addition. Stir in vanilla.
- Alternately add yeast mixture and flour to creamed mixture, mixing well.
- Chill, covered with plastic wrap, overnight.
- Let dough stand at room temperature for 1 hour.
- On lightly-floured pastry cloth, roll dough to form large circle.
- In small mixing bowl, beat egg whites with 1 cup sugar until consistency of marshmallow. Spread meringue on dough.
- Sprinkle cinnamon, walnuts and raisins over meringue.
- Cut dough circle into 6 wedges; roll, jellyroll fashion, and place in greased baking pan, cut side down.
- Let rise at room temperature for about 2 hours.
- Preheat oven to 325°.
- Bake for 1 hour.
- Serve freshly baked or toasted. Coffee cake may be frozen.

Esther H. Salk
Lake Worth, Florida

QUICK AND EASY MONKEY BREAD

Serves: 8 to 10

½ cup chopped nuts
1 (25-ounce) package frozen dinner
  rolls
¾ cup firmly-packed brown sugar
1 teaspoon ground cinnamon

1 (3½-ounce) package vanilla pudding
  mix (not instant)
6 tablespoons butter or margarine,
  melted

- The evening before serving, sprinkle nuts in bottom of greased 10-inch tube or fluted tube pan.
- Place rolls on nuts. Sprinkle with brown sugar, cinnamon and dry pudding mix. Pour melted butter over rolls.
- Let stand, covered with waxed paper, at room temperature overnight.
- Preheat oven to 350°.
- Bake for 30 minutes. Immediately invert on serving plate.
- Serve warm.

Joanne R. Kooden
Savannah, Georgia

BANANA BREAD

Yield: 2 loaves

½ cup vegetable oil
1 cup sugar
2 eggs, beaten until light
1¼ cups all-purpose flour

1 teaspoon baking powder
1 teaspoon baking soda
3 large or 4 small bananas
1 teaspoon ground cinnamon

- Preheat oven to 350°.
- Using electric mixer, beat oil and sugar together for 2 minutes in large mixing bowl.
- Add eggs to oil mixture; beat well.
- Sift flour, baking powder and baking soda together; add to egg mixture and beat for 2 minutes.
- In separate bowl, mash bananas with cinnamon; add to batter and beat until well blended.
- Pour batter into 2 well greased 9x5x3-inch loaf pans.
- Bake for 45 to 50 minutes. Cool 10 minutes in pans, invert and cool on wire rack.
- Serve warm or cold. Bread may be frozen.

Pearl Ansell
Orlando, Florida

CRANBERRY-BANANA QUICK BREAD

Yield: 1 loaf

1 cup pecans
1½ cups fresh or frozen cranberries
2 medium-large ripe bananas, cut in
  pieces
1 cup sugar
¼ cup butter or margarine,
  cut in pieces

¼ cup milk
1 egg
2 (1-inch) strips orange peel
2 cups all-purpose flour
1 tablespoon baking powder
½ teaspoon salt
¾ teaspoon ground cinnamon

- Preheat oven to 350°.
- Using food processor, process pecans with steel blade with on/off until chopped; remove from bowl.
- Process cranberries with on/off until finely chopped; remove and drain excess juice.
- Rinse processor bowl, then combine bananas, sugar, butter, milk, egg and orange peel; process until smooth.
- Combine flour, baking powder, salt and cinnamon; add to processor bowl and mix with 3 on/off turns, just until flour is blended. Do not overmix.
- Place batter in large mixing bowl. Fold in pecans and cranberries.
- Spoon batter into 1 greased 9x5x3-inch loaf pan or 2 greased 5x3x2-inch loaf pans.
- Bake large loaves for 60 minutes or small loaves for 45 minutes. Cool in pan 10 minutes, invert and cool on wire rack.

- Serve warm or cold. Loaves may be frozen.

Lynne Billing
Tampa, Florida

MANGO BREAD

Yield: 2 loaves

2 cups all-purpose flour
1½ cups sugar
2 teaspoons baking soda
½ teaspoon salt
2 teaspoons ground cinnamon

3 eggs, lightly beaten
¾ cup vegetable oil
1 cup chopped walnuts
2 cups diced mango

- Preheat oven to 325°.
- In large mixing bowl, combine flour, sugar, baking soda, salt and cinnamon.
- Add eggs and oil; beat thoroughly.
- Stir in walnuts and mango.
- Spoon batter into 2 greased 9x5x3-inch loaf pans or 4 greased 5x3x2-inch loaf pans.
- Bake for 1 hour or until wooden pick inserted near center comes out clean. Cool in pans 10 minutes, invert and cool on wire rack.
- Serve warm or cold.

Betty Siegel
Delray Beach, Florida

GRAHAM NUT BREAD

Yield: 1 loaf

2⅓ cups finely crushed graham
   cracker crumbs (28 squares)
½ cup sugar
½ teaspoon salt
2½ teaspoons baking powder

1 cup chopped walnuts
3 eggs, beaten
½ cup milk
½ cup melted margarine
2 tablespoons grated orange peel

- Preheat oven to 375°.
- In large mixing bowl, combine cracker crumbs, sugar, salt, baking powder and walnuts.
- In small mixing bowl, combine eggs, milk, margarine and orange peel.
- Add liquid mixture to dry ingredients; stir until blended. Pour batter into greased 9x5x3-inch loaf pan.
- Bake for 45 minutes. Cool in pan 10 minutes, invert and cool on wire rack.
- Serve warm or cold.

Selma Shore
Boca Raton, Florida

DATE NUT BREAD

Yield: 2 or 3 loaves

1 teaspoon baking soda
¾ cup warm water
1 cup chopped walnuts
1 cup dates, cut in thirds

1 egg
¾ cup sugar
1¾ cups sifted all-purpose flour

- Preheat oven to 300°.
- Dissolve soda in warm water in measuring cup.
- In small mixing bowl, combine walnuts and dates; add soda mixture. Let stand, covered.
- Using electric mixer, beat egg. Add sugar and beat until creamy.
- Drain water from walnut-date mixture. Alternately add liquid and flour to egg-sugar mixture. Stir in walnuts and dates.
- Spoon batter into 2 or 3 well greased 16-ounce fruit or vegetable cans, filling about two-thirds full.
- Bake for 45 minutes. Let rest in cans for about 5 minutes. Use knife to release bread from sides of cans. Cool on wire rack.
- Slice into rounds to serve warm or cold. Bread may be frozen.

Rose Wallerstein
West Palm Beach, Florida

PUMPKIN BREAD

Yield: 1 loaf

¼ cup butter, softened
¾ cup firmly-packed light brown sugar
2 eggs
¾ cup puréed pumpkin

1⅔ cups all-purpose flour
1 tablespoon baking powder
½ teaspoon salt
½ teaspoon ground allspice

- Preheat oven to 350°.
- In large mixing bowl, cream butter and sugar until smooth. Add eggs 1 at a time, beating well after each addition. Stir in pumpkin and mix thoroughly.
- Sift flour, baking powder, salt and allspice together. Add to pumpkin mixture and stir just until smooth.
- Spoon batter into 1 well-greased 9x5x3-inch loaf pan or 2 5x3x2-inch loaf pans.
- Bake large loaf for 40 to 50 minutes and small loaves for 35 minutes. Cool 10 minutes in pan, invert and cool on wire rack.
- Serve warm with cream cheese as spread.

Judy Jay
Atlanta, Georgia

LEMON BREAD

Yield: 1 loaf

1½ cups sifted all-purpose flour
1 cup sugar
½ teaspoon salt
1 teaspoon baking powder

2 eggs
½ cup milk
½ cup vegetable oil
1½ teaspoons grated lemon peel

- Preheat oven to 350°.
- In large mixing bowl, combine flour, sugar, salt and baking powder.
- In small mixing bowl, beat eggs, milk, oil and peel together. Add liquids to dry ingredients and mix just until blended.
- Pour batter into greased and floured 9x5x3-inch loaf pan.
- Bake for 45 to 50 minutes or until wooden pick inserted near center comes out clean.

Glaze

4½ teaspoons lemon juice   ⅓ cup sugar

- Combine lemon juice and sugar in small saucepan. Heat until sugar is dissolved.
- After removing bread from oven, poke holes with skewer from top to bottom of loaf. Drizzle hot glaze over loaf, allowing it to soak into bread. Cool in pan for 20 to 30 minutes. Remove and cool on wire rack.
- Serve warm or cold. Bread may be frozen.

Louise Berman
Lauderhill, Florida

PUMPKIN-PECAN BREAD

Yield: 4 loaves

3½ cups all-purpose flour
2 teaspoons baking soda
1½ teaspoons salt
1½ teaspoons ground cinnamon
1 teaspoon ground nutmeg
1 cup sugar

1 cup vegetable oil
4 eggs
⅔ cup water
1 (16-ounce) can pumpkin
1 cup chopped pecans

- Preheat oven to 350°.
- In large mixing bowl, sift flour, baking soda, salt and spices together. Add sugar and blend thoroughly.
- Make a well in center of dry ingredients. Add together the oil, eggs, water and pumpkin. Stir in pecans.
- Spoon batter into 4 greased 8½x4½x3-inch loaf pans, filling each ½ full.
- Bake for 1 hour or until wooden pick inserted near center comes out clean. Cool in pan 10 minutes, invert and cool on wire rack.
- Serve warm or cold.

Dorothy Kodish
Tampa, Florida

ZUCCHINI BREAD

Yield: 2 loaves

3 cups all-purpose flour
1 teaspoon baking powder
1 teaspoon baking soda
1 teaspoon salt
1½ teaspoons ground cinnamon

2 cups sugar
1 cup vegetable oil
3 eggs
2 cups shredded zucchini
1 cup chopped pecans or other nuts

- Preheat oven to 350°.
- In large mixing bowl, sift flour, baking powder, baking soda, salt and cinnamon together.
- Using electric mixer, blend in sugar, oil, eggs and zucchini. Stir in pecans.
- Spoon batter into 2 well-greased 8½x4½x3-inch loaf pans.
- Bake for 1 hour. Cool in pan 10 minutes, invert and slice.
- Serve cold. Bread may be frozen.

Elaine Gruenhut
Atlanta, Georgia

STRAWBERRY BREAD

Yield: 1 loaf

3 cups all-purpose flour
2 cups sugar
1 teaspoon baking soda
1 teaspoon salt
1 teaspoon ground cinnamon
2 (10-ounce) packages frozen
  strawberries, thawed and drained
  with juice reserved

1¼ cups vegetable oil
4 eggs, well beaten
Confectioner's sugar

- Preheat oven to 350°.
- In large mixing bowl, combine flour, sugar, baking soda, salt and cinnamon.
- Add strawberries, oil and eggs; beat thoroughly.
- Pour batter into greased and floured 9x5x3-inch loaf pan.
- Bake for 1 hour, then place "tent" of aluminum foil over loaf, reduce oven temperature to 325° and bake for 15 to 20 minutes.
- Combine strawberry juice and confectioner's sugar to form glaze of pouring consistency; pour over hot loaf in pan. Cool.
- Serve cold. Bread may be frozen.

Louise Berman
Lauderhill, Florida

CHEESE MUFFINS

Yield: 15 to 18

2½ tablespoons melted butter
3 eggs
1 teaspoon vanilla
½ cup biscuit baking mix

¼ to ½ cup sugar
2 (12-ounce) cartons small curd
  cottage cheese
¼ cup sour cream

- Preheat oven to 350°.
- In large mixing bowl, blend butter, eggs and vanilla.
- Stir in biscuit mix and sugar and mix well.
- Add cottage cheese and sour cream.
- Spoon batter into non-stick muffin pans, filling each cup ¾ full.
- Bake for 45 minutes or until golden brown.
- Serve with dollop of sour cream. Muffins may be frozen. Place in toaster oven and heat thoroughly.

Lillian W. Shucard
Delray Beach, Florida

BRAN MUFFINS

Yield: 12

2 bananas, mashed
1 teaspoon baking soda
1 egg
½ cup vegetable oil
Grated peel of 1 orange
¼ cup orange juice

½ to ¾ cup sugar
1 cup all-purpose flour
1 teaspoon baking powder
1 cup bran
½ cup raisins

- Preheat oven to 400°.
- In small mixing bowl, blend bananas and baking soda.
- In another small bowl, combine egg, oil, peel, juice and sugar, beating until smooth.
- In medium-sized mixing bowl, sift flour with baking powder. Stir in bran and raisins. Add banana and egg mixtures to dry ingredients; mix just until blended.
- Spoon batter into paper-lined muffin pans.
- Bake for 20 to 25 minutes or until lightly browned.
- Serve warm or cold.

Dorothy Freistadt
Lake Worth, Florida

WHOLE WHEAT MUFFINS

Yield: 12

1 cup all-purpose flour
¾ cup whole wheat flour
2 teaspoons baking powder
½ teaspoon salt

1 egg, beaten
¼ cup honey
1 cup milk
¼ cup vegetable oil

- Preheat oven to 400°.
- In medium-sized mixing bowl, combine flours, baking powder and salt.
- In small mixing bowl, combine egg, honey, milk and oil; mix thoroughly. Add egg mixture to dry ingredients, stirring just until moistened; do not overmix. Batter will not be smooth.
- Spoon batter into greased muffin pans, filling cups ¾ full.
- Bake for 20 minutes or until lightly browned.
- Remove muffins immediately to cool on wire rack.
- Serve warm.

Carol A. Glazer
Cape Coral, Florida

POPOVERS

Yield: 12

2 eggs
1 cup milk
1 cup all-purpose flour

½ teaspoon salt
1 teaspoon butter

- Preheat oven to 450°.
- In medium-sized mixing bowl, combine eggs, milk, flour and salt; add butter in small bits. Mix just until blended; batter will be lumpy.
- Pour batter into well-greased muffin pans.
- Bake for 30 minutes.
- Serve immediately.

Carol Sue Press
Hollywood, Florida

FRUITED POULTRY STUFFING

Serves: 8 to 10

1 challah loaf, torn in small pieces
Water
1 (6-ounce) package chopped prunes
1 (6-ounce) package dried apples
1 (8-ounce) package dried peaches or apricots or dried mixed fruit

2 quarts boiling water
1 cup coarsely chopped walnuts or pecans
½ cup melted margarine
1 (7-ounce) can clear chicken broth
Salt to taste (optional)

- In large mixing bowl, soak challah in water; squeeze to remove excess moisture.
- Simmer dried fruits in boiling water for 5 minutes. Drain and chop coarsely.
- In large mixing bowl, combine challah, fruit and nuts. Stir in margarine and broth and mix well. Season with salt if desired.
- Spoon stuffing into turkey cavity and roast turkey.
- Stuffing may be baked separately from turkey. Preheat oven to 375°. Spoon mixture into baking dish prepared with non-stick vegetable spray.
- Bake for 30 minutes or until lightly browned. Stuffing freezes well and may be reheated by microwave oven. Different dried or fresh fruits (no simmering required) may be substituted.

Paula Woolf
Miami, Florida

VEGETABLES

BROCCOLI-RICE CASSEROLE

Serves: 6

1 (10-ounce) package frozen chopped broccoli
1 (10-ounce) package yellow rice mix
1 onion, diced
½ green pepper, diced

1 tablespoon butter or margarine
½ (8-ounce) jar pasteurized process cheese spread
1 (10¾-ounce) can cream of mushroom soup, undiluted

• Prepare broccoli and rice according to package directions.
• Preheat oven to 325°.
• In small skillet, sauté onion and green pepper in butter until tender.
• In large mixing bowl, combine broccoli, rice, sautéed vegetables, cheese spread and soup; mix well.
• Pour mixture into 2-quart casserole.
• Bake for 30 minutes.
• Serve hot. Casserole may be assembled several hours before baking.

Wendy Feinberg
Atlanta, Georgia

BROCCOLI SURPRISE

Serves: 6

2 (10-ounce) packages frozen chopped broccoli
1 (10-ounce) package frozen peas
1 (8-ounce) jar pasteurized process cheese spread

1 (10¾-ounce) can cream of mushroom soup, undiluted
1 loaf challah or French bread
½ cup butter or margarine, melted

• Prepare broccoli and peas according to package directions. Drain. Combine in large mixing bowl.
• In saucepan over low heat, melt cheese. Stir in soup, beat until smooth and heat until well blended.
• Add cheese sauce to vegetables and mix well. Pour mixture into 8x8x2-inch baking pan.
• Preheat oven to 350°.
• Tear inside of bread into large chunks, dip in margarine and place on broccoli mixture to form topping.
• Bake, uncovered, for 30 minutes or until browned.
• Serve hot.

Joanne R. Kooden
Savannah, Georgia

BROCCOLI AU GRATIN

Serves: 6

1 large bunch broccoli or 2 (10-ounce) packages frozen broccoli
¼ cup plus 3 tablespoons butter or margarine, divided
¼ cup all-purpose flour
2 cups scalded milk
1 teaspoon salt
Dash of white pepper
½ pound mushrooms, sliced
1 cup grated Parmesan or Cheddar cheese
½ cup dry breadcrumbs

- Cook fresh broccoli in salted boiling water or prepare frozen broccoli according to package directions. Drain.
- In 1-quart saucepan, melt ¼ cup butter. Blend in flour. Cook, stirring constantly, for 2 to 3 minutes. Remove from heat. Add milk and beat with wire whisk to prevent lumping. Cook over low heat, stirring until thickened. Add seasonings. Remove from heat.
- Preheat oven to 350°.
- In small skillet, sauté mushrooms in 2 tablespoons butter for 5 minutes.
- In 2-quart casserole, layer ⅓ each of broccoli, mushrooms, sauce and cheese; repeat layers twice, ending with cheese. Sprinkle with breadcrumbs and dot with 1 tablespoon butter.
- Bake for 20 minutes.
- Serve hot.

Barbara Shulman
Raleigh, North Carolina

CORN AND BROCCOLI BAKE

Serves: 10

2 (10-ounce) packages frozen chopped broccoli, thawed
1 (8-ounce) can cream-style corn
2 eggs, lightly beaten
Salt and pepper to taste
2 tablespoons grated onion
2 cups breadcrumbs, divided
¼ cup plus 2 tablespoons margarine, melted

- Preheat oven to 350°.
- In large mixing bowl, combine broccoli, corn, eggs, salt, pepper, onion, 1 cup breadcrumbs and margarine; mix thoroughly.
- Spread vegetable mixture in greased 13x9x2-inch baking pan. Sprinkle with 1 cup breadcrumbs.
- Bake for 35 minutes.
- Serve hot.

Fay S. Wiegler
Boca Raton, Florida

SWEET AND SOUR RED CABBAGE

Serves: 6 to 8

1 large red onion, sliced
1 tablespoon butter or margarine
4 pounds red cabbage, shredded
1 large tart apple, grated
2 teaspoons sour salt

2 tablespoons firmly-packed brown
  sugar
½ teaspoon freshly-ground pepper
½ cup raisins

- In large skillet, sauté onion in butter until tender.
- Add cabbage, apple, salt, brown sugar, pepper and raisins, mixing with wooden spoon.
- Simmer, covered, for 1 hour.
- Serve hot.

Betty Warner
Boca Raton, Florida

CARROT SOUFFLÉ

Serves: 6

1 pound carrots, steamed until tender
½ cup margarine
½ cup honey
3 eggs
3 tablespoons all-purpose flour
1 teaspoon ground cinnamon

⅛ teaspoon nutmeg
1 teaspoon vanilla
¼ cup corn flakes
3 tablespoons firmly-packed brown
  sugar
¼ cup chopped pecans

- Preheat oven to 350°.
- In blender container or food processor bowl, combine carrots, margarine, honey, eggs, flour, cinnamon, nutmeg and vanilla; blend until smooth.
- Pour carrot mixture into greased 13x9x2-inch baking pan.
- In small mixing bowl, combine corn flakes, brown sugar and pecans. Sprinkle over carrot mixture.
- Bake, uncovered, for 45 minutes.
- Serve hot.

Alison Augenstein
Atlanta, Georgia

BAKED APPLES AND CARROTS

Serves: 6 to 8

3 medium Granny Smith apples, sliced
8 carrots, sliced
¼ cup firmly-packed brown sugar
¼ cup butter or margarine, softened

⅛ teaspoon nutmeg
Salt and pepper to taste
2 tablespoons chopped parsley for
  garnish

- Preheat oven to 350°.
- In large mixing bowl, combine apples, carrots, brown sugar, butter, nutmeg, salt and pepper; mix well. Spread mixture in 2-quart casserole.
- Bake for 1 hour.
- Serve hot, garnished with parsley.

Elise Dolgow
Parkland, Florida

THE BEST CARROT PUDDING

Serves: 8 to 10

1 pound carrots, peeled and cut in
  ½-inch slices, cooked
3 eggs
3 tablespoons matzo cake meal
1 teaspoon baking powder

1 cup sugar
1 teaspoon vanilla
½ cup margarine, melted
⅛ teaspoon cinnamon

- Preheat oven to 350°.
- Place cooked carrots and eggs in food processor bowl; process until smooth.
- Add cake meal, baking powder, sugar, vanilla, margarine and cinnamon; mix for a few seconds.
- Pour batter into greased 9x5x3-inch loaf pan or casserole.

Topping

2 tablespoons margarine, softened
3 tablespoons firmly-packed brown
  sugar

1 tablespoon matzo meal
Dash of cinnamon

- In small mixing bowl, combine margarine, brown sugar, meal and cinnamon with a fork. Sprinkle topping over carrot batter.
- Bake for 45 minutes. Cool in pan 10 minutes, remove and cool on wire rack.
- Serve warm or cold. Pudding may be doubled by increasing carrots to 2 to 3 pounds but use ¾ cup margarine and 1½ cups sugar.

Elaine Gruenhut
Atlanta, Georgia

CARROTS VERONIQUE

Serves: 4 to 6

1 pound carrots, cut in julienne strips
½ cup orange juice, divided
¼ teaspoon salt

2 tablespoons butter or margarine
1½ teaspoons cornstarch
1 cup seedless grape halves

- In 2-quart microwave-safe casserole, combine carrots, ¼ cup orange juice and salt. Cook, covered, on high (100%) for 6 to 8 minutes or until carrots are crisp-tender. Add butter and stir until melted.
- In small mixing bowl, blend cornstarch and ¼ cup orange juice; add to carrots. Cook, uncovered, on high for 2 to 3 minutes or until thickened, stirring every 30 seconds. Stir in grapes.
- Serve immediately.

Cookie Berman
Tamarac, Florida

VEGETABLE EGG FOO YUNG

Serves: 2

4 eggs, beaten
½ teaspoon salt, divided
2 teaspoons soy sauce, divided
1 cup bean sprouts, chopped
1 cup chopped onion, green pepper,
mushrooms, baby corn, water
chestnuts or combination

¼ cup vegetable oil
1 cup beef bouillon or soup stock
1 tablespoon cornstarch

- In medium-sized mixing bowl, combine eggs, ¼ teaspoon salt, 1 teaspoon soy sauce, sprouts and vegetables.
- In wok or small skillet, pour ½ cup egg mixture into hot oil. Cook, pushing edges to form 4-inch cake; when egg is fairly set, turn cake and brown on other side. Remove and keep warm; repeat with remaining egg mixture.
- In small saucepan, combine 1 teaspoon soy sauce, ¼ teaspoon salt, bouillon and cornstarch; whisk until cornstarch is dissolved. Cook over medium heat until sauce is thickened.
- Serve cakes hot with sauce.

Peppe Dragoni
Seminole, Florida

CORN PUDDING

Serves: 8

2 eggs, lightly beaten
1 (16-ounce) can whole kernel corn, drained
1 (16-ounce) can cream-style corn

1 (10-ounce) package corn muffin mix
1 (8-ounce) carton sour cream
¼ cup butter, softened
¼ cup sugar (optional)

- Preheat oven to 350°.
- In large mixing bowl, combine all ingredients. Pour into greased 2-quart casserole.
- Bake for 40 to 50 minutes; pudding should be firm.

Janet Weismark
Nashville, Tennessee

EGGPLANT STRATA

Serves: 12

1 large eggplant, skin removed and sliced
Vegetable oil
1 teaspoon paprika
2 teaspoons dried oregano
1 large onion, cut up
3 green peppers, cut up

3 cloves garlic, crushed
2 tablespoons butter
6 mushrooms (optional)
4 stalks celery, sliced (optional)
6 pods okra, sliced (optional)
1 (15-ounce) can tomato sauce
¼ cup grated Parmesan cheese

- Salt eggplant slices; let stand 1 hour. Rinse to remove salt and remove excess moisture with paper towel.
- In small mixing bowl, combine small amount of oil, paprika and oregano. Rub eggplant slices with paste. Cut slices into quarters.
- In large saucepan, sauté onion, green peppers and garlic in 2 tablespoons butter until tender. Remove from heat. Add eggplant and mix lightly. Add mushrooms, celery and okra.
- Preheat oven to 375°.
- In 2-quart casserole, layer ½ of eggplant mixture, tomato sauce and cheese; repeat layers.
- Bake for 40 minutes or until eggplant is tender.
- Serve hot.

Margaret Newman Stearn
Miami Beach, Florida

EGGPLANT ZITI BAKE

Serves: 4 to 6

1 cup ziti
¼ cup plus 1 tablespoon olive oil,
  divided
1 medium eggplant, diced
1 medium zucchini, diced
1 medium-sized yellow squash, diced
2 red peppers, diced
1 onion, diced

1 clove garlic, crushed
1 cup mushrooms, quartered
1 (15-ounce) can tomato sauce
Pepper to taste
1 tablespoon dried oregano
1 (4-ounce) package shredded
  mozzarella cheese

- Prepare ziti according to package directions. Drain. Add 1 tablespoon olive oil and toss until well coated.
- Preheat oven to 375°.
- In large skillet, cook vegetables in ¼ cup olive oil until crisp-tender. Stir in ziti, tomato sauce and seasonings.
- Pour mixture into 2-quart casserole. Sprinkle with cheese.
- Bake for 15 minutes.
- Serve hot.

Beverly Pechenik
North Miami Beach, Florida

EGGPLANT AFGHANISTAN

Serves: 4

1 medium-sized onion
¼ cup margarine
1 large eggplant, peeled and cut in
  ⅛-inch slices

1 (16-ounce) can stewed tomatoes
1 (8-ounce) carton plain yogurt or
  sour cream
Salt

- Preheat oven to 300°.
- In greased 12x8x2-inch baking dish, sauté onion in margarine in oven.
- Score eggplant slices, place on dry dish towel and lightly salt both sides. Let stand 15 minutes or until towel absorbs moisture from slices.
- Arrange slices over onion in baking dish.
- In small mixing bowl, combine tomatoes and yogurt. Pour over eggplant.
- Bake for 45 minutes or until tender, basting with sauce every 20 minutes.
- Place in serving dish, spooning sauce over eggplant slices, and serve hot.

Freda Majzlin
Boca Raton, Florida

SCALLOPED EGGPLANT

Serves: 4

1 large eggplant, peeled and cubed
Boiling water
2 or 3 onions, diced
1 cup diced green pepper
¼ cup margarine

1 (8-ounce) package Swiss or Cheddar
  cheese or combination, grated
½ cup seasoned breadcrumbs
2 eggs
Salt and pepper to taste

- In 1½-quart saucepan, cook eggplant in boiling water for about 10 minutes. Drain and mash.
- In small skillet, sauté onions and green peppers in margarine for 15 minutes.
- Preheat oven to 300°.
- Reserving small amount of cheese and breadcrumbs, add remainder to eggplant along with sautéed vegetables, eggs, salt and pepper. Spread mixture in greased 12x8x2-inch baking dish. Sprinkle with reserved cheese and breadcrumbs.
- Bake for 30 minutes.
- Serve hot.

Note: For soufflé effect, separate eggs; add yolks to eggplant, beat whites until stiff and fold into eggplant mixture.

Evelyn Savino
Boca Raton, Florida

BARLEY AND MUSHROOMS

Serves: 8

1 pound mushrooms
½ cup plus 3 tablespoons butter or
  margarine, divided
2 large onions, chopped

2 cups medium barley
2 (10½-ounce) cans chicken broth,
  divided

- Preheat oven to 350°.
- In large skillet, cook mushrooms in 3 tablespoons butter until soft; remove from skillet.
- Sauté onions and barley in ¼ cup butter until onions are translucent.
- Add mushrooms and mix well. Pour into 2½-quart casserole. Add 1 can chicken broth.
- Bake, covered, for 30 minutes. Add second can of broth and bake, covered, for 30 minutes.
- Serve hot.

Delcy P. Harber
Dunwoody, Georgia

ARTICHOKES AND MUSHROOMS

Serves: 6 to 8

1 (9-ounce) package frozen artichokes
1 pound mushrooms, halved
2 tablespoons water
¼ cup sliced green onion
2 tablespoons butter or margarine
2 tablespoons all-purpose flour
1 teaspoon chicken bouillon granules

¼ teaspoon dried thyme
Dash of nutmeg
½ (4-ounce) package Swiss cheese, shredded
½ (8-ounce) carton sour cream
½ cup coarsely chopped pecans, toasted

- Place artichokes in colander and rinse with running cold water until separated; drain. Cut in halves lengthwise.
- In 2-quart microwave-safe casserole, combine artichokes, mushrooms and 2 tablespoons water. Cook, covered, on high (100%) for 8 to 10 minutes, stirring twice. Drain liquid.
- In 4-cup glass measuring cup, combine onion and butter. Cook, covered, on high for 2 minutes.
- Stir in flour, bouillon, thyme, nutmeg and ⅔ cup water. Cook, uncovered, on high for 2 to 3 minutes, stirring after each minute.
- Stir in cheese, mixing until melted. Fold in sour cream.
- Add cheese sauce to vegetables. Cook, uncovered, on high for 2 minutes, stirring once. Add pecans.
- Serve hot.

Cookie Berman
Tamarac, Florida

CHEESE STUFFED PEPPERS

Serves: 4

1 egg, beaten
3½ slices bread, crumbled
2 cups creamy cottage cheese
Salt to taste
1 tablespoon sugar or to taste

4 large Italian peppers (do not substitute)
1 (8-ounce) carton sour cream
½ cup cereal flake crumbs
¾ cup melted butter or margarine

- Preheat oven to 375°.
- In large mixing bowl, combine egg and bread. Add cottage cheese, salt and sugar.
- Cut thin slice from top of peppers and remove seeds.
- Spoon cottage cheese filling into peppers. Spread sour cream on top of filling and sprinkle with cereal crumbs. Place in 13x9x2-inch baking pan. Pour butter on and around peppers. Arrange peppers so sides nearly touch.
- Bake, uncovered, for 45 minutes or until peppers are tender.
- Serve hot. Peppers may be assembled in advance and stored in refrigerator until time to bake.

Jean Weiss
Fort Lauderdale, Florida

GRANDMA DIAMOND'S POTATO KUGEL

Serves: 6 to 8

2 large onions, chopped
⅓ cup chicken fat
6 medium potatoes, peeled and grated
3 eggs, beaten

½ cup all-purpose flour
½ teaspoon baking powder
1½ teaspoons salt
½ teaspoon pepper

- In small skillet, brown onions in fat.
- Preheat oven to 350°.
- In large mixing bowl, combine onions, potatoes, eggs, flour, baking powder, salt and pepper; mix thoroughly. Spread mixture in greased 12x8x2-inch baking pan.
- Bake for 1 hour; kugel will be browned.
- Serve hot.

Dana Gilbert
St. Petersburg, Florida

CRISP ONION ROASTED POTATOES

Serves: 4 to 6

4 to 6 potatoes, unpeeled and
  quartered
1 envelope onion soup mix
½ cup olive oil

¼ cup melted margarine
1 teaspoon dried thyme
1 teaspoon marjoram
¼ teaspoon pepper

- Preheat oven to 450°.
- Arrange potatoes in 1 layer in 13x9x2-inch baking pan.
- In small mixing bowl, combine soup mix, oil, margarine and seasonings. Pour over potatoes.
- Bake, uncovered, for 30 minutes; turn potatoes and continue baking for 30 minutes.
- Serve hot.

Alison Augenstein
Atlanta, Georgia

POTATOES DEL MONICA

Serves: 4

6 potatoes, cooked, cooled, peeled and
  diced
1 large onion, chopped
1½ cups half and half
½ cup butter

¾ teaspoon salt
¼ teaspoon pepper
Breadcrumbs
Grated Parmesan cheese

- In large saucepan, combine cooked potatoes, onion, half and half, butter and seasonings. Cook over medium heat, stirring frequently, until sauce is thickened.
- Preheat oven to 375°.
- Pour into greased 13x9x2-inch baking dish. Sprinkle with breadcrumbs and Parmesan cheese.
- Bake for 1 hour; potatoes will be browned.
- Serve hot. Potatoes may be prepared to point of baking, then frozen. Thaw at room temperature before baking.

Lisa Epner
Cary, North Carolina

GRANDMA'S POTATO LATKES

Serves: 10 to 12

1 large onion, diced
1 tablespoon butter or margarine
3 cups grated potatoes
3 eggs
½ cup all-purpose flour

½ teaspoon baking powder
Salt and pepper to taste
Peanut oil
Applesauce
Sour cream

- In small skillet, sauté onions in butter until browned.
- In large mixing bowl, combine onions, potatoes, eggs, flour, baking powder and seasonings; mix well.
- Drop potato mixture by tablespoonfuls into hot peanut oil in large skillet. Fry until brown on each side and crispy. Add oil as necessary.
- Serve hot with applesauce and sour cream.

Dana Gilbert
St. Petersburg, Florida

VIDALIA ONION PIE

Serves: 6

4 cups sliced Vidalia onion
½ cup margarine, divided
1 cup crushed saltine crackers
4 eggs, lightly beaten

1½ cups milk
1 (6-ounce) package Cheddar cheese, shredded

- Preheat oven to 350°.
- In large skillet, sauté onions in ¼ cup margarine until tender and yellow.
- Melt ¼ cup margarine in 10-inch pie plate. Pour crushed crackers into plate and press to form crust. Spoon onions into crust.
- In medium-sized mixing bowl, combine eggs and milk. Pour over onions. Sprinkle with cheese.
- Bake, uncovered, for 30 minutes.
- Serve hot.

Joanne R. Kooden
Savannah, Georgia

SPINACH-BROCCOLI CASSEROLE

Serves: 6

1 (10-ounce) package frozen chopped broccoli
1 (10-ounce) package frozen chopped spinach
2 tablespoons vinegar
1 (10¾-ounce) can cream of mushroom or cream of celery soup, undiluted
½ teaspoon salt
¼ teaspoon pepper
¼ teaspoon dried tarragon
1 (2¾-ounce) can French fried onion rings
2 medium tomatoes, peeled and quartered
½ cup grated Cheddar or American cheese

- Prepare broccoli and spinach according to package directions, adding vinegar to pan liquid. Drain.
- Preheat oven to 325°.
- In large mixing bowl, combine soup and seasonings. Fold in vegetables. Spoon mixture into 12x8x2-inch baking dish. Arrange onions and tomatoes on broccoli-spinach mixture. Sprinkle with cheese.
- Bake for 35 minutes.
- Serve hot.

Phyllis Klain
Coconut Creek, Florida

SPINACH CHEESE PUDDING

Serves: 12 to 18

6 eggs, beaten
Salt and pepper to taste
3 (10-ounce) packages frozen chopped spinach, thawed and well drained
1 medium-sized onion, chopped
2 (15-ounce) cartons ricotta cheese
¼ cup matzo meal
¼ cup vegetable oil

- Preheat oven to 350°.
- In large mixing bowl, combine eggs, salt, pepper, spinach, onion, cheese and meal.
- Prepare a 13x9x2-inch baking pan with oil; add excess oil to spinach mixture. Mix well. Spread mixture in pan.
- Bake for 45 minutes.
- Serve hot. Pudding may be frozen.

Barbara Shulman
Raleigh, North Carolina

SPINACH PIE

Serves: 6 to 8

¼ pound mushrooms, sliced
½ green pepper, chopped
2 tablespoons butter
1 (15-ounce) carton ricotta cheese
1 (4-ounce) package shredded
  mozzarella or Cheddar cheese
2 tablespoons oil

½ teaspoon salt
¼ teaspoon pepper
1 teaspoon onion salt
1 (10-ounce) package frozen chopped
  spinach, thawed and drained
½ cup sliced zucchini
3 eggs, lightly beaten

- In small skillet, sauté mushrooms and green pepper in butter until tender.
- Preheat oven to 350°.
- In large mixing bowl, combine cheeses, oil, seasonings, spinach, zucchini, mushrooms, green pepper and eggs; mix well. Spread mixture in oiled 12x8x2-inch baking dish.
- Bake for 40 minutes. Cool.
- Cut into squares and serve warm or at room temperature.

Rochelle Derman
Atlanta, Georgia

GREEK SPINACH PIE

Serves: 8

1 onion, minced
1 tablespoon vegetable oil
2 (10-ounce) packages frozen chopped
  spinach, thawed and well drained
1 (8-ounce) package farmer cheese
1 (12-ounce) carton cottage cheese
½ cup shredded mozzarella cheese
  (optional)

1 tablespoon plain yogurt (optional)
2 eggs, beaten
Salt and pepper to taste
Dill weed to taste
½ cup grated Parmesan cheese
  (optional)

- In large skillet, cook onion in oil until tender. Stir in spinach and cook for time indicated on package directions.
- Preheat oven to 375°.
- In large mixing bowl, combine cheeses (except Parmesan), yogurt, eggs, seasonings and spinach-onion mixture. Spread in greased 13x9x2-inch baking pan. Sprinkle with Parmesan cheese.
- Bake for 45 minutes or until lightly browned.
- Serve hot.

Eileen Ginzburg
North Miami Beach, Florida

QUICKIE QUICHE

Serves: 6

1 unbaked 9-inch pastry shell
3 tablespoons margarine or butter,
  divided
¼ cup chopped onion
1 (10-ounce) package frozen chopped
  spinach, cooked and drained
1 tablespoon mayonnaise
3 or 4 eggs, beaten
2 tablespoons sour cream

1 (4-ounce) package shredded
  mozzarella, Cheddar, Monterey Jack
  or 1 cup cottage cheese
Salt and pepper to taste
All-purpose seasoning to taste
Nutmeg to taste
1 (2¾-ounce) can French fried onion
  rings or ½ cup cracker crumbs
Grated Parmesan cheese to taste

- Bake pastry shell in 9-inch pie plate according to package directions, piercing bottom with fork tines and spread with 2 tablespoons margarine.
- If necessary, adjust oven temperature to 350°.
- In small skillet, sauté onion in 1 tablespoon butter. Spread onion in bottom of baked shell.
- In large mixing bowl, combine spinach, mayonnaise, eggs, sour cream, shredded cheese and seasonings. Pour over onion layer in shell. Sprinkle with fried onions or crumbs and top with Parmesan cheese.
- Bake for 30 minutes or until bubbly.
- Serve hot.

Nancy Taffel
Atlanta, Georgia

MEATLESS EASY TZIMMES

Serves: 6 to 8

1 (28-ounce) can yams, drained
2 (16-ounce) cans carrots, sliced and
  drained
1 (16-ounce) package pitted prunes

Ground cinnamon
Brown sugar
1 cup orange or pineapple juice
Margarine

- Preheat oven to 350°.
- In greased 10x10x2-inch baking dish, layer yams, carrots and prunes, sprinkling each layer with cinnamon and brown sugar. Pour juice over vegetables and fruit. Dot with margarine.
- Bake, uncovered, for 1 hour.
- Serve hot.

Note: Amounts of yams, carrots and prunes may be varied.

Evie Lehman
Tamarac, Florida

TZIMMES

Serves: 4 to 6

1 pound carrots, sliced
2 pounds sweet potatoes, peeled and
quartered
Salt
Boiling water
1 (16-ounce) can crushed pineapple
with juice

½ to 1 cup pitted prunes
1 cup orange juice
½ cup honey
½ teaspoon salt (optional)
½ teaspoon ground cinnamon
¼ cup margarine

- In large saucepan, cook carrots and sweet potatoes in salted boiling water to cover until vegetables are tender but firm. Drain.
- Preheat oven to 350°.
- Place carrots, sweet potatoes, pineapple and prunes in 2-quart casserole.
- In small mixing bowl, combine orange juice, honey and seasonings; pour over vegetables and fruit. Dot with margarine.
- Bake, covered with aluminum foil, for 30 minutes; stir, then bake, uncovered, for 10 minutes.
- Serve hot. Canned sweet potatoes in syrup may be substituted but reduce amount of honey.

Mildred Rakofsky
Tamarac, Florida

BRANDIED SWEET POTATO-APPLE CASSEROLE

Serves: 8 to 10

1 (28-ounce) can sweet potatoes,
drained
6 baking apples, cut in wedges
½ lemon
1 (11-ounce) can mandarin oranges,
drained

1 (10-ounce) package miniature
marshmallows
½ cup sugar
1 teaspoon ground cinnamon
2 to 3 tablespoons liquid margarine
½ cup brandy

- Preheat oven to 350°.
- In 3-quart casserole, layer ½ of each sweet potato slices or wedges, apples sprinkled with lemon juice, oranges, marshmallows and sugar mixed with cinnamon; repeat with remaining ingredients. Pour margarine over top, then add brandy.
- Bake, covered, for 1 hour.
- Serve hot.

Betty S. Allan
Coral Springs, Florida

AMARETTO SWEET POTATOES

Serves: 12

5 pounds yams
20 gingersnaps, finely crushed or
  ground
¾ cup margarine, divided

¼ cup firmly-packed brown sugar
¼ cup amaretto
¼ cup orange marmalade
½ teaspoon salt

- Preheat oven to 375°. Bake yams until soft.
- In small mixing bowl, combine gingersnap crumbs and ½ cup margarine; mix well and chill.
- When baked yams are cool to touch, scoop out pulp. In large mixing bowl, mash potatoes with ¼ cup margarine, sugar, amaretto, marmalade and salt; beat until creamy. Spread mixture in ovenproof serving dish. Spoon gingersnap crumbs around edges.
- Bake for 30 minutes, then broil for 2 to 3 minutes to brown.
- Serve hot. Potatoes may be prepared a day in advance to point of baking.

Beverly Kamenetzky
West Palm Beach, Florida

SQUASH SOUFFLÉ

Serves: 6

1 (10-ounce) package frozen squash,
  thawed
¼ cup sugar
½ cup all-purpose flour
Dash of salt

3 eggs
2 cups milk
¼ cup margarine, melted
Ground nutmeg

- Preheat oven to 350°.
- In large mixing bowl, combine squash, sugar, flour, salt, eggs, milk and margarine. Beat with whisk until smooth.
- Pour mixture into greased 1-quart casserole. Sprinkle with nutmeg.
- Bake for 1 hour.
- Serve hot. Soufflé should not be frozen.

Frances "Dottie" Sherman
Fort Lauderdale, Florida

STIR-FRY ZUCCHINI AND PEARS

Serves: 6

2 cloves garlic, minced
½ cup thinly sliced onion
½ teaspoon salt
¼ teaspoon crumbled dried oregano
¼ teaspoon crumbled dried basil

1½ tablespoons olive oil
3 cups thinly sliced zucchini
2 medium Bartlett pears, cored and
  sliced
1 teaspoon grated Parmesan cheese

- In 10-inch skillet or wok, stir-fry garlic and onion seasoned with salt, oregano and basil in olive oil for 1 minute. Add zucchini and stir-fry for 5 minutes or until zucchini is tender.
- Add pears to zucchini, mixing gently. Sprinkle with cheese. Steam, covered, for 5 minutes or until pears are thoroughly heated and cheese is melted.
- Serve immediately. Dish may be prepared to point of adding pears and frozen. Thaw at room temperature.

Linda Kahn
Miami, Florida

ZUCCHINI CASSEROLE

Serves: 8

1 large zucchini, cut up
1 onion, sliced
Water
1 large carrot, shredded
1 (10¾-ounce) can cream of
  mushroom soup, undiluted

1 (8-ounce) carton sour cream
Salt and pepper to taste
½ cup margarine
1 (8-ounce) package herb-seasoned
  stuffing mix

- In 2-quart saucepan, simmer zucchini and onion in water to cover for 10 minutes or until tender. Drain well.
- Add carrot, soup, sour cream, salt and pepper to zucchini and onion.
- Preheat oven to 350°.
- In small saucepan, melt margarine. Add stuffing mix and toss until well coated.
- Spoon ½ of stuffing into 11x9x1½-inch baking pan. Spread zucchini mixture over stuffing; sprinkle with remaining stuffing.
- Bake for 15 to 20 minutes until bubbly.
- Serve hot.

Anne Gaynor
Tamarac, Florida

ZUCCHINI QUICHE

Serves: 6

1 medium-sized onion, chopped
2 tablespoons butter
2 medium zucchini, sliced
2 eggs
1 (8-ounce) package shredded
mozzarella cheese

1 (8-ounce) package refrigerated
crescent rolls
Dijon mustard

- In small skillet, sauté onion in butter until browned. Add zucchini and sauté until zucchini is tender.
- Preheat oven to 350 °.
- In medium-sized mixing bowl, combine eggs and cheese. Add vegetables and mix well.
- Place roll dough in 10-inch quiche pan, pressing to close perforations. Spread with mustard. Add vegetable mixture.
- Bake for 20 minutes or until lightly browned.
- Serve hot.

Barbara Kushner
Plantation, Florida

ZUCCHINI PUDDING

Serves: 4

3 or 4 medium zucchini, sliced
1 cup seasoned breadcrumbs
1 (4-ounce) package Parmesan cheese,
crumbled

3 tablespoons margarine
¼ cup grated Romano cheese

- Preheat oven to 350°.
- Layer ⅓ each of zucchini, breadcrumbs, Parmesan cheese and dots of margarine in 8x4x3-inch loaf pan prepared with non-stick vegetable spray; repeat layers twice. Sprinkle with Romano cheese and remaining margarine.
- Bake for 50 minutes.
- Serve hot. Pudding may be assembled in advance and baked just before serving.

Zelda Magid
North Miami Beach, Florida

ZUCCHINI LATKES

Serves: 6 to 8

2 pounds zucchini, grated
1 medium-sized onion, minced
½ cup all-purpose flour
2 eggs, lightly beaten

3 tablespoons grated Parmesan cheese
1 teaspoon salt (optional)
Freshly ground pepper to taste
Vegetable oil

- Place zucchini in colander, cover with plate and press to remove all excess moisture.
- In medium-sized mixing bowl, combine zucchini, onion, flour, eggs, cheese, salt and pepper; mix well.
- In 10-inch skillet, carefully drop batter by large tablespoonfuls into hot oil. Fry until golden, turning when edges are browned. Drain on paper towel.
- Serve immediately. Latkes may be frozen; reheat on brown paper in 350° oven.

Linda Kahn
Miami, Florida

VEGETABLE CUTLETS

Serves: 2

½ cup chopped onion
½ cup chopped green pepper
2 large carrots, grated
2 tablespoons butter or margarine
2 tablespoons grated zucchini

2 cups breadcrumbs
2 eggs, beaten
¼ cup milk
Salt and pepper to taste
Breadcrumbs

- In small skillet, sauté onion, green pepper and carrots in butter until tender. Remove from heat. Stir in zucchini and breadcrumbs.
- Preheat oven to 350°.
- In small mixing bowl, combine eggs, milk and seasoning. Stir into vegetable mixture. Shape into cutlets and coat with breadcrumbs. Place on baking sheet.
- Bake for 30 minutes or until browned.
- Serve hot.

Betty Jackel
Delray Beach, Florida

RATATOUILLE

Serves: 8

1 large onion, chopped
2 cloves garlic, minced
¼ cup olive oil
1 large or 2 medium eggplant, chopped
1 large or 2 medium zucchini, chopped
2 green peppers, chopped
½ cup mushrooms, chopped

4 or 5 large tomatoes or 1 (6-ounce) can tomato paste
Salt and pepper to taste
1 teaspoon dried oregano or marjoram
1 teaspoon dried basil
1 tablespoon chopped parsley or flakes
1 teaspoon sugar

- In 8-quart stockpot, cook onion and garlic in oil until tender.
- In order, add eggplant, zucchini, green peppers, mushrooms and tomatoes to onion-garlic mixture. Season with salt, pepper, oregano, basil, parsley and sugar.
- Simmer vegetables for 45 minutes to 1 hour. 1 (6-ounce) can tomato paste may be added to thicken if necessary; check to determine if more sugar is needed.
- Serve hot or cold.

Sue Rosenbluth
Largo, Florida

SWISS VEGETABLE MEDLEY

Serves: 6

1 (16-ounce) package frozen broccoli-carrots-cauliflower combination, thawed
1 (10¾-ounce) can cream of mushroom soup, undiluted
1 (4-ounce) package Swiss cheese, shredded

⅓ cup sour cream
¼ teaspoon pepper
1 (4-ounce) jar chopped pimentos, drained (optional)
1 (2¾-ounce) can French fried onions

- Preheat oven to 350°.
- In large mixing bowl, combine vegetables, soup, ½ cup cheese, sour cream, pepper, pimentos and ½ of onions. Spread mixture in 1-quart casserole.
- Bake, covered, for 30 minutes. Sprinkle with remaining cheese and onions and bake, uncovered, for 5 minutes.
- Serve hot.

Delcy P. Harber
Dunwoody, Georgia

PASTA
&
RICE

BAKED MANICOTTI WITH CHEESE FILLING

Serves: 8

Sauce

1½ cups minced onion	2 tablespoons chopped parsley
1 clove garlic, crushed	1 tablespoon sugar
⅓ cup olive or vegetable oil	1 teaspoon dried oregano
1 (35-ounce) can Italian tomatoes, undrained	1 teaspoon dried basil
	¼ teaspoon pepper
1 (6-ounce) can tomato paste	1½ cups water

- In 5-quart Dutch oven, cook onion and garlic in oil for 5 minutes. Add remaining ingredients, mashing tomatoes with fork. Bring to a boil, then simmer, stirring occasionally, for 1 hour.

Manicotti

6 eggs or equivalent egg substitute, at room temperature	1½ cups unsifted all-purpose flour
	1½ cups water

- In large bowl of electric mixer, combine eggs, flour and water; beat until smooth. Let stand for 30 minutes or longer.
- Heat 8-inch skillet over medium heat. Pour 3 tablespoons batter into skillet, rotating to spread batter evenly. Cook until surface is dry but down side is not overbrowned. Place on wire rack to cool. Repeat with remaining batter. As manicotti cool, stack with waxed paper sheets to separate.

Filling

2 (15-ounce) cartons ricotta cheese	2 eggs or equivalent egg substitute
1 (8-ounce) package mozzarella cheese, diced	¼ teaspoon pepper
	1 tablespoon chopped parsley
⅓ cup grated Parmesan cheese	Grated Parmesan cheese

- Preheat oven to 350°.
- In large mixing bowl, combine cheeses, eggs, pepper and parsley; beat with wooden spoon until well mixed.
- Spread ¼ cup filling down each manicotti and roll up.
- Spoon sauce into 16x10x2-inch baking pan. Place 10 manicotti rolls, seam side down, in sauce. Add second layer of 6 manicotti and cover with sauce. Sprinkle with Parmesan cheese.

- Bake for 30 minutes or until sauce is bubbly. Manicotti may be baked in two 9x9x2-inch baking pans and frozen.
- Serve hot.

Beverly Pechenik
North Miami Beach, Florida

LASAGNE FLORENTINE

Serves: 5 to 6

1 (15-ounce) carton ricotta cheese or
2 cups cottage cheese
1 (6-ounce) package shredded
mozzarella cheese, divided
1 egg
1 (10-ounce) package frozen chopped
spinach, thawed and drained

1 teaspoon salt
⅛ teaspoon pepper
¾ teaspoon dried oregano
1 (32-ounce) jar spaghetti sauce
1 (16-ounce) package lasagne noodles,
cooked
1 cup water

- In large mixing bowl, combine ricotta cheese, 1 cup mozzarella cheese, egg, spinach and seasonings.
- Preheat oven to 350°.
- Pour ½ cup sauce into 13x9x2-inch baking pan prepared with non-stick vegetable spray. In order, add layer of noodles (do not overlap), ½ of cheese mixture, sauce, noodles, remaining cheese mixture, noodles and remaining sauce. Sprinkle with ½ cup mozzarella.
- Using knife, gently push layers from sides of pan and pour water around edge.
- Bake, covered with aluminum foil, for 1 hour and 15 minutes.
- Let stand 15 minutes before cutting. Serve hot. Lasagne may be frozen.

Betty Jackel
Delray Beach, Florida

SPINACH LASAGNE

Serves: 6

1 (15-ounce) carton ricotta cheese
1 (8-ounce) package shredded
  mozzarella cheese, divided
1 egg
1 (10-ounce) package frozen chopped
  spinach, thawed and drained

1 teaspoon dried oregano
Dash of pepper
1 (32-ounce) jar spaghetti sauce
½ (16-ounce) package lasagne noodles,
  uncooked
1 cup water

- Preheat oven to 350°.
- In large mixing bowl, combine ricotta cheese, 1 cup mozzarella cheese, egg, spinach, oregano and pepper.
- In greased 13x9x2-inch baking pan, pour 1 cup sauce, add single layer of noodles and half of cheese mixture; repeat layers and end with remaining noodles and sauce.
- Sprinkle with 1 cup mozzarella. Pour water around edges of pan.
- Bake, tightly covered with aluminum foil, for 1 hour and 15 minutes.
- Let stand 15 minutes before serving. Lasagne may be assembled in advance and stored in refrigerator until ready to bake or may be frozen.

Anne Rosenberg
Pembroke Pines, Florida

MEATLESS LASAGNE

Serves: 6 to 8

1 (32-ounce) jar meatless spaghetti
  sauce
¼ cup minced onion
1 clove garlic, minced
¾ teaspoon salt
⅛ teaspoon pepper
½ teaspoon dried oregano

2 tablespoons parsley flakes
½ (16-ounce) package lasagne noodles,
  uncooked
¼ cup grated Parmesan cheese
1 (8-ounce) package shredded
  mozzarella cheese
1 (8-ounce) carton ricotta cheese

- In medium-sized mixing bowl, combine sauce, onion, garlic and seasonings.
- In 12x8x2-inch baking dish, layer, in order, ¼ of sauce, ⅓ of noodles, and ⅓ of cheeses; repeat layers twice, ending with sauce.
- Cook, covered with plastic wrap, on high (100%) for 10 minutes; cook on medium (50%) for 30 to 40 minutes.
- Let stand 5 minutes to firm.
- Serve hot.

Clare Klugman
Fort Lauderdale, Florida

VEGETARIAN SPAGHETTI

Serves: 4

½ to 1 cup chopped onion
1 clove garlic, minced
1 tablespoon margarine
1 (8-ounce) can tomato sauce
2 tablespoons tomato paste

½ cup water
½ cup shredded mild Cheddar or
 American cheese
1 (8-ounce) package spaghetti, cooked
 and drained

- In 10-inch skillet, sauté onion and garlic in margarine until vegetables are tender but not browned.
- Stir in tomato sauce and paste and water; simmer, uncovered, for about 10 minutes or until thickened.
- Add cheese to sauce and stir until melted. Add spaghetti and cook, covered, until thoroughly heated.
- Serve hot.

Adrienne B. Stoun
Sarasota, Florida

MARINARA SAUCE WITH SPAGHETTI

Serves: 6 to 8

3 cloves garlic, sliced
3 tablespoons olive oil
1 (28-ounce) can crushed Italian
 tomatoes
½ (8-ounce) can tomato sauce
1½ cups chopped parsley

2 teaspoons dried oregano
3 tablespoons dried basil or 1 cup
 chopped fresh basil
Salt and pepper to taste
1½ (16-ounce) packages spaghetti,
 cooked and drained

- In Dutch oven, cook garlic in oil until fork-tender and slightly browned on edges.
- Add tomatoes, tomato sauce, herbs and seasonings to garlic. Simmer, covered, for 45 minutes.
- Serve hot over spaghetti. Sauce may be prepared 1 day in advance and stored in refrigerator in non-metallic container or frozen.

Paula DiRoma-Luongo
Hallandale, Florida

VEGETABLE ZITI

Serves: 8 to 10

1 (32-ounce) jar marinara sauce
1 (16-ounce) package ziti, cooked and
drained
1 (8-ounce) package mozzarella
cheese, grated and divided
1 (10-ounce) package frozen chopped
spinach, thawed and drained

2 tablespoons chopped parsley
1 (15-ounce) carton ricotta cheese
Salt and pepper to taste
½ cup grated Parmesan cheese, divided

- Preheat oven to 350°.
- In large mixing bowl, combine 2 cups sauce with ziti. Add 1 cup mozzarella cheese, spinach, parsley, ricotta cheese, salt, pepper and ¼ cup Parmesan cheese.
- Pour 1 cup sauce into 13x9x2-inch baking pan prepared with non-stick vegetable spray. Spread ziti mixture in pan, spoon 1 cup sauce over mixture and sprinkle with ¼ cup Parmesan cheese.
- Bake for 25 minutes, add 1 cup mozzarella cheese and bake for 10 to 15 minutes.
- Serve hot.

Arlene Gelber
Boca Raton, Florida

PASTA SALAD DELIGHT

Serves: 6 to 8

1 (16-ounce) package spiral pasta,
cooked, drained and chilled
½ bunch broccoli, cut in florets
3 small zucchini, sliced
3 tomatoes, cubed
3 carrots, sliced
1 large red pepper, sliced
1 large green pepper, sliced

1 large sweet onion, sliced
1 (4-ounce) can black olives
1 (4-ounce) package Swiss cheese,
diced
1 (4-ounce) package American cheese,
diced
1 (8-ounce) bottle Italian dressing
1 hard-cooked egg, diced

- In large mixing bowl, combine pasta, vegetables and cheeses; toss to mix thoroughly.
- Pour dressing over salad and mix well. Pour salad into serving bowl and sprinkle with egg.
- Serve cold with warm garlic bread.

Pearl Belous
North Miami Beach, Florida

SPINACH NOODLE PUDDING
(Parve)

Serves: 8

1 (16-ounce) package medium
  noodles, cooked and drained
¾ cup margarine (parve), melted
1 (16-ounce) carton coffee creamer
5 eggs
2 envelopes onion soup mix

2 (10-ounce) packages frozen chopped
  spinach, thawed and well drained
Breadcrumbs
Paprika
Margarine

- Preheat oven to 375°.
- In large mixing bowl, combine noodles, margarine and creamer. Add eggs, 1 at a time, mixing gently but thoroughly. Add soup mix and spinach.
- Spoon mixture into 3-quart casserole prepared with non-stick vegetable spray. Sprinkle with breadcrumbs and paprika and dot with margarine.
- Bake for 40 minutes. Let stand 10 minutes.
- Serve hot. Pudding may be frozen.

Tillie R. Sidman
Lake Worth, Florida

NOODLES FLORENTINE

Serves: 6

½ (12-ounce) package egg noodles,
  cooked and well drained
2 tablespoons butter
2 tablespoons all-purpose flour
1 cup milk
1 (10-ounce) package frozen chopped
  spinach, thawed and well drained

Dash of hot pepper sauce
Few drops Worcestershire sauce
1 teaspoon salt
⅛ teaspoon freshly ground nutmeg
1 tablespoon chopped parsley
1 to 2 tablespoons dry white wine or
  vermouth

- In 2-quart saucepan over low heat, melt butter. Blend in flour. Gradually add milk, stirring constantly to prevent lumps; cook over medium heat until thickened and smooth. Remove from heat.
- Preheat oven to 350°.
- Add spinach and seasonings to white sauce. Stir in wine and mix gently.
- Pour noodles into buttered 12x8x2-inch baking dish. Pour spinach sauce over noodles and mix lightly.
- Bake for 15 to 20 minutes.
- Serve hot.

Terrie Temkin
Hollywood, Florida

SWISS CHEESE-NOODLE CASSEROLE

Serves: 12

1 (8-ounce) package medium noodles,
  cooked and drained
1 (12-ounce) carton cottage cheese
½ cup chopped scallion greens
1 tablespoon minced celery

2 tablespoons chopped parsley
½ (8-ounce) package Swiss cheese
  slices, torn in small pieces
Parmesan cheese

- Preheat oven to 350°.
- In large mixing bowl, combine noodles, cottage cheese, scallions, celery, parsley and Swiss cheese; mix gently but thoroughly.
- Spread mixture in greased 13x9x2-inch baking dish. Sprinkle generous layer of Parmesan cheese over mixture.
- Bake for 25 to 30 minutes or until browned.
- Serve hot. Casserole may be prepared a day in advance and baked for 15 to 20 minutes. Cool, store in refrigerator and return to room temperature before finishing baking time.

Ellen Goldstein
Atlanta, Georgia

APPLE NOODLE KUGEL

Serves: 10 to 12

1 (16-ounce) package medium noodles
½ cup plus 2 tablespoons margarine or
  butter
4 eggs, lightly beaten
¾ cup sugar
¾ teaspoon ground cinnamon
1 teaspoon vanilla

1 cup orange juice or milk
2 large apples, sliced or diced
½ cup raisins
1 cup crushed sugar-coated cereal
  flakes
Ground cinnamon
Margarine

- Prepare noodles according to package directions but cook for 8 minutes. Drain. Add ½ cup plus 2 tablespoons margarine to noodles and toss until margarine is melted.
- Preheat oven to 350°.
- Add eggs, sugar, cinnamon, vanilla and juice to noodles; mix gently but thoroughly. Fold in apples and raisins.
- Spread noodle mixture in greased 13x9x2-inch baking pan. Sprinkle with cereal and cinnamon. Dot with margarine.
- Bake on center oven shelf for 1 hour; noodles will be browned.
- Serve warm.

Sylvia Kowal
Pembroke Pines, Florida

MANDARIN KUGEL

Serves: 8 to 10

1 (8-ounce) package very thin noodles
1 (8-ounce) carton sour cream
½ cup butter
½ cup sugar
1 teaspoon vanilla
4 eggs

1 (8-ounce) can crushed pineapple, drained
1 (11-ounce) can mandarin oranges, drained
Ground cinnamon
Sugar

- Prepare noodles according to package directions.
- While noodles cook, combine sour cream, butter, sugar, vanilla and eggs in large mixing bowl, blending until smooth and creamy.
- Preheat oven to 350°.
- Drain noodles and add to creamed mixture; mix well. Fold in pineapple and oranges.
- Spread noodle mixture in 12x8x2-inch baking dish. Sprinkle with cinnamon and sugar.
- Bake for 45 minutes or until browned crust forms at edge.
- Serve warm.

Wendy J. Katz
Sarasota, Florida

UPSIDE DOWN NOODLE BAKE

Serves: 16

1 (16-ounce) package medium noodles, cooked, rinsed and drained
1 (8-ounce) carton sour cream
⅓ cup sugar
Pinch of salt
4 eggs, beaten

1 cup cottage cheese
1 teaspoon vanilla
¼ cup butter or margarine
1 cup firmly-packed brown sugar
1 cup pecans

- In large mixing bowl, combine noodles, sour cream, sugar, salt, eggs, cottage cheese and vanilla; mix well.
- Preheat oven to 350°.
- In 13x9x2-inch baking pan, melt butter. Sprinkle brown sugar over margarine and press pecans into sugar layer.
- Carefully pour noodle mixture into pan to avoid disturbing pecans.
- Bake for 1 hour. Cool in pan 15 minutes, then invert on serving plate and cool 10 minutes.
- Serve warm. Pudding may be frozen.

Eve Saks
Plantation, Florida

PINEAPPLE NOODLE KUGEL

(Parve)

Serves: 16

1 (16-ounce) package medium
   noodles, cooked and drained
8 eggs
½ cup honey
½ cup sugar
1 (16-ounce) can crushed pineapple,
   drained

¾ cup melted margarine (parve)
Salt and pepper to taste
½ cup corn flake crumbs
1 teaspoon ground cinnamon
4 teaspoons sugar
¼ cup margarine (parve)

- Preheat oven to 350°.
- In large mixing bowl, combine noodles, eggs, honey, ½ cup sugar, pineapple, melted margarine, salt and pepper. Spread mixture in greased 13x9x2-inch baking pan.
- Sprinkle crumbs, then mixture of cinnamon and 4 teaspoons sugar over noodle mixture. Dot with margarine.
- Bake, uncovered, for 1 hour. Cool slightly before cutting in squares.
- Serve warm. Baked pudding may be frozen; reheat, covered with aluminum foil, at 325° for 35 to 45 minutes, removing foil for last 10 minutes.

Perry Stevens
Orlando, Florida

PINEAPPLE BREAD PUDDING

Serves: 6

5 slices fresh bread, torn in pieces
¼ cup melted butter or margarine
½ cup sugar
½ teaspoon salt

3 eggs, well beaten
1 (20-ounce) can crushed pineapple
   with juice

- Preheat oven to 350°.
- In large mixing bowl, combine bread, butter, sugar and salt; mix well.
- Stir in eggs and pineapple; blend thoroughly.
- Spread mixture in buttered 1-quart casserole.
- Bake for 1 hour.
- Serve warm.

Clare Klugman
Fort Lauderdale, Florida

DAIRY NOODLE PUDDING

Serves: 8 to 10

½ cup butter or margarine
1 (8-ounce) package medium noodles,
  cooked and drained
1 teaspoon salt
¾ cup sugar
4 eggs, lightly beaten

1 (8-ounce) carton sour cream.
2 cups cottage cheese
1 (8-ounce) package cream cheese,
  cubed
1 teaspoon vanilla
1 (21-ounce) can cherry pie filling

- Preheat oven to 375°.
- Melt margarine in 13x9x2-inch baking dish in oven; turn to evenly coat sides and bottom of pan.
- In large mixing bowl, pour excess margarine from baking dish over noodles; mix gently but thoroughly. Stir in salt, sugar, eggs, sour cream, cottage cheese, cream cheese and vanilla.
- Spread mixture in baking dish.
- Bake, covered with aluminum foil, for about 1 hour. Cool, then store in refrigerator until a few hours before serving.
- Preheat oven to 375°.
- Spoon pie filling over pudding surface and bake for 30 minutes.
- Serve hot or warm. Pudding may be prepared through first baking several days in advance and stored in refrigerator.

Harriet Kotler
Tamarac, Florida

RICE PUDDING

Serves: 4 to 6

3 eggs, beaten
½ cup sugar
2 cups scalded milk

1½ cups cooked rice
1 cup raisins
1 teaspoon vanilla

- Preheat oven to 325°.
- In large mixing bowl, combine eggs and sugar. Slowly add milk, mixing thoroughly. Stir in rice, raisins and vanilla.
- Pour into 1½-quart casserole. Place in baking pan; add water to pan to 1-inch depth.
- Bake for 1½ hours.
- Serve warm.

Frances Rutstein
Delray Beach, Florida

ORZO CASSEROLE

Serves: 6

1 (8-ounce) package orzo pasta
Water
1 envelope onion soup mix
½ cup slivered almonds
1 (4-ounce) can mushrooms

1 (6-ounce) can water chestnuts
¼ cup water
1 tablespoon chopped parsley
½ teaspoon pepper

- Prepare orzo according to package directions, cooking for 10 minutes. Drain.
- Preheat oven to 350°.
- In large mixing bowl, combine orzo, soup mix, almonds, mushrooms, water chestnuts, water, parsley and pepper. Spread mixture in greased 10x10x2-inch baking dish.
- Bake, covered, for 30 minutes.
- Serve hot. May be prepared in advance and stored in refrigerator or frozen.

Nadine King
Memphis, Tennessee

RICE JOAN

Serves: 10 to 12

1 (12-ounce) package thin noodles
1 cup margarine (parve)
3 (10½-ounce) cans chicken broth
1½ cups water

1½ envelopes onion soup mix
3 cups instant rice
1 (8-ounce) can sliced water chestnuts
1 (8-ounce) can sliced mushrooms

- In Dutch oven over medium heat, sauté noodles in margarine until golden brown.
- Stir in chicken broth and water; bring to a boil.
- Add soup mix, rice, water chestnuts and mushrooms. Simmer, covered, stirring occasionally, until liquid is absorbed.
- Serve hot.

Lesley J. Roth
Coral Springs, Florida

SPANISH RICE

Serves: 4

1½ cups instant rice
½ cup butter or margarine
1 medium-sized onion, grated

1 (10¾-ounce) can vegetable soup, diluted

- In large skillet, sauté rice in butter for 5 to 10 minutes or until rice is golden brown. Add onions and cook for a few minutes.
- Stir in diluted vegetable soup, remove from heat and let stand, covered, for 15 minutes.
- Serve hot. Rice may be prepared in advance and heated in oven.

Birdie Grace
Miami, Florida

DAVID'S PANCAKES

Serves: 2 to 4

½ cup all-purpose flour
½ cup milk
2 eggs, lightly beaten
Pinch of nutmeg

¼ cup butter
2 tablespoons confectioner's sugar
Juice of ½ lemon

- Preheat oven to 425°.
- In medium-sized mixing bowl, combine flour, milk, eggs and nutmeg; beat lightly, leaving batter slightly lumpy.
- In ovenproof 12-inch skillet, melt butter. Pour batter into skillet.
- Bake for 15 to 20 minutes or until golden brown.
- Sprinkle with confectioner's sugar and bake for a few minutes to melt sugar.
- Sprinkle with lemon juice. Serve hot with jelly, jam or marmalade.

Caroline Singer
Fort Lauderdale, Florida

CHALLAH SOUFFLÉ

Serves: 10

1 challah loaf, sliced
Butter
1 (12-ounce) package Monterey Jack cheese, grated
1 (12-ounce) package Cheddar cheese, grated

1 medium-sized onion, chopped
1 green pepper, diced
½ pound mushrooms, sliced
6 eggs
1 cup milk

- Spread butter on both sides of each challah slice. Place half the slices to form one layer in bottom of large buttered baking dish.
- Combine cheeses, then sprinkle half over bread slices; top with remaining bread.
- Combine onion, green pepper and mushrooms; spoon mixture over bread layer.
- In medium-sized mixing bowl, beat eggs; stir in milk and beat until thoroughly blended. Pour egg mixture over vegetable layer in baking dish.
- Chill, covered, for 12 to 24 hours.
- Bake at 350° for 1 to 1½ hours.
- Serve hot.

Robyn Haber
Miami, Florida

HEALTHY EATING

CHICKEN BOMBAY

Serves: 6

1 cup uncooked rice
1 (6-ounce) package dried mixed fruit
½ cup chopped onion
2 teaspoons curry powder, divided
1 teaspoon sugar or granulated sugar
substitute

2 cups water
1 (3-pound) broiler-fryer, skin
removed and cut in pieces
2 tablespoons vegetable oil
½ teaspoon paprika
Chopped parsley for garnish

- Preheat oven to 375°.
- In 12x8x2-inch baking dish, combine rice, fruit, onion, 1 teaspoon curry powder, sugar and water; mix thoroughly.
- Arrange chicken pieces over rice mixture.
- In small bowl, blend oil, paprika and 1 teaspoon curry powder. Brush sauce over chicken pieces.
- Bake, tightly covered with aluminum foil, for 1 hour or until chicken is tender and most of liquid is absorbed.
- Serve hot, garnished with parsley.

Cecilia Lieberman
Wesley Chapel, Florida

LITE CHICKEN

Serves: 4

1 (2½ to 3-pound) broiler-fryer, skin
removed and cut in 8 pieces
2 tablespoons fresh or reconstituted
lemon juice
Lite or low-salt soy sauce

½ teaspoon garlic powder
½ teaspoon onion powder
½ teaspoon paprika
1 tablespoon brown sugar substitute

- Place chicken pieces on broiler pan, meatier side down.
- Sprinkle, in order, with half of lemon juice, soy sauce, garlic powder and onion powder. Sprinkle generously with paprika. Sprinkle with brown sugar substitute.
- Broil for 15 to 20 minutes. Turn chicken pieces and repeat seasonings in same order. Broil for 10 minutes.
- Serve hot.

Florence Dash
Coral Springs, Florida

ISRAELI ORANGE CHICKEN

(Low Calorie)

Serves: 4 to 5

1 (3-pound) broiler-fryer, cut in pieces
¼ cup lemon juice
½ cup orange juice
1 teaspoon grated lemon or orange peel
¼ teaspoon dried tarragon

¼ teaspoon dried thyme
Salt and pepper to taste
1 teaspoon garlic powder
2 teaspoons paprika

- Preheat oven to 450°.
- Place chicken in single layer, skin side down, in shallow roasting pan.
- Bake for 20 to 25 minutes or until skin is crisp and rendered of all fat. Drain and discard excess fat.
- In small mixing bowl, combine juices, peel, tarragon and thyme; pour over chicken. Sprinkle with salt, pepper, garlic powder and paprika.
- Reduce oven temperature to 325°. Bake, basting occasionally with pan juices, for 20 to 30 minutes or until chicken is tender.
- Spoon sauce over chicken to serve.

Mildred Rakofsky
Lauderhill, Florida

PITA TACOS

Serves: 4

1 cup diced onion
1 cup diced green pepper
2 tablespoons margarine (parve)
1½ pounds ground turkey
1 (1¼-ounce) package taco seasoning
1 tablespoon minced garlic in oil
1 (8-ounce) can tomato sauce

4 rounds onion pita bread
Lettuce salad (optional)
Cole slaw (optional)
Diced raw onion (optional)
Diced tomato (optional)
Diced squash (optional)

- In skillet, sauté onion and green pepper in margarine until slightly soft. Add ground turkey and cook until turkey loses pink color and is well mixed with vegetables.
- Stir in taco seasoning, garlic and tomato sauce. Cook, covered, for about 20 minutes.
- Slice pita bread in half-circles and warm in toaster until halves open easily. Spoon 2 tablespoons meat mixture into each bread half; fill with choice of salad or vegetables.

Roz Beck
Coconut Creek, Florida

MEATLOAF

(Low Calorie)

Serves: 3

1 pound ground turkey
½ cup unsweetened applesauce
Crumbs of 2 slices lite bread (40
  calories per slice)

½ teaspoon rosemary
1 teaspoon minced onion (optional)
1 tablespoon gravy mix or tomato
  sauce

- In medium-sized mixing bowl, combine turkey, applesauce, breadcrumbs, rosemary and onion. Place in microwave-safe tube or muffin pan.
- Drizzle gravy mix or tomato sauce over meat mixture.
- Cook, uncovered, on high for 20 minutes for tube pan or 15 minutes for muffin pan, turning once or twice.
- Serve hot. Meatloaf may be doubled; extend cooking time by 10 minutes for tube pan and 5 minutes for muffins. If frozen, reheat at 60% power.

Lee Engel
Boca Raton, Florida

STUFFED TURKEY CABBAGE

Serves: 6

1 large head cabbage
Boiling water
2 onions, sliced
2 tablespoons vegetable oil
3 cups canned tomatoes
½ teaspoon pepper
1 pound ground turkey

3 tablespoons uncooked rice
¼ cup grated onion
2 tablespoons egg substitute
3 tablespoons cold water
3 tablespoons honey
¼ cup lemon juice
¼ cup seedless raisins

- Place cabbage in deep bowl or pan, cover with boiling water and let soak 15 minutes. Drain. Carefully remove 12 leaves; if leaves are small, use more.
- In deep saucepan, lightly brown sliced onions in oil. Add tomatoes and pepper. Simmer for 30 minutes.
- In small mixing bowl, combine turkey, rice, grated onion, egg substitute and water. Place portion of mixture on each cabbage leaf, fold side edges of cabbage over turkey and carefully roll, securing with wooden pick. Place stuffed rolls in tomato sauce and simmer, covered, for 1½ hours.
- Add honey, lemon juice and raisins to sauce and simmer additional 30 minutes.
- Serve hot, reminding diners of wooden picks. Cabbage rolls may be frozen.

Ruth Klein
Tampa, Florida

BAKED TOFU WITH CHEESE AND WINE

Serves: 4 to 6

2 medium-sized onions, minced
4 cloves garlic, crushed
3 tablespoons vegetable oil
1⅓ tablespoons margarine
1 pound mushrooms, chopped
½ teaspoon salt
½ teaspoon dried thyme

2 (16-ounce) packages tofu, drained
and pressed
1 (12-ounce) package Monterey Jack
or mild Cheddar cheese, grated
½ cup Rhine wine
1 tablespoon Worcestershire sauce
1 tablespoon sesame seeds

- Preheat oven to 350°.
- In large skillet, sauté onion and garlic in oil and margarine until translucent. Add mushrooms and salt; cook for 5 minutes, add thyme and cook for 5 minutes.
- Cut tofu into ½-inch cubes. Place half of cubes in bottom of oiled 2-quart casserole. Add layer of half of onion-mushroom mixture and cheese; repeat layers with remaining tofu, onion-mushroom mixture and cheese, reserving 2 to 3 tablespoons of cheese.
- Pour wine and Worcestershire sauce over layered ingredients and mix gently. Sprinkle with reserved cheese and sesame seeds.
- Bake, uncovered, for 20 minutes to warm tofu and melt cheese.
- Serve hot.

Barbara Robinson Feifer
Coral Springs, Florida

TOFU CASSEROLE

Serves: 4

1 large onion, chopped
1 green pepper, diced
2 tablespoons margarine
1 (16-ounce) package tofu, drained

Salt and pepper to taste
Garlic powder to taste
1 (15¾-ounce) jar spaghetti sauce
½ cup Parmesan cheese

- In large skillet, sauté onion and green pepper in margarine until soft.
- Add tofu to vegetables. Season with salt, pepper and garlic powder. Add spaghetti sauce, mixing well. Stir in cheese.
- Cook, covered, for 10 minutes.
- Serve hot as side dish or over spaghetti noodles or spaghetti squash as a main dish.

Debbie Lieberman
Palm Harbor, Florida

TOFU SALAD

Serves: 6

2 green onions
2 large cloves garlic
2 tablespoons lemon juice
2 tablespoons tehina

2 tablespoons tamari
1 (16-ounce) package tofu, well
drained and cut in large chunks

- Place onions, garlic, lemon juice, tehina and tamari in food processor bowl. Process, using metal blade, until well blended.
- Add tofu to onion mixture; process briefly.
- Serve with pita bread, lettuce and tomatoes or as a dip with vegetables or corn chips.

Florence Abramson
Sarasota, Florida

SWEET AND SOUR CABBAGE

(Low Sodium/Low Sugar)

Serves: 6 to 8

1 medium head cabbage
Boiling water
2 pounds ground turkey
¾ cup uncooked rice
1½ cups low sodium tomato sauce,
divided
¾ cup plus 3 tablespoons low sugar
catsup, divided

¼ onion, chopped
3 cups water
1 cup brown sugar substitute
1 tablespoon powdered sugar
substitute

- Remove core from cabbage and cook leaves in boiling water until pliable.
- In medium-sized mixing bowl, combine turkey, rice, ½ cup tomato sauce, 3 tablespoons catsup and onion. Spoon 1 tablespoon meat mixture on cabbage leaf, roll up and secure with wooden pick; repeat with remaining ingredients.
- In stockpot, combine 1 cup tomato sauce, water, brown sugar substitute, ¾ cup catsup and sugar substitute; heat thoroughly.
- Place cabbage rolls in sauce, along with any extra cabbage leaves.
- Simmer, covered, for 2 hours.
- Serve hot with sauce, reminding diners of wooden picks in rolls. Rolls may be baked, then frozen. Veal or beef may be substituted for turkey.

Nadine King
Memphis, Tennessee

SPICY RED CABBAGE
(No Fat)

Serves: 3 or 4

4 cups shredded red cabbage
½ cup unsweetened apple juice
1 teaspoon salt
½ teaspoon ground cinnamon
¼ teaspoon ground allspice

⅛ teaspoon ground nutmeg
2 large or 3 medium apples, peeled and shredded
2 packets granulated sugar substitute

- In 3-quart saucepan, combine cabbage, apple juice and seasonings. Cook, covered, over medium heat for 15 minutes, tossing several times.
- Add apples to cabbage mixture. Cook, covered, for 5 minutes. If more liquid is required during cooking, add 2 to 3 tablespoons water; all moisture should be evaporated at end of cooking time.
- Remove cabbage mixture from heat and stir in sugar substitute.
- Serve cold as a salad or warm as a vegetable side dish. Cabbage may be stored in refrigerator for 3 to 4 days.

Marlene Packler
Clearwater, Florida

EGGPLANT GOULASH

Serves: 4 to 6

2 cloves garlic, diced
2 onions, sliced
3 tablespoons olive oil
3 stalks celery, chopped
3 carrots, sliced in circles
2 potatoes, cut in chunks
1 cup cauliflower florets (optional)
½ teaspoon sea salt
½ teaspoon garlic powder

½ teaspoon dried oregano
½ teaspoon dried basil
2 green peppers, chopped
2 eggplants, peeled and cut into bite-sized pieces
½ cup green peas or ½ cup sliced green beans
1 (8-ounce) can tomato sauce

- In large skillet over medium heat, cook garlic and onions in oil for 4 to 5 minutes.
- Add celery, carrots, potatoes and cauliflower to garlic and onions.
- Combine seasonings in measuring cup; add 1 teaspoon mixture to vegetables. Cook, covered, for 10 minutes.
- Add green pepper, eggplant, peas, tomato sauce and remaining seasonings to vegetables. Simmer, covered, for 3 to 4 minutes.
- Serve immediately. Goulash may be served over rice or noodles.

Joyce Portner
Delray Beach, Florida

SPINACH STUFFED SHELLS
(Low Cholesterol)

Serves: 4

1 (10-ounce) package frozen chopped spinach, thawed and well drained
½ cup lowfat ricotta cheese or 1% lowfat cottage cheese
½ cup shredded lowfat mozzarella cheese
1 tablespoon grated Parmesan cheese

1 egg, well beaten, or equivalent egg substitute or 2 egg whites
⅛ teaspoon pepper
⅛ teaspoon ground nutmeg
16 jumbo pasta shells, cooked
1 (15¾-ounce) jar spaghetti sauce, divided

- Preheat oven to 350°.
- In large mixing bowl, combine spinach, cheeses, egg and seasonings; set aside.
- Prepare pasta according to package directions. Drain well.
- Pour ½ cup spaghetti sauce into 9x9x2-inch baking pan.
- Spoon 1 tablespoon spinach mixture into each shell; place shells in single layer on sauce in pan. Pour remaining sauce over shells.
- Bake for 20 to 30 minutes or until thoroughly heated.
- Serve hot.

June Klein
Marietta, Georgia

HOUMMUS

Yield: 2 cups

1 (15-ounce) can chickpeas, drained
½ cup tehina
1 clove garlic, crushed

Salt to taste
2 tablespoons lemon juice
Ground red pepper to taste

- Place chickpeas in food processor bowl; process with metal blade until well ground.
- Add tehina, garlic, salt and lemon juice; process thoroughly.
- Season with red pepper.
- Serve with pita bread.

Patti Hershorin
Sarasota, Florida

APPLESAUCE OAT BRAN MUFFINS

Yield: 12

¾ cup buttermilk
1 tablespoon baking powder
1 teaspoon salt
2 tablespoons peanut oil
3 tablespoons firmly-packed brown
sugar

½ cup frozen apple juice concentrate
½ cup applesauce
2¼ cups oat bran
4 egg whites, beaten

- Preheat oven to 400°.
- In measuring cup, blend buttermilk with baking powder; let stand 5 minutes.
- In large mixing bowl, combine salt, oil, brown sugar, apple juice, applesauce and buttermilk liquid; mix thoroughly.
- Fold oat bran into applesauce mixture. Gently fold bran mixture into egg whites.
- Spoon batter into paper-lined muffin pans or pans prepared with non-stick vegetable spray.
- Bake for 20 minutes. Cool in pan for 5 minutes.
- Serve warm or cold.

Marian Pressman
Tamarac, Florida

PEAR BRAN MUFFINS

Yield: 12

2¼ cups oat bran
1 tablespoon baking powder
¼ cup golden raisins
2 tablespoons vegetable oil
1 cup evaporated skim milk

2 egg whites
1 (16-ounce) can water-packed pears, peaches or fruit cocktail, drained and diced

- Preheat oven to 425°.
- In large mixing bowl, combine bran, baking powder and raisins.
- In medium-sized mixing bowl, blend oil, milk and egg whites. Add liquid mixture to dry ingredients, mixing just until well moistened. Stir in pears. If batter is too stiff, add small amount of liquid drained from pears.
- Spoon batter into paper-lined muffin pan, filling cups nearly full.
- Bake for 17 minutes or until wooden pick inserted in center of muffin comes out clean.
- Serve warm or cold. Muffins may be frozen.

Hortense Kalet
Lake Worth, Florida

BANANA OAT BRAN MUFFINS

Yield: 12

2 cups oat bran
¼ cup firmly-packed brown sugar
2 teaspoons baking powder
1 cup skim milk

2 egg whites, lightly beaten
2 tablespoons vegetable oil
½ cup raisins
1 banana, mashed

- Preheat oven to 425°.
- In medium-sized mixing bowl, combine bran, brown sugar and baking powder.
- Stir in milk, egg whites and oil, mixing just until dry ingredients are moistened.
- Fold in raisins and banana.
- Spoon batter into paper-lined muffin pans (or pans in which cup bottoms only have been prepared with non-stick vegetable spray), filling nearly full.
- Bake for 15 to 17 minutes.
- Serve warm or cold. Muffins may be frozen for up to 3 months.

Nina Indianer
Miami, Florida

BANANA NUT OAT BRAN MUFFINS

Yield: 12 to 15

2¼ cups oat bran
1 tablespoon baking powder
¼ cup firmly-packed brown sugar
¼ cup chopped walnuts or pecans
¼ cup raisins (optional)

1¼ cups skim milk, apple juice or
  other fruit juice
2 or 3 very ripe bananas
2 egg whites
2 tablespoons vegetable oil

- Preheat oven to 425°.
- In large mixing bowl, combine bran, baking powder, brown sugar, nuts and raisins.
- Using electric blender or mixing by hand, blend milk or juice, bananas, egg whites and oil. Add liquid mixture to dry ingredients and mix just until well moistened.
- Spoon batter into paper-lined muffin pans, filling cups nearly full.
- Bake for 17 minutes. Muffins should be stored in refrigerator because no preservatives are used. Muffins may be frozen.
- Serve warm or cold.

Esther Schwedock
North Miami Beach, Florida

MIGHTY MUFFINS

Yield: 12

2 cups whole wheat flour
½ cup grapenut cereal
½ cup firmly-packed brown sugar
1 tablespoon baking powder
¼ teaspoon salt

1 egg, beaten
1 cup milk
¼ cup sunflower oil
½ cup chopped dates (optional)

- Preheat oven to 400°.
- In small mixing bowl, combine flour, cereal, brown sugar, baking powder and salt.
- In medium-sized mixing bowl, blend egg, milk and oil. Add dry ingredients and dates; mix well.
- Spoon batter into greased muffin pan, filling cups nearly full.
- Bake for 20 to 25 minutes.
- Serve warm or cold.

Cathy Abrams
Atlanta, Georgia

ORANGE BRAN MUFFINS

Yield: 12

1 cup whole wheat flour
¾ cup wheat bran
¾ teaspoon baking soda
⅛ teaspoon salt
1 tablespoon grated orange peel

1 egg white
1 tablespoon vegetable oil
2 tablespoons dark molasses
1 cup buttermilk
½ cup raisins (optional)

- Preheat oven to 350°.
- In small mixing bowl, combine flour, bran, baking soda, salt and orange peel.
- In large mixing bowl, beat egg white; whip in oil, molasses and buttermilk.
- Add dry ingredients to liquid mixture, mixing just until moistened. Fold in raisins.
- Spoon batter into paper-lined muffin pans or pans prepared with non-stick vegetable spray.
- Bake for 25 minutes.
- Serve warm or cold.

Eileen Sidlow
Miami Beach, Florida

THREE GRAIN MUFFINS

(Sugar Free)

Yield: 12

1 cup oat bran
½ cup bran
½ cup wheat germ
½ cup all-purpose flour
2½ teaspoons baking powder
1 teaspoon baking soda
½ teaspoon salt (optional)
½ teaspoon ground cinnamon
2 ripe bananas

2 chopped apples
2 tablespoons all fruit spread
⅓ cup vegetable oil
1 egg
1 cup lowfat milk
½ cup raisins (optional)
½ cup chopped walnuts or pecans
  (optional)

- Preheat oven to 350°.
- In small mixing bowl, combine brans, wheat germ, flour, baking powder, baking soda, salt and cinnamon.
- In electric mixer bowl, beat bananas until mashed. Add apples, fruit spread, oil, egg, milk, raisins and nuts.
- Add dry ingredients to fruit mixture; beat at medium speed for 3 minutes.
- Spoon batter into greased muffin pans, filling cups ¾ full.
- Bake for 15 to 20 minutes or until wooden pick inserted near center of muffin comes out clean.
- Serve warm or cold.

Dorothy Scheinberg
Hollywood, Florida

RAISIN SPICE MUFFINS

(Dietetic)

Yield: 12

2 cups all-purpose flour
2 teaspoons baking powder
¼ teaspoon salt
¾ teaspoon ground cinnamon
¼ cup sugar substitute
¼ cup margarine, melted

2 eggs, well beaten
1 cup skim milk
1 teaspoon vanilla
1 cup cornflakes
1 cup raisins

- Preheat oven to 400°.
- In large mixing bowl, sift flour, baking powder, salt and cinnamon together. Stir in sugar substitute. Make a well in center of dry ingredients and pour margarine into well.
- In small mixing bowl, combine eggs, milk and vanilla. Add to dry ingredients and stir just until moistened. Fold in cornflakes and raisins.
- Spoon batter into lightly-greased muffin pans.
- Bake for 15 to 20 minutes or until lightly browned and wooden pick inserted near center of muffin comes out clean.
- Serve warm.

Esther Manor
Boca Raton, Florida

NUT BREAD

(Low Cholesterol)

Yield: 2 loaves

1 cup all-purpose unbleached flour
2 cups whole wheat flour
1 tablespoon baking powder
½ teaspoon baking soda

1½ cups skim milk
1 cup firmly-packed dark brown sugar
1 cup coarsely chopped walnuts

- Preheat oven to 300°.
- In large mixing bowl, sift flours, baking powder and baking soda together.
- Stir milk and sugar into dry ingredients, mixing thoroughly. Add nuts.
- Pour batter into 2 greased 8½x4½-inch loaf pans.
- Bake for 1 hour. Cool in pan 10 minutes, invert and cool on wire rack.
- Serve cold, thinly sliced and spread with butter or jam.

Helen Brownfeld
Orlando, Florida

APPLE PINEAPPLE PIE

(Dietetic)

Serves: 6

¼ cup orange juice
½ cup pineapple juice
½ cup cold water
2 envelopes unflavored gelatin
2 packets sugar substitute

5 large apples, coarsely grated
1 (20-ounce) can crushed pineapple in
 natural juices
½ cup skim milk powder
½ teaspoon ground cinnamon

- Preheat oven to 350°.
- In electric blender container, combine orange and pineapple juices, water, gelatin and sugar substitute; blend thoroughly.
- Place apples and pineapple in 9-inch pie plate prepared with non-stick vegetable spray.
- Mix milk powder and cinnamon together; sprinkle over fruit. Pour juice mixture over fruit.
- Bake for 1 hour.
- Serve cold.

Zelda Magid
North Miami Beach, Florida

APPLE CAKE

Serves: 8

1 cup sugar
3 medium apples, peeled and diced
1 egg, lightly beaten
1 cup all-purpose flour

1 teaspoon baking soda
1 teaspoon ground cinnamon
¼ cup wheat germ, divided

- In large mixing bowl, sprinkle sugar over apples; let stand 30 minutes.
- Preheat oven to 375°.
- Add egg, flour, baking soda, cinnamon and 3 tablespoons wheat germ to apples; blend thoroughly.
- Spread batter in greased 8x8x2-inch baking pan. Sprinkle with 1 tablespoon wheat germ.
- Bake for 30 minutes or until wooden pick inserted near center comes out clean. Cool on wire rack.
- Serve warm or at room temperature.

Belle North
Boca Raton, Florida

CHOCOLATE CAKE

(Low Cholesterol)

Serves: 8

1½ cups all-purpose flour
1 cup sugar
1 teaspoon baking soda
¼ cup unsweetened cocoa

1 cup water
1 tablespoon vinegar
¼ cup plus 2 tablespoons vegetable oil
1 teaspoon vanilla

- Preheat oven to 350°.
- In large mixing bowl, combine flour, sugar, baking soda and cocoa.
- Using wooden spoon, stir in water, vinegar, oil and vanilla; mix just until batter is smooth.
- Pour batter into greased 8x8x2-inch baking pan.
- Bake for 25 to 30 minutes or until wooden pick inserted near center comes out clean.

Elaine Dickstein
Boca Raton, Florida

CHEESE PIE

(Low Calorie)

Serves: 6

1 egg
½ cup pineapple juice
5 packets sugar substitute
1 envelope unflavored gelatin
1 tablespoon vanilla

2 cups cottage cheese
1 cup unsweetened, drained crushed
  pineapple
Ground cinnamon

- Preheat oven to 350°.
- In electric blender container or food processor bowl, combine egg, pineapple juice, sugar substitute, gelatin and vanilla. Blend or process for 2 minutes.
- Add cottage cheese and pineapple; blend until well mixed.
- Pour mixture into 9-inch aluminum pie pan. Sprinkle with cinnamon.
- Bake for 30 minutes. Cool before cutting.
- Serve cold.

Cookie Berman
Tamarac, Florida

MOCK CHEESECAKE

(No Cheese or Eggs)

Serves: 6 to 8

1 baked 9-inch graham cracker crust
1 pound tofu
1½ tablespoons lemon juice
¼ teaspoon salt

¼ cup honey
¼ cup vegetable oil
1½ teaspoons vanilla
½ cup sugar

- Preheat oven to 375°.
- Place tofu, lemon juice, salt, honey, oil, vanilla and sugar in electric blender container; blend until smooth and creamy. Pour mixture into crust.
- Bake for 40 minutes. Cool, then chill.
- Serve cold with fresh strawberries, sliced kiwi or other fruit.

Gertrude Durst
Nashville, Tennessee

CHEESECAKE

(Low Calorie)

Serves: 6 to 8

1 (15-ounce) carton ricotta cheese
1 egg
1 teaspoon vanilla
1 (8-ounce) can crushed pineapple, drained

6 packets sugar substitute
1 envelope unflavored gelatin
Ground cinnamon

- Preheat oven to 400°.
- In large mixing bowl, combine cheese, egg, vanilla, pineapple, sugar substitute and gelatin, blending thoroughly.
- Pour mixture into 9-inch pie pan prepared with non-stick vegetable spray. Sprinkle with cinnamon.
- Bake for 40 minutes. Turn oven off, leave door ajar but do not remove cheesecake for 30 minutes.
- Serve cold.

Zelda Magid
North Miami Beach, Florida

ORANGE CAKE

(No Cholesterol)

Serves: 8 to 10

1½ cups sifted all-purpose flour
1 cup sugar
2 teaspoons baking powder
¼ teaspoon salt
½ cup corn oil

½ cup orange juice
1 teaspoon vanilla
2 teaspoons grated orange peel
4 egg whites

- Preheat oven to 350°.
- In large mixing bowl, combine flour, sugar, baking powder and salt.
- Add oil, juice and vanilla to dry ingredients. Stir in orange peel.
- Using electric mixer, beat egg whites in small bowl at high speed until stiff peaks form. Fold into batter.
- Pour batter into 9x5x3-inch loaf pan prepared with bottom greased and floured.
- Bake for 50 minutes or until top of cake springs back when lightly touched. Cool on wire rack.
- Serve at room temperature. Cake may be frozen.

Nan Eckstein
Boynton Beach, Florida

RAISIN CAKE

(No Cholesterol)

Serves: 9

1 cup water
1 cup sugar
½ cup peanut or vegetable oil
1 teaspoon ground cinnamon

1 cup raisins
2 cups sifted all-purpose flour
1 teaspoon baking soda
½ teaspoon salt

- In 1½-quart saucepan, combine water, sugar, oil, cinnamon and raisins. Bring to a boil, then boil for 5 minutes. Allow mixture to cool.
- Preheat oven to 350°.
- Sift flour, baking soda and salt together. Stir into cooled raisin mixture.
- Pour batter into greased 8x8x2-inch baking pan.
- Bake for 40 to 45 minutes or until wooden pick inserted near center comes out clean. Cool on wire rack.
- Serve warm or cold. Cake may be frozen.

Eve Bornstein
Sarasota, Florida

SUGAR COOKIES

(Low Cholesterol)

Yield: 84 to 90

1 cup low cholesterol margarine or 1
scant cup vegetable oil
1 cup sugar
2 eggs or equivalent egg substitute
1 teaspoon vanilla

1 tablespoon orange juice
3 cups all-purpose flour
2 teaspoons baking powder
Sugar
Ground cinnamon

- Preheat oven to 350°.
- In large mixing bowl, combine margarine, sugar, egg substitute, vanilla and orange juice.
- Stir in flour with baking powder and mix thoroughly.
- Form walnut-sized balls of dough or drop by teaspoonfuls about 2 inches apart on baking sheets prepared with non-stick vegetable spray. Sprinkle with mixture of sugar and cinnamon.
- Bake for 15 to 20 minutes or until brown on edges. Remove from baking sheet and cool on wire rack. Store in plastic container.

Ruth Yaeger
Boca Raton, Florida

CRANBERRY FRUIT MOLD

Serves: 24

2 (⅓-ounce) packages red fruit sugar-
free gelatin
2 cups boiling water
1 cup sugar-free cherry lemon-lime
soda
1 cup sugar (½ cup optional)
1 cup water

1 (12-ounce) package cranberries
½ cup chopped celery
½ apple, unpeeled and chopped
Grated peel of 2 large oranges
1½ oranges, peeled and chopped
¾ cup coarsely chopped walnuts

- In large mixing bowl, dissolve gelatin in boiling water. Stir in soda. Chill until partially firm.
- In 2-quart saucepan, dissolve sugar in water. Bring to a boil, add cranberries, return to boil, then simmer for 10 minutes or until cranberries burst. Cool in pan, then chill.
- Add celery, apple, peel, oranges and walnuts to cranberry sauce. Stir fruit mixture into thickened gelatin. Pour into 10-cup mold and chill until firm.
- Invert mold on serving plate. Mold must be prepared 12 hours in advance and may be prepared several days before serving.

Flo Don
Sarasota, Florida

MANDELBRODT

(Sugar Free)

Yield: 36

¾ cup margarine
3 eggs
15 packets sugar substitute
¼ cup orange juice
1 teaspoon vanilla
1 teaspoon lemon extract

2½ cups all-purpose flour
1 tablespoon baking powder
1 cup chopped walnuts, pecans or
 almonds
Ground cinnamon

- Preheat oven to 350°.
- In large mixing bowl, cream margarine, eggs and sugar substitute until smooth. Add orange juice and flavorings; beat until thoroughly mixed.
- Add flour and baking powder to creamed mixture and blend well. Stir in nuts.
- Form dough into 4 rolls and place on greased baking sheet.
- Bake for 25 minutes. Remove from oven and let cool 5 minutes. Cut into slices 1½-inches thick, arrange on baking sheet, sprinkle with cinnamon and sugar substitute. Bake additional 10 minutes to toast.

Temmie Schwarz
North Miami Beach, Florida

MANDELBRODT

(Low Cholesterol)

Yield: 40 to 45

1 cup sugar
½ cup corn oil margarine
¾ cup egg substitute
1 teaspoon vanilla
3 cups all-purpose flour

1 tablespoon baking powder
1 cup chopped nuts
1 cup raisins or chocolate chips
(optional)

- Preheat oven to 350°.
- Using electric mixer, cream sugar, margarine and egg substitute until smooth. Beat in vanilla.
- Gradually add flour with baking powder to creamed mixture, beating well.
- Stir in nuts and raisins or chocolate chips.
- Knead dough to form a ball, then divide in 3 portions. On lightly-floured surface, roll each to form 15x1¾-inch strip and place on greased baking sheet.
- Bake for 25 minutes or until lightly browned. Remove from oven, cut rolls in 1-inch slices, arranging on baking sheet. Bake 10 minutes, turn, and bake 10 minutes to toast on both sides. Cool on wire rack.

Ruth Novick
North Miami Beach, Florida

PASSOVER

CHAROSIS
(Israeli)

Yield: 5 cups

1 apple, chopped
3 bananas, mashed
Juice of 1 orange
15 dates, chopped

1 cup chopped almonds or peanuts
1 teaspoon ground cinnamon
½ cup red wine
Honey or sugar to taste

- In medium-sized mixing bowl, combine fruit, nuts, cinnamon and wine. Sweeten to taste. Mixture may be thickened with matzo meal.

(Greek)

Yield: 4 cups

20 large dates, chopped
¾ cup walnuts, ground
1 cup raisins, chopped

½ cup almonds, chopped
Trace of grated lemon peel
Red wine to taste

- In medium-sized mixing bowl, combine dates, nuts, raisins, lemon peel and wine.
- Chill before serving.

(Sephardic)

Yield: 4 cups

½ cup shredded coconut
½ cup golden raisins
1 (6-ounce) package mixed dried fruit
    bits
½ cup chopped walnuts

¼ cup sugar
2 teaspoons ground cinnamon
Water
½ (8-ounce) jar cherry preserves
⅓ cup blackberry wine

- In 1½-quart saucepan, combine fruit, nuts, sugar and cinnamon. Add water to cover. Simmer, covered, for 1 hour or until thickened.
- Stir in preserves and wine.
- Chill before serving.

Dottie Stevens
Sarasota, Florida

ORANGE GLAZED CORNISH HENS WITH FRUIT STUFFING

Serves: 10 to 12

1 cup diced celery
1 cup chopped onion
¼ cup margarine
1½ cups sliced mushrooms
1½ cups chicken stock
½ teaspoon dried dill
½ teaspoon salt
Pepper to taste
2 tablespoons chopped parsley

¼ teaspoon ground sage
1 (12-ounce) package matzo farfel
½ cup chopped mixed dried fruit
2 eggs, beaten
4 to 6 kosher cornish hens
Margarine, melted
½ cup orange marmalade
½ cup orange juice
½ cup cranberries

- Preheat oven to 350°.

- In large skillet, sauté onion, celery and mushrooms in margarine for about 5 minutes or until tender.

- Stir in chicken stock and seasonings; simmer for a few minutes.

- In large mixing bowl, combine matzo farfel and dried fruit. Add onion mixture and mix well. Stir in eggs. Stuffing should be moist but not soggy; if too dry, add small amount of chicken stock.

- Spoon stuffing into cornish hens. Place hens breast side up in large shallow baking dish. Brush with margarine and sprinkle with additional seasoning of choice. Cover loosely with aluminum foil.

- Bake for 45 minutes. While hens bake, prepare sauce. In small saucepan, combine marmalade, orange juice and cranberries; simmer for 1 minute.

- Baste partially baked hens with sauce. Bake for additional 1½ hours or until golden brown, basting frequently.

- Cool hens slightly, cut in halves and serve warm. For use year-round, substitute bread for matzo farfel.

Nancy Gillen Doyle
North Miami Beach, Florida

SCHNAPSY SEDER CHICKEN

Serves: 8

2 (2½ to 3-pound) broiler fryers,
  cut up
½ cup peanut oil
2½ teaspoons salt
1½ teaspoons pepper
½ teaspoon garlic powder
1 teaspoon onion powder
2 teaspoons paprika

2 chicken bouillon cubes, crushed
3 ripe tomatoes, chopped
1 (10½-ounce) can tomato sauce with
  mushrooms
2 large onions, sliced
5 medium zucchini, sliced
1½ cups Passover red wine

- In Dutch oven over medium heat, brown chicken in oil, turning as necessary.
- Sprinkle chicken with seasonings and bouillon.
- Add tomatoes, tomato sauce, onion, zucchini and wine. Simmer, covered, for 30 minutes. Remove cover and simmer for 15 minutes or until liquid is reduced and chicken is tender.

Flo Harris
Hollywood, Florida

MATZO LASAGNA

Serves: 6 to 8

1 large onion, chopped
1 tablespoon vegetable oil
3 pounds ground turkey or beef
2 eggs

Salt and pepper to taste
6 to 8 matzos, dampened and wrapped
  in towel
Chicken broth

- Preheat oven to 350°.
- In large skillet, cook onion in oil over medium heat until onion is lightly browned. Stir in meat and cook until lightly browned. Add eggs and mix thoroughly.
- Cover bottom of 8x8x2-inch baking dish with matzos; top with layer of meat mixture. Repeat layers until matzos and meat mixture are used, ending with matzos. Pour broth to cover matzo layer.
- Bake for 45 minutes to 1 hour or until slightly dry on surface.
- Serve hot.

Annette Hirsch
Sarasota, Florida

FRUIT MUFFINS

Yield: 24

6 eggs
1 cup sugar
1 cup chopped dates

1 cup raisins
1 cup shredded coconut
1 cup chopped nuts

- Preheat oven to 350°.
- In large mixing bowl, combine eggs and sugar. Add fruit and nuts and mix well.
- Spoon batter into miniature muffin pans, filling cups nearly full.
- Bake for 25 to 30 minutes.
- Serve warm or cold. Muffins may be frozen.

Dale Flam
North Miami Beach, Florida

FRUITY MUFFINS

Yield: 24

1 cup chopped dates
1 cup ground walnuts
½ cup chopped dried apricots

½ cup chopped prunes
6 egg whites
3 tablespoons safflower oil

- Preheat oven to 350°.
- Using food processor, chop fruit and nuts together.
- In small bowl, combine egg whites and oil; add to fruit-nut mixture and process until well blended.
- Spoon batter into miniature muffin pans, filling cups nearly full.
- Bake for 20 minutes.
- Serve warm or cold. Muffins may be frozen.

Sonny Lipschultz
Largo, Florida

DATE NUT MINI-MUFFINS

Yield: 12

2 egg whites
½ cup raisins

8 pitted dates
½ cup chopped nuts

- Place egg whites, raisins and dates in blender container or food processor bowl; blend until raisins and dates are coarsely chopped. Add nuts, mixing with fork.
- Place teaspoon of mixture in each cup of styrofoam egg carton.
- Microwave on high for 2 to 3 minutes or until almost dry.
- Let cool slightly. Close carton, tap with finger, open and invert to remove muffins.
- Serve warm.

Rita Templer
North Miami Beach, Florida

BAGELACH

Yield: 12

1 cup boiling water
½ cup margarine
½ teaspoon salt

2 teaspoons sugar
1 cup matzo meal
3 eggs

- In 1½-quart saucepan, combine boiling water, margarine, salt and sugar. When margarine is melted, quickly stir in matzo meal just until blended. Cool.
- Preheat oven to 350°.
- Add eggs, 1 at a time, to cooled mixture, beating after each addition until batter is smooth.
- Drop batter by tablespoonful on greased baking sheet. Use water-moistened fingertip to poke hole in center of each bagelach.
- Bake for 40 minutes or until golden brown.

Lil Rosenblatt
Miami Beach, Florida

WORLD'S BEST MATZO BALLS

Yield: 7

4 eggs, well beaten
¾ cup matzo meal
½ teaspoon salt

¼ cup vegetable oil or chicken fat
Boiling water
Salt

- In medium-sized mixing bowl, combine eggs, meal, salt and oil; mix well. If batter is too thin, add small amount of meal.
- Chill batter, uncovered, overnight.
- In stockpot, bring water to boil; season with salt.
- Moisten hands and form ball of chilled batter; drop into boiling water. Matzo balls will rise to surface. Simer, covered, for 30 minutes.

Barbara Ginsberg
West Palm Beach, Florida

MOM'S CHICKEN SOUP

Serves: 4 to 6

1 (3½-pound) broiler-fryer chicken, quartered
4 carrots, cut in thirds
4 stalks celery with leaves, cut in quarters
3 medium-sized onions, quartered

½ fresh parsnip, cup in ½-inch slices
1 bunch parsley, chopped
8 to 10 sprigs fresh dill
10 peppercorns
Cold water
Salt to taste

- Place chicken, vegetables, dill and peppercorns in 8-quart stockpot.
- Add cold water just to cover chicken and vegetables. Bring to a boil, reduce heat and simmer, covered, for about 2 hours.
- Drain soup liquid through colander into large container. Vegetables may be retained to serve in soup. Remove chicken from bones and serve separately or serve in soup.
- Chill soup, allowing fat to rise to top and solidify; remove fat.
- Serve hot. Use within 3 or 4 days. Soup may be frozen but flavor will be slightly diminished.

Elaine Gruenhut
Atlanta, Georgia

MATZO STUFFING

Serves: 3 to 4

6 matzos, soaked in water and drained
3 eggs, beaten
1 cup diced onion
1 cup diced celery

2 tablespoons margarine
2 cups chicken bouillon
2 teaspoons salt
¼ teaspoon pepper

- Preheat oven to 350°.
- In large mixing bowl, combine matzos and eggs.
- In skillet, sauté onion and celery in margarine until tender.
- Add onion, celery, bouillon, salt and pepper to matzo-egg mixture.
- Spoon into 3-quart casserole.
- Bake, uncovered, for 1 hour and 30 minutes.
- Serve hot. Stuffing may be frozen and reheated.

Ruth Reich Capell
North Miami Beach, Florida

MA NISHTANAH STUFFING

Serves: 5 to 6

¾ cup minced onion
¾ cup vegetable shortening or chicken
fat
10 matzos, finely broken
1 teaspoon salt
¼ teaspoon pepper
½ teaspoon garlic powder

1 tablespoon paprika
1 egg
1½ (10¾-ounce) cans condensed clear
chicken soup, undiluted
Chopped pecans or mushrooms or
chicken livers

- In large skillet, cook onion in shortening until tender but not browned.
- Add matzos, seasonings, egg and soup.
- Stir in pecans, mushrooms or livers.
- Spoon stuffing into cavity of 10 to 12 pound fowl. Roast according to directions for fowl.

Note: This is a dry stuffing. For a moister stuffing, increase soup to 2 cans.

Flo Harris
Hollywood, Florida

MATZO CHRIMSEL

(Fritters)

Serves: 8

6 matzos
Water
4 eggs, separated
2 tablespoons honey

2 tablespoons lemon or orange juice
½ cup matzo meal
½ cup chopped nuts
2 tablespoons vegetable oil

- Soak matzos in water for about 10 minutes, squeeze to remove excess liquid and drain in colander.
- In medium-sized mixing bowl, combine egg yolks, honey, juice, meal and nuts. Stir in soaked matzos.
- In small mixing bowl, beat egg whites until stiff but not dry. Fold into matzo mixture.
- Drop large tablespoons of mixture into hot oil in non-stick 10-inch skillet, frying until browned on both sides. Cook up to 6 chrimsels in a skillet at one time using more oil as necessary; use 2 skillets to speed preparation.
- If chrimsels are to be served immediately, cover loosely and simmer for about 5 minutes. If served later, place in baking dish and warm in 350° oven for 10 to 15 minutes.
- Serve with stewed fruit. Chrimsels may be frozen.

Greta Friedhoff
Clearwater, Florida

MATZO BREI

Serves: 2

3 regular matzos, broken in
  ½-inch pieces
Warm water
½ cup smooth creamy cottage cheese

2 eggs, lightly beaten
1 teaspoon salt
2 tablespoons margarine, butter or
  vegetable oil

- Place matzos in 1-quart bowl, add warm water, then squeeze to remove excess liquid.
- Add cottage cheese to matzos; toss lightly.
- Combine eggs and salt; add to matzo mixture.
- Prepare 7-inch skillet with non-stick vegetable spray. Heat margarine in skillet over medium heat until sizzling.
- Pour matzo mixture into skillet. Fry for 10 minutes. Turn like a pancake or crumble mixture and continue cooking until browned.
- Serve immediately.

Pat Kimmel
Plantation, Florida

COTTAGE CHEESE PANCAKES

Serves: 4

3 eggs
1 cup milk
1 cup cottage cheese
1 tablespoon sugar

1 cup matzo meal
¾ teaspoon salt
½ teaspoon ground cinnamon

- Combine all ingredients in electric blender container; blend until smooth.
- Drop batter by teaspoonfuls on hot well greased griddle. Brown on one side; turn and brown on second side.
- Serve hot.

Dana Gilbert
St. Petersburg, Florida

CARROT RING

Serves: 12

3 cups sliced carrots
1 bay leaf
1 onion, quartered
Salt to taste
Boiling water
1 tablespoon ground cinnamon
½ teaspoon ground ginger

1 teaspoon salt
Freshly ground pepper to taste
5 eggs, separated
1 cup sugar
½ cup matzo meal
1 cup ground walnuts

- In large saucepan, combine carrots, bay leaf, onion and salt with boiling water to cover. Bring to a boil, then simmer, covered, for about 20 minutes or until carrots are tender. Remove onion and bay leaf; drain liquid.
- Mash carrots until smooth. Stir in cinnamon, ginger, 1 teaspoon salt and pepper.
- Preheat oven to 350°.
- In large mixing bowl, beat egg yolks with sugar until lemon colored and thick. Add carrot mixture and mix well.
- In medium-sized mixing bowl, beat egg whites until stiff but not dry. Alternately fold egg whites and matzo meal with nuts into carrot mixture.
- Spread mixture in 10- to 12-cup ring mold. Place in baking pan of boiling water.
- Bake for 40 minutes or until firm.
- Serve hot.

Mimi Gardner
Fort Lauderdale, Florida

TZIMMES

Serves: 6

1 pound carrots, sliced
1 pound yams, thinly sliced
Water
3 tablespoons potato starch

Salt and pepper to taste
2 tablespoons margarine
1 cup honey
½ cup raisins

- In 2-quart saucepan, combine carrots and yams with salted water to cover; cook for 25 minutes. Drain, reserving ½ cup cooking liquid.
- Gradually add potato starch to reserved liquid, blending until smooth. Season with salt and pepper.
- Preheat oven to 350°.
- Melt margarine in 13x9x2-inch baking dish. Add carrots and yams and toss thoroughly to coat.
- Add honey to potato starch mixture; pour over carrots and yams. Stir in raisins.
- Bake for 1 hour and 30 minutes.
- Serve hot.

Sari F. Rutt
Fort Myers, Florida

SPINACH SOUFFLÉ

Serves: 10

2 (10-ounce) packages frozen chopped spinach, thawed and well drained
6 matzos, soaked in water and well drained
7 eggs, divided

1 (4-ounce) package feta cheese
1 (8-ounce) package farmer cheese
½ cup vegetable oil
1½ teaspoons salt

- Preheat oven to 350°.
- In large mixing bowl, combine spinach, matzos, 6 eggs, cheeses, oil and salt.
- Grease 13x9x2-inch baking pan and heat for 30 seconds over stove burner. Spread spinach mixture in pan as soon as oil is hot.
- In small bowl, beat 1 egg; brush on top of spinach mixture.
- Bake, uncovered, for 1 hour.
- Serve hot. Soufflé may be prepared in advance.

Lena Sami
Maitland, Florida

SPINACH MATZO CASSEROLE

Serves: 6 to 8

1 large onion, chopped
1 tablespoon butter
2 tablespoons chopped parsley
2 tablespoons chopped chives
5 matzos, broken, soaked and drained
1 (8-ounce) carton sour cream
½ (8-ounce) package cream cheese, softened

1 egg, beaten
Salt and pepper to taste
1 (10-ounce) package frozen chopped spinach, cooked and drained
1 (4-ounce) package Muenster cheese, cut in chunks

- Preheat oven to 350°.
- In small skillet, sauté onion in butter with parsley and chives until tender.
- In medium-sized mixing bowl, combine matzos, sour cream, cream cheese, egg, salt, pepper, onion, spinach and cheese. Pour into greased 12x9x2-inch baking dish.
- Bake for 30 to 40 minutes.
- Serve hot.

Dana Gilbert
St. Petersburg, Florida

BARBARA'S SWEET FARFEL PUDDING

Serves: 6

3 cups farfel
Hot water
½ cup sugar
½ teaspoon salt
2 apples, peeled and thinly sliced
½ cup golden raisins

1 (8-ounce) can crushed pineapple, undrained
1 teaspoon vanilla
2 eggs, well beaten
3 tablespoons vegetable oil
Ground cinnamon

- Preheat oven to 350°.
- In large mixing bowl, moisten farfel with water. Add sugar, salt, apples, raisins, pineapple, vanilla and eggs.
- Heat oil in 2-quart casserole. Pour fruit mixture over oil; sprinkle with cinnamon.
- Bake, covered, for 1 hour.
- Serve hot. Pudding may be frozen and reheated in microwave oven. Tastes better a day after preparation.

Shirley Alderman
Boynton Beach, Florida

MATZO PUDDING

Serves: 6

4 matzos
Boiling water
3 eggs, beaten
½ teaspoon salt
¼ cup sugar, divided

5 tablespoons melted butter
1 cup chopped walnuts
3 apples, peeled and thinly sliced
½ teaspoon cinnamon

- Break matzos in thin strips and place in colander. Pour boiling water over matzos, drain and let cool.
- Preheat oven to 350°.
- In medium-sized mixing bowl, combine matzos, eggs, salt, 3 tablespoons sugar and melted butter. Pour half of mixture into 1½-quart casserole.
- Place nuts and apples on matzo mixture. Sprinkle with cinnamon and 1 tablespoon sugar. Top with remaining matzo mixture.
- Bake for 30 minutes.

Kim G. Cohen
Atlanta, Georgia

PRIZE KUGEL

Serves: 8 to 10

6 matzos
1 (8-ounce) can crushed pineapple,
  drained and juice reserved
Water
1 egg plus 5 egg whites

1 tablespoon canola oil
1 teaspoon ground cinnamon
Pinch of nutmeg
¾ cup chopped pecans
¾ cup raisins

- Preheat oven to 350°.
- Break matzos in medium-sized mixing bowl; add pineapple juice to moisten with enough water to make matzos spongy in consistency.
- In large mixing bowl, beat eggs, oil and spices together. Stir in nuts, pineapple, raisins and matzos.
- Pour mixture into lightly oiled 11x8x1½-inch baking pan.
- Bake for 45 minutes or until browned to preference.
- Serve warm. Kugel may be assembled and stored in refrigerator up to 24 hours before baking.

Diana Reinhardt
Marietta, Georgia

CHEESE BLINTZES

Serves: 6 to 10

3 eggs
¾ cup matzo cake meal

1½ cups water
½ teaspoon salt

- In medium-sized mixing bowl, beat eggs. Alternately add cake meal and water to make a thin batter. Add salt.
- Pour 3 tablespoons batter in well greased skillet. Fry until brown. Place on tea towel, browned side up.

Filling

2 cups (16 ounces) dry cottage cheese
1 egg
½ teaspoon salt
½ teaspoon sugar
1 tablespoon whipping cream

Margarine
Sugar
Ground cinnamon
Sour cream

- In medium-sized mixing bowl, combine cottage cheese, egg, salt, sugar and whipping cream; mix well. Spread portion of filling on browned side of each wrapper, tuck ends and roll up.
- Brown blintzes in margarine in skillet.
- Serve hot with sugar, cinnamon and sour cream.

Dana Gilbert
St. Petersburg, Florida

PHARAOH'S PEARS

Serves: 4

½ cup sugar
2 cups water
1½ teaspoons ground cinnamon

1 tablespoon lemon juice
8 medium pears, peeled
1 cup Passover red wine

- In 3-quart saucepan, combine sugar, water, cinnamon and lemon juice; bring to a boil, then maintain moderate boil.
- Poach pears in syrup for about 20 minutes or until tender.
- Add wine and cook for 10 to 15 minutes or until pears are color of wine. Remove pears from syrup.
- Cook syrup until reduced by ⅓.
- Place pears on slices of Passover sponge cake; spoon syrup over pears and cake.
- Serve warm.

Flo Harris
Hollywood, Florida

DELICIOUS MATZO CHARLOTTE

Serves: 12

4 egg matzos
½ cup butter or margarine, softened
½ cup sugar
3 eggs, separated
2 tablespoons lemon juice
1 teaspoon salt

3 tablespoons apricot preserves
2 tablespoons Grand Marnier
1 teaspoon ground cinnamon
3 large apples, grated
½ cup chopped nuts
½ cup raisins

- Soak matzos in cold water for 5 minutes; drain and crush.
- Preheat oven to 350°.
- In large mixing bowl, cream butter and sugar until light and fluffy. Add matzos, egg yolks, lemon juice, salt, apricot preserves, Grand Marnier, cinnamon, apples, nuts and raisins; mix well.
- In small mixing bowl, beat egg whites until stiff; fold into matzo mixture.
- Pour batter into well greased 13x9x2-inch baking pan.
- Bake for 40 to 45 minutes or until medium brown.
- Cool slightly in pan; cut squares and place on individual serving plates while still warm. Serve with warm lemon sauce.

Sauce

1 cup sugar
2 tablespoons butter or margarine

Juice and grated peel of 2 lemons
3 eggs, well beaten

- In medium-sized mixing bowl, cream butter and sugar. Add lemon juice and peel. Transfer to 1-quart saucepan.
- In small mixing bowl, beat eggs.
- Heat creamed mixture, then add small amount to eggs; mix well and add remainder to eggs. Heat, stirring constantly, until mixture coats a spoon.
- Pour lemon sauce over warm Matzo Charlotte.

Lois Spielberg
Coral Springs, Florida

BANANA SPONGE CAKE

Serves: 12

9 eggs, divided
1½ cups sugar, divided
½ teaspoon salt

½ cup mashed banana
1 teaspoon grated lemon peel
1 cup sifted potato starch

- Preheat oven to 350°.
- Separate 7 eggs, placing whites in electric mixer bowl and yolks in large mixing bowl. Beat whites until soft peaks form. Gradually add ½ cup sugar, beating until very stiff peaks form.
- Combine yolks, 2 whole eggs, 1 cup sugar, salt, banana, lemon peel and potato starch. Gently fold in egg whites.
- Pour batter into ungreased 10-inch tube pan.
- Bake 50 to 55 minutes or until wooden pick inserted near center comes out clean and dry. Invert pan on wire rack and cool before removing from pan.
- Slice and serve.

Nettie Goldstein
Tamarac, Florida

APRICOT UPSIDE DOWN CHARLOTTE

Serves: 9 to 12

½ cup melted margarine, divided
⅓ cup firmly-packed brown sugar
8 canned apricots, drained and juice
  reserved
4 matzos, broken

1½ cups apricot juice
3 eggs
¼ cup sugar
¼ teaspoon salt
½ cup chopped nuts

- In bottom of 9-inch round springform or baking pan, combine 3 tablespoons margarine and brown sugar; spread evenly in pan.
- Cut apricots in halves. Place 1 apricot half, cut side down, in center of pan; allowing ½-inch space from center apricot, arrange remaining halves in circle.
- Preheat oven to 350°.
- In large mixing bowl, soak matzos in apricot juice for 15 minutes.
- Add 5 tablespoons margarine, eggs, sugar, salt and nuts to matzos; beat thoroughly and spread mixture over fruit in pan.
- Bake for 40 minutes.
- Use knife to separate cake from sides of pan and invert immediately on plate. Chill.
- Serve cold.

Dana Gilbert
St. Petersburg, Florida

CHOCOLATE CARROT CAKE

Serves: 12

Butter
5 eggs, separated
¾ cup sugar, divided
½ (8-ounce) package semisweet
  chocolate, melted

⅓ cup matzo meal
1 cup grated unpeeled carrots
1½ cups finely ground toasted almonds
Pinch of salt

- Preheat oven to 350°.
- Prepare 9x3-inch springform pan by buttering bottom and sides, lining bottom with waxed paper, buttering the waxed paper and dusting bottom and sides with matzo meal.
- In small mixing bowl, combine egg yolks and ½ cup sugar. Using electric mixer, beat at high speed for 2 to 3 minutes or until pale lemon-colored and creamy. Add cooled chocolate and beat on low speed just until mixed. Transfer mixture to large mixing bowl and stir in matzo meal, carrots and almonds.
- Clean small bowl and beaters. Beat egg whites with salt until soft peaks form. Gradually add ¼ cup sugar, beating on medium speed, then beat on high speed until soft peaks form (must not be stiff or dry).
- In 4 additions, fold egg whites into chocolate mixture.
- Pour batter into springform pan, rotating briskly to level surface of batter.
- Bake for 1 hour and 5 to 10 minutes or until wooden pick inserted near center comes out clean and dry and sides of cake begin to release from pan. Use knife to separate cake from pan sides, invert on wire rack and remove pan and paper lining, cover with another wire rack and invert again. Freeze on rack until firm. Cake will be about 2 inches high.
- Place on cake plate. Slice and serve at room temperature. Cake may be frozen.

Paula Woolf
Miami, Florida

CHOCOLATE WALNUT SPONGECAKE

Serves: 12

9 eggs, separated, at room temperature
1½ cups sugar, divided
2 tablespoons fresh orange juice
1 tablespoon fresh lemon juice
⅓ cup potato starch

⅓ cup matzo meal
⅓ cup unsweetened cocoa
¼ teaspoon salt
½ cup ground walnuts

- Preheat oven to 325°.
- In large bowl of electric mixer, beat egg yolks until thickened. Gradually add 1 cup sugar, beating until very thick. Add juices and beat well.
- Sift potato starch, meal and cocoa together; gradually beat into egg mixture, beating just until combined.
- In separate bowl with clean beaters, beat egg whites with salt until soft peaks form. Gradually add ½ cup sugar, beating until stiff peaks form.
- Stir 1 cup egg whites into chocolate mixture; fold in remaining whites. Fold in walnuts.
- Pour batter into ungreased 10-inch tube pan with removable bottom.
- Bake for 55 to 60 minutes or until wooden pick inserted near center comes out clean.
- Invert pan on bottle neck to cool. Use knife to separate cake from sides, tube and bottom of pan. Place on serving plate.

Sandy Listokin
Boca Raton, Florida

AUNT BESSIE'S SPONGE CAKE

Serves: 8

7 eggs, separated, at room temperature
1 cup sifted sugar
Juice of 1 lemon

Grated peel of ½ lemon
½ cup matzo cake meal
1 tablespoon potato starch

- Preheat oven to 325°.
- In medium-sized mixing bowl, beat egg yolks, sugar, lemon juice and peel together until thick and lemon colored.
- Sift meal and starch together three times.
- In medium-sized mixing bowl, beat egg whites until soft peaks form.
- Fold dry ingredients into egg yolk mixture, then fold egg whites into batter.
- Spread batter in 9x3-inch round baking pan which has been oiled and lined with waxed paper.
- Bake for 1 hour or until wooden pick inserted near center comes out clean.
- Invert pan on wire rack and cover with towel until cool.
- Invert cooled cake on serving plate. Cake may be frozen.

Frances Simon Low
West Palm Beach, Florida

WALNUT TORTE

Serves: 12

6 eggs, separated
1⅓ cups sugar
¼ cup orange juice
2 tablespoons grated orange peel

½ cup matzo cake meal
½ cup potato starch
1 cup walnuts, chopped
Confectioner's sugar

- Preheat oven to 325°.
- In large bowl of electric mixer, beat egg yolks until very thick.
- Gradually add sugar to yolks, beating well after each addition. Add orange juice, peel, cake meal and starch; mix well.
- In separate bowl, beat whites until soft peaks form. Stir 1 cup whites into yolk mixture, then fold in remaining whites. Gently fold in nuts.
- Pour batter into ungreased 9-inch tube pan with removable bottom.
- Bake in center of oven for 55 to 60 minutes.
- Invert pan on bottle neck to cool. Use knife to separate cake from sides and bottom of pan.
- Place on serving plate and dust with confectioner's sugar.

Erika Brodsky
Boca Raton, Florida

ENGLISH TRIFLE

Serves: 10 to 12

1½ inch-thick layer stale sponge cake
1 (8-ounce) jar raspberry jam
12 macaroons
1 cup Passover wine
2 to 3 cups fresh fruit such as
   strawberries or blueberries
2 cups milk
6 egg yolks, lightly beaten

¾ cup sugar, divided
Grated peel of ½ lemon
¼ teaspoon salt
1 cup whipping cream
1 (3-ounce) package raspberry or
   strawberry Passover gelatin
Slivered almonds
Whole strawberries

- Arrange spongecake to cover bottom of trifle bowl. Spread with generous layer of jam. Layer macaroons over jam. Pour wine over macaroons. Add layer of fresh fruit. Chill.
- In 2-quart saucepan, bring milk to a boil.
- In top pan of double boiler, combine egg yolks, ½ cup sugar, lemon peel and salt. Gradually add milk to egg mixture, stirring constantly. Place over hot water, stirring constantly, until mixture is thickened. Cool, beat well and chill.
- In electric mixer bowl, whip cream and ¼ cup sugar until stiff. Chill 2 hours.
- Prepare gelatin according to package directions. Pour over fruit in trifle bowl. Spoon custard over fruit and top with whipped cream. Sprinkle with almonds and garnish with strawberries.
- Serve immediately.

Molly G. Lipschultz
Delray Beach, Florida

CHOCOLATE MOUSSE CAKE

Serves: 8

8 eggs, separated
⅛ teaspoon salt
1 (8-ounce) package semisweet
  chocolate
¼ cup boiling water

1 tablespoon instant coffee granules
⅔ cup sugar
1 teaspoon vanilla
Whipped cream

- In large mixing bowl, beat egg whites with salt until stiff; set aside.
- In small bowl, melt chocolate in boiling water with coffee granules; set aside to cool slightly.
- In large mixing bowl, beat egg yolks until thickened; add sugar and beat 5 minutes or until very thick.
- Add vanilla and chocolate mixture to egg yolks; blend well. Fold in half of egg whites, then fold chocolate mixture into remaining egg whites. Reserve 4 cups of mixture as mousse; chill.
- Spoon remaining mixture into 9-inch pie plate which has been greased and dusted with matzo meal.
- Bake for 20 minutes. Turn oven off but do not remove cake for 5 minutes. Cool.
- Spoon chilled mousse in center of cake. Chill until ready to serve.
- Serve with whipped cream.

Ada Friedkin
Hallandale, Florida

SPICED WINE CAKE

Serves: 16

¾ cup matzo cake meal
½ cup potato starch
2 tablespoons finely ground almonds
½ teaspoon salt
8 eggs, separated

1½ cups sugar
⅓ cup kosher red wine
⅓ cup orange juice
1 teaspoon grated lemon peel
Confectioner's sugar

- Preheat oven to 325°.
- In small mixing bowl, combine meal, starch, almonds and salt.
- In large mixing bowl, beat egg yolks until thick and lemon colored. Gradually add sugar, beating until thick and light.
- Add wine, orange juice and lemon peel to egg yolks; beat at medium speed for 4 minutes.
- Fold dry ingredients into egg yolk mixture.
- In medium-sized mixing bowl, beat egg whites until soft peaks form. Fold whites into wine batter; do not overmix.
- Pour batter into greased 10-inch tube pan.
- Bake for 1 hour and 30 minutes.
- Invert pan on bottle neck to cool. Place cake on serving plate and dust with confectioner's sugar.

Carol A. Glazer
Cape Coral, Florida

FARFEL COOKIES

Yield: 72

2 cups matzo farfel
2 cups matzo meal
1½ cups sugar
1 teaspoon ground cinnamon

½ teaspoon salt
4 eggs, beaten
⅔ cup vegetable oil
2 cups chopped pecans

- In large mixing bowl, combine farfel, meal, sugar, cinnamon and salt. Add eggs and oil; beat well. Stir in pecans.
- Preheat oven to 325°.
- Shape dough into walnut-sized balls, dampening fingertips and palm of hand to ease handling and keep dough together; place balls ¾-inch apart on ungreased baking sheets.
- Bake for 25 minutes. Cool on baking sheets.

Suzanne Piha Mack
Atlanta, Georgia

BROWNIES

Yield: 16 to 20

1 cup vegetable shortening, melted
  and cooled
2¼ cups sugar
½ cup plus 1 tablespoon cocoa

1½ cups matzo cake meal
¼ cup potato starch
7 eggs
1½ cups chopped nuts

- Preheat oven to 350°.
- In large mixing bowl, beat shortening and sugar together.
- Combine cocoa, cake meal and starch; add to sugar mixture.
- Add eggs, 1 at a time, beating well after each addition.
- Stir in nuts.
- Pour batter into greased 13x9x2-inch baking pan.
- Bake for 30 to 35 minutes.

Barbara Moritz
North Miami Beach, Florida

ALMOND MACAROONS

Yield: 24 to 36

4 teaspoons matzo cake meal
1 (16-ounce) package finely ground
blanched almonds
4 cups confectioner's sugar

Grated peel of 2 lemons
5 egg whites
Cake meal

- Preheat oven to 350°.
- In large mixing bowl, combine 4 teaspoons matzo cake meal, almonds, sugar and peel.
- In medium-sized mixing bowl, beat egg whites until stiff and dry. Fold into almond mixture.
- Dust greased baking sheet with cake meal. Drop almond mixture by rounded teaspoonfuls or tablespoonfuls about ½-inch apart on baking sheet.

- Bake until golden brown.

Barbara Moritz
North Miami Beach, Florida

MERINGUE COOKIES

Yield: 24

3 egg whites at room temperature
⅞ cup sugar
¼ teaspoon vinegar
1 teaspoon vanilla or 1 teaspoon grated
lemon peel

½ cup crushed walnuts
½ (6-ounce) package semisweet
chocolate morsels

- Preheat oven to 400°.
- In large bowl of electric mixer, beat egg whites until soft peaks form.
- Add sugar, vinegar and vanilla to egg whites; beat until stiff.
- Fold in walnuts and chocolate morsels.
- Drop meringue by rounded teaspoonfuls on greased baking sheet.
- Reduce oven temperature to 250°.
- Bake for 1 hour.

Kay Freedman
Boca Raton, Florida

CAKES
&
PIES

APPLE CAKE

Serves: 12

2 cups all-purpose flour
2 teaspoons baking powder
¼ teaspoon salt
1 cup sugar, divided
½ cup vegetable oil or shortening
2 eggs plus 1 egg yolk, divided

2 teaspoons grated lemon peel or
  2 teaspoons vanilla flavoring
3 pounds apples, thinly sliced
1 teaspoon ground cinnamon
1 teaspoon lemon juice

- In large mixing bowl, combine flour, baking powder, salt, ½ cup sugar, oil, 2 eggs and peel. Mix to form dough, adding ¼ to ½ cup additional flour if necessary.
- On lightly floured surface, roll dough to ⅛-inch thickness. Press in bottom and against sides of lightly oiled 9-inch springform pan. If preferred, do not roll dough but take small portions and press against bottom and sides, smoothing with fingertips. Reserve excess dough.
- In large mixing bowl, combine apples, cinnamon, ½ cup sugar and lemon juice. Place in dough-lined pan.
- Preheat oven to 325°.
- Roll remaining dough into pencil-thin strips and weave lattice-style over apples. Brush strips with egg yolk.
- Bake for 1½ to 1¾ hours. Cool in pan to room temperature before releasing sides.

Harriet Kotler
Tamarac, Florida

BLUEBERRY CUPCAKES

Yield: 18 to 24

½ cup butter, softened
1 cup plus 2 teaspoons sugar, divided
2 eggs
2 cups all-purpose flour
2 teaspoons baking powder

½ teaspoon salt
½ cup milk
1 teaspoon vanilla
2½ cups blueberries

- In large mixing bowl, combine butter and 1 cup sugar; using electric mixer, cream until fluffy. Add eggs, 1 at a time, beating until thoroughly blended.
- Sift flour, baking powder and salt together on waxed paper. Alternately add dry ingredients and milk with vanilla to creamed mixture. Stir in blueberries.
- Grease cups and surface of muffin pans. Spoon batter into cups, filling nearly full. Sprinkle with remaining sugar.
- Bake for 30 minutes. Cool in pans for 30 minutes.

Edith Cohen
Tamarac, Florida

BEST COCONUT CAKE EVER

Serves: 12

Cake

1½ cups butter or margarine, softened	5 eggs or equivalent egg substitute
½ teaspoon salt	3 cups sifted all-purpose flour
¾ teaspoon almond extract	1 teaspoon baking powder
2 teaspoons vanilla	1 cup milk
2 cups sugar	1 (7-ounce) can flaked coconut

- In large mixing bowl, combine butter, salt and flavorings. Using electric mixer, gradually blend in sugar, beating at medium speed for 5 minutes.
- Add eggs to creamed mixture, 1 at a time, beating after each addition.
- Sift flour and baking powder together on waxed paper. Alternately add dry ingredients, ½ cup at a time, with milk to egg mixture; mix by hand.
- Fold coconut into batter. Pour batter into well greased and lightly floured 10-inch tube pan.
- Bake in 300° oven (not preheated) for 2 hours or until wooden pick inserted near center comes out clean. Prepare glaze before cake is finished baking.

Glaze

1 cup sugar	3 tablespoons butter or margarine
½ cup water	½ teaspoon vanilla
¼ cup light corn syrup	

- In small saucepan, combine sugar, water, syrup and butter. Bring to a boil, then boil gently for 5 minutes. Stir in vanilla.
- Spoon hot glaze over hot cake.
- Cool cake in pan. Invert on serving plate. Store in airtight container.

Arlene Klinger
Roswell, Georgia

DUMP CAKE

Serves: 16

Cake

2 cups all-purpose flour
½ cup sugar
2 teaspoons baking soda
½ teaspoon salt
2 eggs

1 teaspoon vanilla
1 cup chopped walnuts
1 (20-ounce) can crushed pineapple
   with juice

- Preheat oven to 350°.
- In large mixing bowl, combine all ingredients, mixing by hand until flour is absorbed. Pour into ungreased 13x9x2-inch baking pan.
- Bake for 25 to 30 minutes. Cool in pan. Frost cooled cake. Store in refrigerator or freeze.

Frosting

1 (8-ounce) package cream cheese, softened
½ cup margarine, softened

1 teaspoon vanilla
1½ cups confectioner's sugar
Grated peel of 1 orange

- In medium-sized mixing bowl, combine cream cheese, margarine and vanilla; cream until smooth.
- Add sugar and orange peel to creamed mixture and blend thoroughly. Spread on cooled cake.

Harriet Berger
Coconut Creek, Florida

APPLE CAKE

Serves: 16 to 20

Cake

⅔ cup vegetable oil	1 teaspoon salt
1 teaspoon vanilla	1½ teaspoons baking soda
2 eggs	½ teaspoon ground cinnamon
2 cups all-purpose flour	1 (21-ounce) can apple pie filling
1 cup sugar	½ cup chopped nuts

- Preheat oven to 350°.
- In large mixing bowl, combine oil, vanilla and eggs; beat until smooth.
- Combine flour, sugar, salt, baking soda and cinnamon on waxed paper. Add to egg mixture and mix thoroughly.
- Stir in pie filling and nuts.
- Pour batter into 13x9x2-inch baking pan prepared by greasing and flouring bottom only.
- Bake for 30 minutes. Pierce hot cake with fork at ½-inch intervals. Cool before glazing.

Glaze

½ cup sugar	¼ teaspoon baking soda
½ (8-ounce) carton sour cream	¼ cup chopped nuts

- In small saucepan, combine sugar, sour cream and baking soda. Cook over medium heat, stirring constantly, until glaze is light and foamy. Pour over cooled cake. Sprinkle cake with nuts.

Leona Brachfeld
Lake Worth, Florida

G.G.'S 1-2-3-4 CAKE

Serves: 12

1 cup butter, softened
2 cups sugar
4 eggs
3 cups all-purpose flour

2 teaspoons baking powder
1 cup milk
1 teaspoon vanilla
1 teaspoon lemon extract

- Preheat oven to 350°.
- In large mixing bowl, combine butter and sugar; beat with electric mixer until creamy.
- Add eggs to creamed mixture, 1 at a time, beating well after each addition.
- Combine flour and baking powder; add dry ingredients alternately with milk to egg mixture. Stir in flavorings.
- Pour batter into 10-inch tube pan.
- Bake for 1 hour.

Karen Felder
West Palm Beach, Florida

BUBBE LIZZIE'S CHERRY CAKE

Serves: 12

3 cups all-purpose flour
1½ cups sugar
4 teaspoons baking powder
1 teaspoon salt

⅔ cup vegetable shortening
1 (8-ounce) jar maraschino cherries
⅔ cup milk
3 eggs

- Preheat oven to 350°.
- In large mixing bowl, sift flour, sugar, baking powder and salt together.
- Add shortening, ⅓ cup cherry juice, chopped cherries and milk. Using electric mixer, beat for 2 minutes.
- Add eggs to batter and beat for 2 minutes.
- Pour batter into greased and floured 10-inch tube pan.
- Bake for 35 to 40 minutes or until wooden pick inserted near center comes out clean. Cool in pan for 15 minutes.

Gail Sheiman
Parkland, Florida

SOUR CREAM CHOCOLATE CAKE

Serves: 12

Cake

3 (1-ounce) squares chocolate
1 cup boiling water
1¼ teaspoons baking soda
½ cup unsalted butter
1½ cups sugar
3 eggs, separated

2½ cups all-purpose flour
½ teaspoon salt
1 (8-ounce) carton sour cream
1 teaspoon red food coloring
1 teaspoon vanilla

- In saucepan over very low heat, melt chocolate. Mix with boiling water. Cool slightly. Stir in baking soda.
- In large mixing bowl, cream butter and sugar until smooth. Beat in egg yolks.
- Combine flour and salt on waxed paper; alternately add with sour cream to egg mixture.
- Stir in chocolate liquid, food coloring and vanilla.
- In small mixing bowl, whip egg whites. Fold into chocolate mixture.
- Spread batter in 10-inch tube pan.
- Bake for 55 minutes. Cake may be frozen.

Frosting

⅔ cup sugar
2 tablespoons cornstarch
2 (1-ounce) squares unsweetened
  chocolate

½ cup water
½ cup coffee
1 teaspoon vanilla
1 tablespoon butter

- In 1-quart saucepan, combine all ingredients. Cook over low heat, stirring constantly, until thickened and bubbly.
- Cool for a few minutes before frosting cake.

Wilma Monsky
Tamarac, Florida

FUDGE RIBBON CAKE

Serves: 12

Filling

1 (8-ounce) package cream cheese,
  softened
¼ cup sugar

1 egg
½ teaspoon vanilla

- In small mixing bowl, combine cream cheese and sugar; using electric mixer, beat at medium speed until creamy. Add egg and vanilla; beat at medium speed until well blended. Set aside.

Batter

2 cups unsifted all-purpose flour
1½ cups sugar
1 teaspoon baking powder
½ teaspoon baking soda
1 teaspoon salt
1 teaspoon vanilla

½ cup vegetable shortening
3 (1-ounce) packets melted
  unsweetened chocolate
1⅓ cups milk
2 eggs

- Preheat oven to 350°.
- In large mixing bowl, combine flour, sugar, baking powder, baking soda and salt. Stir in vanilla, shortening, chocolate, milk and eggs. Beat at medium speed for 3 minutes.
- Pour ½ of batter into 13x9x2-inch baking pan prepared by greasing bottom only. Spoon cream cheese mixture evenly over batter. Pour remaining batter over cheese layer.
- Bake for 35 to 40 minutes.
- Cool before frosting. Cake may be frozen.

Susan Laplante
Seminole, Florida

CHOCOLATE CHIP CAKE

Serves: 12

1 (18½-ounce) package yellow butter cake mix
1 (3½-ounce) package instant vanilla pudding mix
1 cup milk
1 cup vegetable oil
4 eggs
1 (6-ounce) package semisweet chocolate morsels
1 (8-ounce) bar German chocolate
Confectioner's sugar

- Preheat oven to 350°.
- In large mixing bowl, combine cake mix, pudding mix, milk, oil and eggs; mix well.
- Stir in chocolate morsels. Grate 5 squares chocolate and add to batter.
- Pour batter into greased and floured fluted tube pan.
- Bake for 1 hour.
- Cool in pan 10 to 15 minutes, invert on wire rack and complete cooling. Sprinkle top with confectioner's sugar; grate 3 squares chocolate and sprinkle on cake. Cake may be frozen.

Ann B. Stillman
Nashville, Tennessee

KAHLUA CHOCOLATE CAKE

Serves: 12

1 (18½-ounce) package devils food cake mix
1 (8-ounce) carton sour cream
1 cup Kahlua or any coffee liqueur
¾ cup vegetable oil
4 eggs
1 (6-ounce) package semisweet chocolate morsels

- Preheat oven to 350°.
- In large mixing bowl, combine cake mix, sour cream, Kahlua, oil and eggs. Using electric mixer, beat at low speed to blend, then at medium speed for 4 minutes and finally at high speed for 8 minutes.
- Stir in chocolate morsels by hand.
- Pour batter into greased and floured 10-inch tube pan.
- Bake for 55 to 60 minutes or until wooden pick inserted near center comes out clean.
- Cool in pan 30 minutes. Invert on wire rack to complete cooling.

Bea Fox
Tamarac, Florida

FRENCH CHOCOLATE CAKE

Serves: 16 to 20

Cake

1 cup butter	2½ teaspoons baking powder
2 cups sugar	1 cup cocoa
4 eggs	1 cup strong coffee, cooled
2¾ cups all-purpose flour	1 teaspoon vanilla

- Preheat oven to 350°.
- In large mixing bowl, cream butter and sugar together until smooth. Add eggs, 1 at a time, beating well after each addition.
- Combine flour, baking powder and cocoa on waxed paper; add to creamed mixture and beat thoroughly.
- Add coffee and vanilla; mix well.
- Pour batter into greased and floured 10-inch tube pan.
- Bake for 1 hour or until wooden pick inserted near center comes out clean.
- Cool cake in pan for 10 to 15 minutes; invert on wire rack and complete cooling before frosting. Cake may be frozen.

Frosting

3 (1-ounce) squares unsweetened chocolate	1 (14-ounce) can sweetened condensed milk
1 tablespoon butter	1 teaspoon vanilla

- In top of double boiler over simmering water, melt chocolate and butter together; mix well. Add milk, stirring constantly.
- When spreading consistency, add vanilla and mix until blended.
- Use regular dinner knife to spread on cooled cake.

Rheta Okun
Clarksdale, Mississippi

ORIGINAL MIXED FRUIT-NUT CAKE

Serves: 8

½ cup margarine, softened
½ cup sugar
½ cup firmly-packed brown sugar
2 eggs
1 banana, mashed
1 apple, peeled and chopped
4 slices canned pineapple, chopped

¾ cup unbleached flour
¾ cup whole wheat flour
¼ teaspoon salt
1 teaspoon baking soda
5 tablespoons sour cream
1 teaspoon vanilla
½ cup chopped walnuts

- Preheat oven to 350°.
- In large mixing bowl, cream margarine and sugars until smooth. Add eggs, one at a time. Blend in banana, apple and pineapple; mix well.
- Sift flours, salt and baking soda together on waxed paper; add dry ingredients alternately with sour cream. Stir in vanilla and walnuts.
- Pour batter into greased 9x5x3-inch loaf pan.
- Bake for 1 hour or until wooden pick inserted near center comes out clean.
- Cool in pan for 15 minutes; invert on wire rack to complete cooling.

Roslyn Dworkin
Boca Raton, Florida

GRAHAM CRACKER CAKE

Serves: 8

¼ cup butter or margarine, softened
¾ cup sugar
1 egg
2 cups finely crushed graham cracker crumbs

2 teaspoons baking powder
1 cup finely chopped nuts
1 cup milk

- Preheat oven to 350°.
- In large mixing bowl, cream butter. Gradually add sugar, beating until light and fluffy. Add egg and beat well.
- Combine crumbs, baking powder and nuts on waxed paper. Alternately add with milk to creamed mixture, beating thoroughly after each addition.
- Pour batter into well-greased and floured 8x8x2-inch baking pan.
- Bake for 45 minutes or until top springs back when touched lightly with fingertips.
- Cool cake in pan. Serve plain or with nut frosting.

Clara Hirshon
North Miami Beach, Florida

PEACH POUND CAKE

Serves: 10 to 12

1 cup butter or margarine, softened
3 cups sugar
6 eggs
3 cups all-purpose flour
¼ teaspoon baking soda
¼ teaspoon salt

½ (8-ounce) carton sour cream
2 cups peeled, chopped fresh or frozen
   peaches, drained
1 teaspoon vanilla extract
1 teaspoon almond extract

- In large mixing bowl, cream butter and sugar until smooth. Add eggs, 1 at a time, beating after each addition.
- Combine flour, baking soda and salt on waxed paper. In small mixing bowl, combine sour cream and peaches. Alternately add with dry ingredients to creamed mixture, beginning and ending with dry ingredients.
- Stir in flavorings.
- Pour batter in greased and floured 10-inch tube pan.
- Bake for 1 hour and 15 to 20 minutes or until wooden pick inserted near center comes out clean.
- Cool for 15 minutes in pan; invert on wire rack to complete cooling.

Leslie Feldman Abrahams
Atlanta, Georgia

SOUR CREAM CAKE

Serves: 10 to 12

1 cup butter, softened
2¾ cups sugar
6 eggs
1 teaspoon vanilla
½ teaspoon almond extract

3 cups cake flour
¼ teaspoon baking soda
¾ teaspoon salt
1 (8-ounce) carton sour cream

- Preheat oven to 350°.
- In large mixing bowl, cream butter and sugar until light. Add eggs, 1 at a time, beating after each addition. Stir in flavoring.
- Sift flour, baking soda and salt together on waxed paper. Alternately add dry ingredients and sour cream to creamed mixture, ending with dry ingredients.
- Pour batter into buttered and floured 10-inch fluted tube pan.
- Bake for 1 hour and 15 minutes.
- Cool in pan for 15 minutes; invert on wire rack to cool completely. Cake may be frozen.

Erika Brodsky
Boca Raton, Florida

ORANGE CAKE VIENNA

Serves: 10 to 12

1 cup unsalted butter or margarine
1 cup sugar
3 eggs, separated
2 cups all-purpose flour
1 teaspoon baking soda
1 teaspoon baking powder
1 (8-ounce) carton sour cream

Grated peel of 1 orange
½ cup chopped walnuts
¼ cup orange juice
⅓ cup Grand Marnier or other orange
  liqueur
Confectioner's sugar

- Preheat oven to 350°.
- In large mixing bowl, cream butter and sugar until light and fluffy. Beat in egg yolks.
- Sift flour, baking soda and baking powder together on waxed paper. Alternately add with sour cream to creamed mixture. Stir in orange peel and walnuts.
- In medium-sized mixing bowl, beat egg whites until stiff. Fold into batter.
- Spread mixture in 9-inch fluted tube pan prepared by greasing and dusting with sugar.
- Bake for 45 to 55 minutes or until wooden pick inserted near center comes out clean.
- Cool in pan for 15 minutes; invert on wire rack and complete cooling.
- In small mixing bowl, combine orange juice and liqueur. Pour over cooled cake on serving plate. Dust with confectioner's sugar.

Marion Last Silver
Lake Worth, Florida

POPPYSEED CAKE

Serves: 12 to 14

1 (18½-ounce) package yellow cake
  mix
1 (3¾-ounce) package instant French
  vanilla pudding mix
5 eggs

1 (8-ounce) carton sour cream
½ cup vegetable oil
½ cup cream sherry or Kahlua
⅓ cup poppyseeds

- Preheat oven to 350°.
- In large mixing bowl, combine all ingredients. Beat by hand until well blended or beat with electric mixer for 5 to 6 minutes.
- Pour batter into greased 10-inch fluted tube pan.
- Bake for 1 hour.
- Cool for 15 minutes; invert on wire rack to complete cooling.

Marcia Kosofsky
Pompano, Florida

BUTTERMILK PRUNE CAKE

Serves: 12 to 16

1 cup cut-up pitted prunes
Boiling water
¾ cup vegetable oil
1½ cups sugar
3 eggs
2 cups all-purpose flour
1 teaspoon baking soda

Dash of salt
1 teaspoon nutmeg
1 teaspoon ground cinnamon
1 cup buttermilk
1 teaspoon vanilla
½ cup chopped walnuts

- Soften prunes in boiling water; let stand while preparing batter.
- Preheat oven to 350°.
- In large mixing bowl, combine oil and sugar; beat until creamy. Add eggs, 1 at a time, beating well after each addition.
- Sift flour, baking soda, salt, nutmeg and cinnamon together on waxed paper. Alternately add with buttermilk to creamed mixture. Stir in vanilla, nuts and drained prunes; mix well.
- Spread batter in greased and floured 10-inch fluted tube pan.
- Bake for 55 minutes.
- Cool in pan; invert on wire rack to complete cooling. Dust with confectioner's sugar or cover with glaze.

Mirian Weipris
Palm Beach, Florida

PINEAPPLE CAKE

Serves: 8

1 (8-ounce) can crushed pineapple
  with juice
2 eggs
2 cups all-purpose flour

1 tablespoon baking powder
½ teaspoon salt
1 cup sugar
½ cup vegetable shortening

- Preheat oven to 375°.
- In medium-sized mixing bowl, combine pineapple and eggs; mix well.
- In large mixing bowl, sift flour, baking powder, salt and sugar together. Cut in shortening until mixture forms crumbs. Reserve ¾ cup for topping.
- Add pineapple-egg mixture to dry ingredients and mix well. Pour into buttered 8x8x2-inch baking pan. Sprinkle with reserved crumbs.
- Bake for 35 minutes or until top springs back when lightly touched with fingertips.
- Cool in pan.

Edith Cohen
Tamarac, Florida

CHEESECAKE

Serves: 10

2 (8-ounce) packages cream cheese,
softened
1 scant cup sugar
3 tablespoons all-purpose flour,
divided

5 eggs, separated
Juice of ¼ small lemon
1 teaspoon vanilla
1 cup milk

- Preheat oven to 375°.
- In large mixing bowl, combine cream cheese and sugar; cream until smooth. Add egg yolks, 1 at a time, beating well after each addition.
- Add 2 tablespoons flour, lemon juice and vanilla to creamed mixture. Add milk and beat thoroughly.
- In medium-sized mixing bowl, beat egg whites until stiff. Fold into batter.
- Spread batter in 8 or 9-inch springform pan prepared by buttering sides and bottom and sprinkling with 1 tablespoon flour.
- Bake for 10 minutes; reduce oven temperature to 325° and bake for 50 minutes. Turn oven off, position door ajar and allow cake to cool in oven.

Vera Spear
Pembroke Pines, Florida

CHEESELESS CHEESECAKE

Serves: 6 to 8

1 (16-ounce) carton sour cream
⅓ cup sugar
2 eggs, separated

1 teaspoon vanilla
1 unbaked 9-inch graham cracker
crust

- Preheat oven to 350°.
- In large mixing bowl, combine sour cream and sugar; blend until smooth. Add egg yolks and mix well. Stir in vanilla.
- In small mixing bowl, beat egg whites until stiff. Fold into yolk mixture.
- Spread batter in crust.
- Bake for 35 to 45 minutes or until golden brown. Turn oven off; do not open oven door. Let stand in oven for 1 hour. Remove and chill.

Betty M. Siegel
Delray Beach, Florida

DYNAMITE FEATHERLIGHT CHEESECAKE

Serves: 12

4 (8-ounce) cartons whipped cream
   cheese, softened
½ cup sweet butter, softened
1 (16-ounce) carton sour cream, at
   room temperature

2 tablespoons cornstarch
1¼ cups sugar
1¼ teaspoons vanilla
1 teaspoon lemon juice
5 eggs, at room temperature

- Preheat oven to 375°.
- In large mixing bowl, combine cream cheese, butter and sour cream. Using electric mixer, beat until smooth.
- Add cornstarch, sugar, vanilla and lemon juice to creamed mixture; beat at high speed until well blended. Add eggs, 1 at a time, beating after each addition.
- Pour batter into greased 9-inch springform pan. Place pan in large pan half filled with warm water.
- Bake for 1 hour or until golden brown. Turn oven off; let cheesecake stand in oven with door closed for 1 hour. Open door and let stand for 30 minutes. Remove from oven and cool at room temperature for 1 hour. Chill, covered.

Sheila Fuchs
Delray Beach, Florida

CREAM CHEESECAKE

Serves: 12

5 (8-ounce) packages cream cheese,
   softened
6 eggs

1 tablespoon vanilla
1 (16-ounce) carton sour cream
1¾ cups sugar

- Preheat oven to 400°.
- In large mixing bowl, combine all ingredients. Using electric mixer, beat until smooth.
- Pour batter into greased 10-inch springform pan. Place pan in roasting pan containing 1 inch water.
- Bake for 1 hour. Cool for 30 minutes before chilling.

Bea Sonnenreich
Delray Beach, Florida

BAVARIAN APPLE TORTE

Serves: 8

Pastry

½ cup margarine, softened
⅓ cup sugar

¼ teaspoon vanilla
1 cup all-purpose flour

- In medium-sized mixing bowl, cream margarine, sugar and vanilla until smooth. Blend in flour.
- Spread dough evenly on bottom and sides of 9-inch springform pan.

Filling

1 (8-ounce) package cream cheese, softened
¼ cup sugar

1 egg
½ teaspoon vanilla

- In medium-sized mixing bowl, combine cream cheese and sugar; beat until smooth. Add egg and vanilla; mix thoroughly.
- Pour filling into dough-lined pan.

Topping

⅓ cup sugar
½ teaspoon cinnamon

4 cups sliced peeled apples
¼ cup sliced almonds

- Preheat oven to 450°.
- In large mixing bowl, combine sugar, cinnamon, apples and almonds; toss to coat evenly. Arrange on filling in pan.
- Bake for 10 minutes at 450°; reduce oven temperature to 400° and bake for 25 minutes.
- Cool in pan. Torte may be stored in refrigerator or frozen.

Carol Brull
Dunwoody, Georgia

CHOCOLATE TORTE

Serves: 16

Cake

¾ cup sugar
¾ cup butter, softened
6 eggs, separated

6 (1-ounce) squares semisweet
   chocolate, melted
¾ cup ground almonds

- In large mixing bowl, cream sugar and butter until light and fluffy. Add egg yolks, 3 at a time, beating well and scraping sides of bowl after each addition.
- Stir in chocolate and mix thoroughly. Blend in almonds.
- Preheat oven to 375°.
- In medium-sized mixing bowl, beat egg whites until stiff. Fold into chocolate batter; do not overmix.
- Pour batter into greased and floured 9-inch springform pan.
- Bake for 20 minutes at 375°; reduce oven temperature to 350° and bake for 45 minutes; do not overbake.
- Cool in pan for 30 minutes. Chill for 1½ to 2 hours before frosting. Cake may be frozen unfrosted; thaw before frosting.

Frosting

5 (1-ounce) squares unsweetened
   chocolate
½ cup butter

1 cup evaporated milk
3 cups confectioner's sugar
1 teaspoon vanilla

- In 1-quart saucepan over low heat, melt chocolate and butter. Add milk, sugar and vanilla; beat until smooth. Cool before spreading on cake.

Rhoda Sue Ambach
Boca Raton, Florida

SACHER TORTE

Serves: 12

Cake

½ cup plus 2 tablespoons unsalted
  butter, softened
¾ cup sugar, divided
8 eggs, separated
6 (1-ounce) squares semisweet
  chocolate, melted

1¼ cups cake flour, sifted
¼ cup plus 2 tablespoons apricot jam,
  strained

- Preheat oven to 300°.
- In large mixing bowl, cream butter and ¼ cup sugar until ribbons form. Add 2 egg yolks at a time, beating after each addition.
- In separate bowl, beat egg whites until fluffy. Gradually add ½ cup sugar and beat until stiff but not dry.
- Alternately add melted chocolate and egg whites to yolk mixture. Carefully fold in flour. Pour batter into well-greased and floured 10-inch springform pan.
- Bake for 50 minutes or until wooden pick inserted near center comes out clean.
- Cool in pan on rack. Remove sides of pan, then brush jam on cooled cake. Pour slightly cooled glaze over cake.

Glaze

½ cup unsalted butter
¼ cup plus 1 tablespoon strong brewed
  coffee
¼ cup plus 1 tablespoon light corn
  syrup

8 (1-ounce) squares semisweet
  chocolate, melted

- In small saucepan, combine butter, syrup and coffee; bring to a boil. Remove from heat and add chocolate, stirring to dissolve.

Erika Brodsky
Boca Raton, Florida

MERINGUE COFFEE CAKE

Serves: 12

2 cakes compressed yeast
½ cup warm (105° to 115°) milk
1 cup butter or margarine, softened
1¼ cups sugar, divided
3 eggs, separated
½ teaspoon vanilla

4 cups sifted all-purpose flour
½ (8-ounce) carton sour cream
2 tablespoons ground cinnamon
½ cup chopped nuts
½ cup raisins

- Dissolve yeast in milk.
- In large mixing bowl, cream butter and ¼ cup sugar until smooth. Add egg yolks and vanilla; mix well.
- Alternately add flour with dissolved yeast and sour cream. Chill, covered with towel, overnight.
- On lightly-floured surface, roll dough to 15x12-inch rectangle.
- In small mixing bowl, beat egg whites with 1 cup sugar until stiff. Spread on dough.
- Combine cinnamon, nuts and raisins on waxed paper; sprinkle evenly over dough.
- Roll dough, jellyroll fashion. Cut in 6 slices and place, cut side up, in greased 10-inch tube pan. Filling will seep from dough.
- Let rise, covered with towel, for 2 hours.
- Preheat oven to 350°.
- Bake for 1 hour. Cool in pan for 15 minutes; invert on serving plate. Coffee cake may be frozen.

Ethel Slovin
Lake Worth, Florida

COFFEE CAKE

Serves: 16

1 cup butter or margarine, softened
3 cups sugar, divided
2 teaspoons vanilla
4 eggs
4 cups all-purpose flour
2 teaspoons baking powder
2 teaspoons baking soda

1 (16-ounce) carton sour cream
Ground cinnamon
1 (16-ounce) package walnuts, finely
   chopped
1 (12-ounce) package semisweet
   chocolate morsels

- In large mixing bowl, cream butter, 2 cups sugar, vanilla and eggs until smooth.
- Combine flour, baking powder and baking soda on waxed paper. Gradually add to creamed mixture, beating thoroughly. Add sour cream, a small amount at a time to moisten, then remainder and mix well.
- Preheat oven to 350°.
- Spread ½ of dough evenly in greased 13x9x2-inch baking pan. Sprinkle with cinnamon. Sprinkle ½ of walnuts, ½ of chocolate morsels and ½ cup sugar over dough; press with palm of hand. Add remaining dough by spoonfuls, spreading to cover evenly. Repeat with cinnamon, walnuts, chocolate morsels and sugar.
- Bake for 1 hour or until wooden pick inserted near center comes out clean.
- Cool in pan.

Florence Schwartzberg
Coconut Creek, Florida

CHOCOLATE CHIP
SOUR CREAM COFFEE CAKE

Serves: 10 to 12

Topping

½ cup firmly-packed light brown sugar
2 tablespoons all-purpose flour
½ cup chopped walnuts

¾ (6-ounce) package semisweet
   chocolate morsels
1 teaspoon ground cinnamon

- In small mixing bowl, combine topping ingredients.

Note: 1 (8-ounce) package chopped dates or figs or 1 cup favorite preserves may be substituted for chocolate morsels.

Batter

½ cup butter or margarine, softened
1 cup sugar
2 eggs
1 (8-ounce) carton sour cream
1 teaspoon vanilla

2 cups all-purpose flour
1 teaspoon baking powder
1 teaspoon baking soda
½ teaspoon salt

- Preheat oven to 350°.
- In large mixing bowl, cream butter and sugar until smooth. Add eggs and vanilla and beat well. Blend in sour cream and vanilla, mixing until creamy.
- Combine flour, baking powder, baking soda and salt. Add to creamed mixture.
- Pour ½ of batter in greased and floured 10-inch tube pan; sprinkle with ½ of topping; repeat layers.
- Bake for 40 to 60 minutes or until wooden pick inserted near center comes out clean.
- Cool in pan for 10 minutes; invert on serving dish to complete cooling.

Phyllis Halio
Delray Beach, Florida

STRAWBERRY CREAM CHEESE COFFEE CAKE

Serves: 16

1 (8-ounce) package cream cheese, softened
½ cup margarine, softened
¾ cup sugar
1 cup milk
2 eggs, beaten
1 teaspoon vanilla
2 cups all-purpose flour
1 teaspoon baking powder
½ teaspoon baking soda
¼ teaspoon salt
1 (18-ounce) jar quality strawberry preserves
1 tablespoon lemon juice
¼ cup firmly-packed brown sugar
½ cup chopped pecans

- Preheat oven to 350°.
- In large mixing bowl, combine cream cheese, margarine and sugar; cream until smooth. Add milk, eggs and vanilla; beat until smooth.
- Sift flour, baking powder, baking soda and salt together on waxed paper; add to creamed mixture.
- Spread ½ of batter in 13x9x2-inch baking pan.
- In small mixing bowl, combine preserves and lemon juice. Spoon mixture on batter, spreading carefully to cover. Pour remaining batter over preserves. Sprinkle with brown sugar and pecans.
- Bake for 40 minutes.
- Serve from pan. Store in refrigerator.

Celia Burack
Delray Beach, Florida

ANNIE'S APPLE-CRANBERRY CAKE

Serves: 12

1 cup vegetable shortening
¾ cup sugar
2 eggs
4 cups plus 2 tablespoons all-purpose flour, divided
2 teaspoons baking powder
½ teaspoon salt

½ cup orange juice
6 apples, grated
1 (16-ounce) can whole cranberry sauce
½ teaspoon ground cinnamon
1 teaspoon grated lemon peel
1 tablespoon sugar

- In large mixing bowl, cream shortening and sugar until smooth. Add eggs and beat thoroughly.
- Combine 4 cups flour, baking powder and salt on waxed paper; alternately add with orange juice to creamed mixture and mix to form dough.
- Divide dough in 2 portions. Wrap in waxed paper and chill for 2 hours.
- Preheat oven to 375°.
- Press ½ of dough on greased 17x12x1-inch baking sheet.
- In large mixing bowl, combine apples, cranberry sauce, cinnamon, lemon peel, sugar and 2 tablespoons flour. Spread mixture evenly on dough-lined baking sheet.
- On lightly floured surface, roll remaining dough to ⅛-inch thickness and cut in ¼-inch strips. Place over fruit filling, weaving for lattice effect.
- Bake for 1 hour.
- Cool before cutting.

Carolyn Kerner Stein
North Miami Beach, Florida

"LIMON" PIE

Serves: 6 to 8

1 (9-inch) graham cracker crust
1 (14-ounce) can sweetened
  condensed milk
1 (8-ounce) carton frozen non-dairy
  whipped topping, thawed

¼ cup lime juice
¼ cup lemon juice

- In large mixing bowl, blend milk and whipped topping. Add juices and mix thoroughly.
- Pour filling into crust. Chill overnight. Pie may be frozen.
- Garnish servings with additional topping, strawberries and kiwi slices, if desired.

Charlotte Shara
Hallandale, Florida

FRESH STRAWBERRY PIE

Serves: 8

1 baked 9-inch pastry shell
1½ quarts fresh strawberries
3 tablespoons cornstarch

1 cup sugar
2 tablespoons lemon juice
Whipped cream or topping

- Reserving ½ of best berries, mash remainder in saucepan (or use food processor, chopping with metal blade). Blend in cornstarch and sugar.
- Cook over medium heat, stirring frequently; bring to a boil. Mixture should thicken and become clear. Cool.
- Reserving a few for garnish, add whole berries to cooled filling. Pour into pastry shell. Spread cream over filling and garnish with whole berries.
- Serve immediately or chilled.

Pepi Dunay
Boca Raton, Florida

CHOCOLATE MOUSSE PIE

Serves: 8

Pastry

2 cups sifted all-purpose flour
½ teaspoon salt

¾ cup vegetable shortening
Ice water

- Preheat oven to 400°.
- In medium-sized mixing bowl, combine flour and salt. Using two knives or pastry blender, cut shortening into dry ingredients. Add enough ice water to form moist, workable dough.
- Divide dough in 2 portions. On floured waxed paper, roll each portion to fit 9-inch pie pan with ½-inch excess.
- Place dough in pans. Flute or crimp edges. Pierce bottom with fork tines.
- Bake for 10 to 15 minutes or until shell is lightly browned and crisp; check several times during baking for bubbles, piercing with fork to remove. Cool to room temperature.

Filling

1 (12-ounce) package semisweet chocolate morsels
¼ cup hot coffee
1 (16-ounce) carton dairy or parve whipping cream
½ (3¾-ounce) package instant vanilla or chocolate pudding mix (optional)

2 tablespoons brandy or liqueur (optional)
¼ teaspoon ground cinnamon (optional)

- Combine chocolate and coffee in top of double boiler over hot water; stir until chocolate is melted. Cool.
- In large mixing bowl, whip cream until foamy. Add pudding mix and whip until stiff.
- Fold in liqueur and cinnamon. Fold in cooled chocolate liquid. Pour filling into baked pastry shell.
- Chill for at least 1 hour before serving. If desired, garnish with maraschino cherry at center or with chocolate shots around edge.

Marion Zeiger
Chapel Hill, North Carolina

SWEDISH APPLE PIE

Serves: 6

4 or 5 large baking apples, peeled and
  thinly sliced
¾ cup plus 2 tablespoons sugar,
  divided
1 teaspoon ground cinnamon

2 tablespoons lemon juice
1 cup all-purpose flour
1 egg, beaten
½ cup butter or margarine, melted

- Preheat oven to 350°.
- Place apple slices in 9-inch pie plate
- In small mixing bowl, combine 2 tablespoons sugar, cinnamon and lemon juice. Pour over apples.
- In small mixing bowl, combine ¾ cup sugar, flour, egg and margarine. Spread mixture over apples.
- Bake for 45 to 60 minutes.
- Serve warm or cold with ice cream.

Kay Freedman
Boca Raton, Florida

KAHLUA PECAN PIE

Serves: 8

1 unbaked 9-inch pastry shell
½ cup butter, softened
1 cup firmly-packed brown sugar
3 jumbo eggs
1 teaspoon Kahlua

1 cup light corn syrup
1 cup chopped pecans
⅔ (6-ounce) package semisweet
  chocolate morsels
Whipped cream

- Preheat oven to 450°.
- In large mixing bowl, cream butter and brown sugar until fluffy. Add eggs, 1 at a time, beating after each addition until light and fluffy.
- Stir in Kahlua and syrup; blend well. Add pecans and chocolate morsels; mix thoroughly.
- Pour filling into shell.
- Bake for 10 minutes at 450°; reduce oven temperature to 325° and bake for 30 minutes.
- Cool. Spoon dollops of whipped cream on individual servings.

Sari T. Addicott
Miami, Florida

CHEESE PIE

Serves: 10

Pastry

1½ cups cinnamon graham cracker
  crumbs

½ cup sugar
½ cup margarine, softened

- In small mixing bowl, combine crumbs, sugar and margarine. Press crumbs in bottom and on sides of 9-inch pie pan.

Filling

2 (8-ounce) packages cream cheese,
  softened
2 eggs, at room temperature
⅔ cup plus 2 tablespoons sugar,
  divided

1 tablespoon plus 1 teaspoon vanilla,
  divided
1 (8-ounce) carton sour cream

- Preheat oven to 375°.
- In large mixing bowl, combine cream cheese, eggs, ⅔ cup sugar and 1 teaspoon vanilla. Using electric mixer, beat until smooth.
- Pour filling into crust.
- Bake for 20 minutes. Cool for 15 minutes. Reset oven temperature to 425° and bake for 10 minutes.
- In small mixing bowl, blend sour cream, 2 tablespoons sugar and 1 tablespoon vanilla. Spread over partially cooled pie.
- Cool, then chill overnight before serving. Pie may be frozen.

Jean Levine
Lauderhill, Florida

ZWETSCHGENKUCHE FRUIT PIE

Serves: 16

Pastry

1 cup butter or margarine, softened
4½ cups sifted all-purpose flour
Pinch of salt

1 cup water
2 tablespoons vegetable oil
2 tablespoons sugar (optional)

- In large mixing bowl, combine butter with flour and salt. Add water, oil and sugar, mixing with pastry blender until dough forms.
- Chill dough for 24 hours or dough may be frozen until needed.

Filling

2½ pounds fresh plums, pitted and cut
to form fan OR 6 large fresh
peaches, sliced OR 4 to 6 large
apples, sliced

- Preheat oven to 400°.
- Roll dough to fit two 12-inch pie plates. Place ½ of fruit in each pastry shell, overlapping slices.
- Bake for 15 to 20 minutes, brush fruit with glaze, and continue baking for 20 minutes.
- Cool. Sprinkle additional sugar over glazed fruit. If desired, decorate pie by piping whipped cream around edge or serve dollops of cream on individual pieces.

Glaze

1 teaspoon cornstarch
1 cup water

1 tablespoon sugar
2 or 3 eggs

- In small saucepan, mix cornstarch with water. Cook over low heat, stirring constantly. Remove from heat. Add sugar and eggs; mix well.
- Brush glaze over fruit halfway through baking time.

Margrit Schechtman
Sarasota, Florida

PUMPKIN PIE

Serves: 8

1 baked 9-inch pastry shell
1 (16-ounce) can pumpkin
¾ cup firmly-packed brown sugar
1 teaspoon ground cinnamon
½ teaspoon ground ginger

½ teaspoon ground cloves
½ teaspoon ground allspice
¼ teaspoon ground nutmeg
2 eggs
1 cup evaporated milk

- In large mixing bowl, combine pumpkin, sugar and spices.
- In small mixing bowl, beat eggs and milk together. Stir into pumpkin mixture.
- Pour filling into baked shell.
- Bake on medium (50%) for 25 to 30 minutes or until filling is set. Let stand 10 to 15 minutes. Cool at room temperature.

Marilyn Prevor
Atlanta, Georgia

PARVE PASTRY DOUGH

4½ cups all-purpose flour
2 teaspoons baking powder
1 teaspoon salt
2 cups vegetable shortening

Grated peel of 1 lemon and/or orange
½ cup sugar
1 cup orange juice
4 egg yolks

- In large mixing bowl, combine flour, baking powder and salt. Make well in center of dry ingredients.
- Add shortening, peel, sugar, orange juice and egg yolks; mix, then knead until dough leaves sides of bowl.
- Wrap in waxed paper and store in refrigerator or freeze; dough may be refrozen.
- Dough may be used for Purim, may be rolled thin for knish or frankfurter appetizers, used for pastry shells or for rugelach: roll thin, spread with layer of apricot preserves, sugar, ground cinnamon, raisins and nuts; sliced and baked at 375° for 20 to 30 minutes.

Harriet Kotler
Tamarac, Florida

COOKIES
&
DESSERTS

THIN BUTTER COOKIES

Yield: 24

1 cup butter
1½ cups sugar
2 eggs
1½ teaspoons vanilla
Few drops yellow food coloring

3 cups sifted all-purpose flour
½ teaspoon baking powder
½ teaspoon salt
¼ cup milk
Colored sugar, sprinkles or nuts

- In large mixing bowl, cream butter and sugar until smooth. Add eggs, vanilla and food coloring; beat thoroughly.
- Combine flour, baking powder and salt on waxed paper. Alternately add dry ingredients and milk to creamed mixture. Mix to form soft dough. Chill dough, covered, for 2 hours.
- Preheat oven to 425°.
- On lightly floured surface, roll dough to ⅛-inch thickness. Cut with cookie cutters and place on greased baking sheet. Decorate with colored sugar, sprinkles or nuts.
- Bake for 5 to 7 minutes.

Carolyn Kerner Stein
North Miami Beach, Florida

CHEESE BITES

Yield: 36

1 egg yolk
1 (8-ounce) package cream cheese, softened
½ cup sugar, divided

18 slices white bread, crusts removed
½ cup butter, melted
¼ teaspoon ground cinnamon

- Preheat oven to 350°.
- In medium-sized mixing bowl, combine egg yolk, cheese and ¼ cup sugar; beat until smooth.
- Roll bread slices as thin as possible. Spread sweetened cream cheese on each slice and roll up. Cut each roll in half.
- Dip rolls in butter and place on baking sheet.
- In small bowl, combine ¼ cup sugar and cinnamon. Sprinkle over rolls.
- Bake for 30 minutes.

Marilyn Friedman
Delray Beach, Florida

MILLION DOLLAR CHOCOLATE CHIP COOKIES

Yield: 60

2 cups butter or margarine
2 cups sugar
2 cups firmly-packed brown sugar
4 eggs
2 teaspoons vanilla
4 cups all-purpose flour
5 cups oatmeal, ground in blender

2 teaspoons baking powder
2 teaspoons baking soda
1 teaspoon salt
1 (12-ounce) package semisweet
  chocolate morsels
1 (8-ounce) chocolate bar, grated

- Preheat oven to 375°.
- In large mixing bowl, cream butter and sugars until smooth. Add eggs and vanilla; beat thoroughly.
- In another large bowl, combine flour, oatmeal, baking powder, baking soda and salt. Stir into creamed mixture and mix well.
- Add chocolate to dough, mixing to distribute evenly throughout dough.
- Shape dough into 1-inch balls (or slightly larger) and place on ungreased baking sheet.
- Bake for 10 to 12 minutes.

Carolyn Ring
West Palm Beach, Florida

JELLY COOKIES

Yield: 50

1 cup butter or margarine (parve)
½ cup confectioner's sugar
1 egg

1 tablespoon vanilla
2¼ cups all-purpose flour
Jelly

- Preheat oven to 375°.
- In large mixing bowl, cream butter and sugar until smooth. Add egg and vanilla; mix thoroughly.
- Add flour to creamed mixture; mix well. Chill for 2 hours or longer.
- Shape dough into small balls and place on baking sheet. With thumb, press center to form well; fill with ¼ teaspoon jelly.
- Bake for 30 minutes or until lightly browned.

Bernice E. Jacobson
Lake Worth, Florida

CHOCOLATE NUT TOPPED COOKIES

Yield: 48

¾ cup margarine
¾ cup sugar
1 egg
1½ teaspoons vanilla
2 cups all-purpose flour

1 teaspoon salt
1 (12-ounce) package semisweet
  chocolate morsels
1 tablespoon shortening
2 cups chopped nuts

- Preheat oven to 350°.
- In large mixing bowl, cream margarine until light. Gradually add sugar, beating until fluffy. Add egg and vanilla; mix thoroughly.
- Combine flour and salt on waxed paper; add to creamed mixture.
- Stir ½ cup chocolate morsels into dough, if desired.
- Shape level measuring teaspoonfuls of batter into log shapes on ungreased baking sheets.
- Bake for 10 to 12 minutes. Transfer cookies to wire racks to cool.
- In top of double boiler over hot water, melt 1½ cups chocolate morsels with shortening. Dip ends of cookies in chocolate, then in nuts and place on wire rack to cool.

Harriett Hesselson
Tamarac, Florida

MADELEINES

Yield: 36

1 cup butter or margarine, softened
2½ cups sifted confectioner's sugar
4 eggs

2 cups unsifted all-purpose flour
¼ teaspoon almond extract

- Preheat oven to 350°.
- Place butter in large mixing bowl; using electric mixer, beat until fluffy. Gradually add sugar, beating thoroughly. Add eggs, 1 at a time, beating at high speed after each addition.
- Mix in flour and flavoring; beat well.
- Spoon 1½ tablespoons batter into buttered and floured madeleine cups.
- Bake for 20 to 25 minutes or until lightly browned. Invert pans on wire rack to remove madeleines.
- Store in airtight container for up to 1 week or freeze.

Andrea Sander
Memphis, Tennessee

RAS-LB-ADWAY

Yield: 36

Cookie

2 cups all-purpose flour
1 cup unsalted margarine, softened
1 cup semolina

1 tablespoon vegetable oil
¼ to ½ cup warm water

- In large mixing bowl, combine flour, margarine, semolina and oil. Gradually add water, mixing until blended. Cover.

Filling

1 pound pitted dates
½ cup water
2 tablespoons margarine (optional)
½ cup chopped walnuts

1 teaspoon grated orange or lemon peel
1 teaspoon ground cinnamon
Confectioner's sugar

- In 2-quart saucepan over medium heat, cook dates with water for 15 minutes or until dates are soft. If using margarine, cook dates for 10 minutes, add margarine and cook for 5 minutes. Remove from heat and mash with potato masher until smooth.
- Add walnuts, peel and cinnamon to dates. Cool.
- Preheat oven to 350°.
- Working with ⅓ of dough at a time, shape dough into walnut-sized balls. Flatten each to 2-inch circle. Place 1 teaspoon date filling in center of circle, roll into a log and place on ungreased baking sheet, bending to form crescent. Repeat with remaining dough and filling.
- Bake for 15 to 20 minutes or until down side of cookies are lightly browned.
- Cookies may be frozen. Sprinkle with confectioner's sugar just before serving.

Ruth Mizrahi
North Miami Beach, Florida

HUNGARIAN CRESCENTS FROM POZSON

Yield: 48

Dough

4 cups unsifted all-purpose flour
Pinch of salt
1 teaspoon sugar
2 cups butter or 2 cups shortening
  plus 1 teaspoon butter flavoring

1 egg
2 egg yolks, divided
1 (8-ounce) carton sour cream
Confectioner's sugar

- In large mixing bowl, combine flour, salt and sugar. Using pastry blender cut butter into dry ingredients.
- Add egg, 1 egg yolk and sour cream. Blend with fingertips until dough holds together. Divide into 3 portions, wrap in waxed paper and chill until ready to fill.

Filling

1 (8-ounce) package walnuts, ground
1 cup sugar

1 teaspoon vanilla
Scalded milk

- Preheat oven to 375°.
- Beat 1 egg yolk.
- In medium-sized mixing bowl, combine walnuts and sugar. Stir in vanilla. Gradually add milk until consistency of paste.
- Working with ⅓ of dough at a time, roll to ⅛-inch thickness. Cut into 3-inch squares. Place ½ teaspoon walnut filling on each. Bring top and bottom edges to center, overlapping slightly. Place on ungreased baking sheet, seam side down, curving slightly to form crescent. Brush with egg yolk.
- Bake for 20 minutes. Cool on wire racks.
- Just before serving, dust with confectioner's sugar. Cookies may be stored in airtight container for several days or frozen.

Note: Vanilla sugar may be substituted for confectioner's sugar. To make, place a vanilla bean, slit to release flavor, into sugar shaker; fill with confectioner's sugar.

Elsie K. Sokol
West Palm Beach, Florida

NEAPOLITAN COOKIES

Yield: 96

Dark Dough

1 cup butter, softened
1½ cups firmly-packed brown sugar
2 eggs
3 cups all-purpose flour
¼ teaspoon salt

½ teaspoon ground cinnamon
½ teaspoon ground cloves
1 cup chopped nuts
½ (12-ounce) package miniature
    semisweet chocolate morsels

Light Dough

½ cup butter, softened
¾ cup sugar
1 egg
1 teaspoon vanilla extract
½ teaspoon almond extract
2 cups all-purpose flour

½ teaspoon salt
¼ teaspoon baking soda
2 tablespoons water
¾ cup chopped raisins
12 candied cherries, chopped

- Prepare both doughs same way, beginning with light dough.
- In large mixing bowl, cream butter and sugar until smooth. Beat in eggs. Add dry ingredients and any additional liquids; blend well.
- Add last two ingredients; mix well.
- Line 2-pound loaf pan with waxed paper, extending edges 2 inches over rim of pan.
- Press ½ of dark dough into pan. Cover with all of light dough and top with remaining dark dough. Chill overnight or at least 4 hours.
- Preheat oven to 400°.
- Use waxed paper edges to lift chilled dough from pan. Slice lengthwise into 3 equal parts. Cut each section into ¼-inch slices. Place on ungreased baking sheet.
- Bake for 10 minutes.

Carol A. Glazer
Cape Coral, Florida

PEANUT BUTTER MACAROONS

Yield: 48

2 egg whites
1 cup sugar
¼ teaspoon almond extract

2 cups crispy rice cereal
⅓ cup peanut butter

- Preheat oven to 375°.
- In large mixing bowl, beat egg whites until stiff. Fold in sugar. Add almond extract by drops, mixing gently. Fold in cereal and peanut butter.
- Drop dough by teaspoonfuls on greased baking sheet.
- Bake for 12 minutes. Remove from pan immediately and cool on wire rack.

Ethel Slifkin
Delray Beach, Florida

PEANUT BUTTER COOKIES

Yield: 18

1 (14-ounce) can sweetened
  condensed milk
1 cup smooth or chunky peanut butter

1 (6-ounce) package semisweet
  chocolate morsels

- Preheat oven to 375°.
- In medium-sized mixing bowl, combine milk and peanut butter; blend until smooth. Stir in chocolate morsels.
- Drop dough by teaspoonfuls on lightly greased baking sheets.
- Bake for 7 to 10 minutes.

Lillian Diamond
Coconut Creek, Florida

PEANUT BUTTER BALLS

Yield: 150

1 (40-ounce) jar chunky peanut butter
½ cup plus 2 tablespoons margarine
4¾ cups confectioner's sugar
2½ cups chopped nuts

7 cups crushed crispy rice cereal
2½ (12-ounce) packages semisweet
  chocolate morsels

- In large mixing bowl, combine peanut butter, margarine, sugar, nuts and cereal. Chill dough.
- In top of double boiler over hot water, melt chocolate morsels.
- Roll cereal mixture into balls, dip in chocolate and place on baking sheets. Chill.

Mary Ellen Peyton
Miami, Florida

PEANUT BUTTER KISS COOKIES

Yield: 48

4 dozen foil wrapped semisweet
  chocolate candy kisses
½ cup margarine, softened
½ cup smooth peanut butter
¼ cup plus 3 tablespoons sugar,
  divided

¾ cup firmly-packed brown sugar
1 egg
1 teaspoon vanilla
¼ teaspoon salt
1¾ cups all-purpose flour
1 teaspoon baking soda

- Remove foil from candy kisses.
- Preheat oven to 375°.
- In medium-sized mixing bowl, beat margarine, peanut butter, ¼ cup sugar, brown sugar, egg, vanilla and salt together until smooth.
- Add flour mixed with baking soda; beat until fluffy.
- Shape dough into 48 balls; roll each in 3 tablespoons sugar. Place 2 inches apart on ungreased baking sheet.
- Bake for 8 to 9 minutes. Immediately top each cookie with a chocolate, pressing to bond. Serve immediately or store in refrigerator.

Randi Eisenband
Boca Raton, Florida

HAMANTASHEN
(For Purim)

Yield: 24

8 cups all-purpose flour
6 eggs
1½ cups vegetable oil
1½ cups sugar
1 tablespoon baking powder
Pinch of baking soda

1 teaspoon lemon juice
Pinch of salt
1 egg, beaten
1 pound lekvar or prune jelly or 1
  (21-ounce) can cherry pie filling

- Preheat oven to 350°.
- In large mixing bowl, make a well in flour. Using wire whisk, slowly beat in eggs, oil, sugar, baking powder, baking soda, lemon juice and salt until dough forms.
- On lightly floured surface, roll ⅓ dough to ⅛-inch thickness. Cut circles with 3-inch cutter. Place about 2 teaspoons of filling in center of each dough circle. Pull edges of circle together over filling to form triangle. Pinch corners and brush with beaten egg. Repeat with remaining dough and filling.
- Bake for 10 minutes.

Bertha Herskowitz
Pembroke Pines, Florida

NUTTY NUGGETS

Yield: 28

½ cup butter or margarine, softened
¼ cup sugar
1 teaspoon vanilla

1½ cups all-purpose flour
¾ cup broken walnuts, pecans or
  other nuts

- Preheat oven to 350°.
- In large mixing bowl, cream butter and sugar until smooth; add vanilla. Stir in flour and nuts; mix thoroughly.
- Shape small pieces of dough into nuggets and place on ungreased baking sheet.
- Bake for 20 minutes or until lightly browned.
- Cool cookies. Roll in confectioner's sugar.

Note: Semisweet chocolate morsels may be substituted for nuts.

Mimi Weiner
Inverrary, Florida

BUTTERHORNS

Yield: 32

Dough

1 cup butter, softened
1 (8-ounce) package cream cheese, softened

2 egg yolks
3 cups all-purpose flour
2 tablespoons sugar

- In medium-sized mixing bowl, combine butter and cream cheese; beat until smooth. Blend in egg yolks.
- Add flour and sugar to creamed mixture.
- Chill dough overnight.

Filling

1 cup chopped nuts
1 cup sugar

¼ cup chopped raisins
1 tablespoon lemon juice

- In small mixing bowl, combine all ingredients.
- Preheat oven to 350°.
- Divide dough into 4 balls. Roll each into a circle. Cut into wedges about 3 inches apart at wide edge. Place small amount of filling on triangles and, starting at wide edge, roll up. Place on baking sheet.
- Bake for 20 to 25 minutes.

Ida Janovsky
North Miami Beach, Florida

RUGELACH

Yield: 48

Dough

3 cups all-purpose flour
1 package dry yeast
1 cup butter
3 egg yolks

½ pint whipping cream or 1 (8-ounce) carton sour cream
1 teaspoon vanilla

- In large mixing bowl, combine flour and yeast. Using pastry blender, cut butter into dry ingredients.
- Add egg yolks, cream and vanilla; mix well.
- Divide dough into 6 balls and chill overnight.

Filling

1 cup sugar
1 tablespoon ground cinnamon

1 cup chopped nuts

- In small mixing bowl, combine sugar, cinnamon and nuts.
- Preheat oven to 350°.
- Working with 1 ball of dough at a time, roll into circle on lightly-floured surface. Sprinkle with some of filling mixture.
- Cut circles into wedges. Starting at wide edge, roll up and place on greased and floured baking sheet.
- Bake for 30 minutes.

Frances Rutstein
Delray Beach, Florida

RAISIN RUGELACH

Yield: 48

Dough

1 cup butter, softened
1 (8-ounce) package cream cheese, softened

2 cups all-purpose flour
Confectioner's sugar

- In large mixing bowl, blend butter, cheese and flour with hands.
- Divide dough into 4 balls. Chill, covered, overnight.

Filling

2 tablespoons jelly
1 cup raisins, rinsed and dried
2 tablespoons lemon juice

2 teaspoons ground cinnamon
¼ cup sugar
½ cup ground walnuts

- In small mixing bowl, combine filling ingredients; mix well.
- Preheat oven to 350°.
- Working with 1 ball of dough at a time, roll into circle. Cut into 12 wedges. Spoon small amount of filling on each wedge. Starting at wide edge, roll up and place on ungreased baking sheet.
- Bake for 20 minutes. Roll in confectioner's sugar.

Leona Fuss
Port St. Lucie, Florida

FROZEN DOUGH RUGELACH

Yield: 50

Dough

1 cup butter, softened	2 eggs
1 (8-ounce) package cream cheese, softened	1 teaspoon vanilla
	3½ cups all-purpose flour
1 cup sugar	1 teaspoon baking powder

- In large mixing bowl, combine butter and cheese; beat until smooth. Add sugar, eggs and vanilla; mix well. Blend in flour and baking powder.
- Shape dough into log, enclose in plastic wrap and freeze overnight or until ready to prepare rugelach.

Filling

1 (7-ounce) package flaked coconut	1 (16-ounce) jar apricot jam
1 (15-ounce) package raisins	Ground cinnamon to taste
1 cup chopped walnuts	
1 (6-ounce) package semisweet chocolate chip morsels	

- In large mixing bowl, combine all filling ingredients.
- Preheat oven to 350°.
- Working with small chunks of frozen dough, knead and flatten into circle on lightly-floured surface. Spoon small amount of filling into center of circle, roll up tightly and place in baking pan. Cut small slits on top of roll.
- Bake for 45 minutes.

Rose Goldman
Tamarac, Florida

SCOTCH SHORTBREAD

Yield: 24

1 cup all-purpose flour	Pinch of salt
¼ cup sugar	½ cup butter

- In medium-sized mixing bowl, combine flour, sugar and salt. Using 2 table knives or pastry blender, cut butter into dry ingredients; mix with hands to form dough.
- Divide dough into 3 portions. Roll each into log. Chill for 30 minutes or longer.
- Preheat oven to 350°.
- Cut dough logs into ¼-inch slices and place on greased baking sheet. Pierce with fork tines.
- Bake for 20 to 25 minutes or until browned on edges. Cookies may be frozen.

Irene S. Krell
Boca Raton, Florida

DOUBLE RAISIN MANDELBRODT

Yield: 70

4 eggs, beaten	½ cup golden raisins
1 cup sugar	3½ cups all-purpose flour
1 teaspoon vanilla	2 teaspoons baking powder
½ cup ground nuts	Pinch of salt
½ cup dark raisins	¾ cup vegetable oil

- Preheat oven to 350°.
- In large mixing bowl, combine eggs, sugar and vanilla; beat until smooth. Stir in nuts and raisins.
- Combine flour, baking powder and salt on waxed paper. Alternately add with oil to creamed mixture, ending with dry ingredients.
- Shape dough into 4 strips, placing 2 each on lightly oiled and floured baking sheets.
- Bake for 25 minutes. Cut into slices, arrange on baking sheets and bake until lightly browned. Cool. Slices may be stored in covered tins for several weeks.

Ida Gelsky
Hollywood, Florida

ALMOND MANDELBRODT

Yield: 80

4 eggs, beaten
1 cup sugar
1 cup vegetable oil
1 teaspoon vanilla

2 teaspoons almond extract
4 cups all-purpose flour
2 teaspoons baking powder
½ cup slivered almonds

- In large mixing bowl, combine eggs and sugar. Alternately add oil with flavorings and flour mixed with baking powder; dough will become very thick. Stir in almonds.
- Chill dough overnight.
- Preheat oven to 350°.
- Shape dough into 8 logs and place on ungreased baking sheet.
- Bake for 30 minutes or until lightly browned.
- Slice logs, place slices on baking sheet and bake until lightly browned on both sides.

Kathryn A. Koffs
West Palm Beach, Florida

EASY MANDELBRODT

Yield: 60

3 eggs
1 cup oil
1 teaspoon vanilla
1 cup sugar

3 cups all-purpose flour
2 teaspoons baking powder
1 cup chopped walnuts

- Preheat oven to 350°.
- In large mixing bowl, beat eggs, oil, vanilla and sugar together until smooth.
- Add flour mixed with baking powder. Stir in walnuts.
- Shape dough into logs and place on greased baking sheet.
- Bake for 30 minutes or until lightly browned.
- Slice logs. Slices may be toasted.

Frances Rutstein
Delray Beach, Florida

RAISIN MANDELBRODT

Yield: 38

2 eggs, beaten
½ cup sugar
½ cup margarine, melted
1½ teaspoons vanilla or almond
    extract

2 cups all-purpose flour
1½ teaspoons baking powder
Pinch of salt
½ cup raisins
½ cup nuts (optional)

- In medium-sized mixing bowl, combine eggs, sugar, margarine and vanilla; mix by hand.
- In large mixing bowl, combine flour, baking powder and salt. Pour egg mixture into dry ingredients and mix thoroughly. Add raisins and nuts. Let dough stand 10 minutes.
- Preheat oven to 400°.
- Form dough in two strips 2 inches wide by ½-inch high on baking sheet.
- Bake for 25 minutes. Immediately cut into slices and place on baking sheet. Sprinkle with sugar and cinnamon. Bake for 1 to 2 minutes or until lightly browned; turn and bake until second side is lightly browned.

Pearl S. Kay
Pembroke Pines, Florida

CHEESECAKE TARTS

Yield: 24

2 (8-ounce) packages cream cheese,
    softened
¾ cup sugar
2 eggs
1 tablespoon lemon juice

1 teaspoon vanilla
24 vanilla wafers
1 (21-ounce) can cherry or blueberry
    pie filling

- In large mixing bowl, combine cream cheese, sugar, eggs, lemon juice and vanilla; beat until fluffy.
- Preheat oven to 375°.
- Place paper liners in cups of miniature muffin pans. Place 1 wafer in each liner and fill ⅔ full with cream cheese mixture.
- Bake for 15 to 20 minutes. Top each tart with 1 tablespoon pie filling. Chill until ready to serve.

Joyce Portner
Delray Beach, Florida

BLINTZES

Yield: 20 to 24

Batter

1 cup cold milk	2 cups sifted all-purpose flour
1 cup cold water	¼ cup butter
4 eggs	Butter
½ teaspoon salt	

- In large mixing bowl, combine milk, water, eggs, salt, flour and ¼ cup butter; beat until smooth. Use electric blender to mix ingredients. Let stand for 1 to 2 hours.
- In small skillet, melt butter to coat bottom. Drop 3 tablespoons batter into hot pan, tip to spread batter thinly over entire surface and cook just until top is dry and starts to blister. Invert on board or cloth. Repeat with remaining batter.
- Place 1 tablespoon filling at edge of pancake, fold once, then fold sides and continue folding until rectangle shape.
- Fry rolled blintzes in butter until browned on both sides.
- Serve with sour cream or jelly. Blintzes may be prepared to point of frying, then frozen.

Cheese Filling

2 (4-ounce) packages farmer cheese	1 egg yolk
	¼ cup sugar
1 (3-ounce) package cream cheese, softened	1 teaspoon lemon juice
	Ground cinnamon to taste

- In medium-sized mixing bowl, mix with fork until light.

Potato Filling

1 large onion, chopped	1 egg yolk
Butter	Salt and pepper to taste
4 potatoes, cooked and mashed	

- In small skillet, sauté onion in butter until soft.
- In medium-sized mixing bowl, combine onion, potatoes, egg yolk, salt and pepper; mix to paste consistency.

Sheila Singer
Delray Beach, Florida

BROWNIES

Yield: 12

½ cup butter, softened
1 cup sugar
2 eggs
1 teaspoon vanilla

½ cup all-purpose flour
Pinch of salt
¼ cup cocoa
1 cup chopped nuts

- Preheat oven to 325°.
- In medium-sized mixing bowl, cream butter and sugar until smooth. Blend in eggs and vanilla.
- Add flour mixed with salt, cocoa and nuts; mix thoroughly.
- Spread batter in 8x6x2-inch baking pan.
- Bake for 25 minutes. Frost while warm.

Frosting

2 tablespoons butter
1 cup confectioner's sugar
2 tablespoons cocoa

1 teaspoon vanilla
1 cup miniature marshmallows

- In small mixing bowl, combine butter and sugar; mix in cocoa and vanilla. Add marshmallows.
- Spread frosting on warm brownies. Cool before cutting into squares.

Pearl Warner
Margate, Florida

THE BEST BROWNIES

Yield: 48

4 (1-ounce) squares unsweetened
  chocolate
1 cup butter
2 cups sugar
2 teaspoons vanilla

4 eggs
1 cup all-purpose flour
1 (6-ounce) package semisweet
  chocolate morsels

- Preheat oven to 350°.
- In top of double boiler over hot water, melt chocolate and butter together; blend until smooth. Cool.
- In large mixing bowl, combine sugar and vanilla. Add eggs, 1 at a time, beating after each addition. Stir in flour and chocolate-butter liquid.
- Pour batter into well-greased 13x9x2-inch baking pan. Sprinkle with chocolate morsels.
- Bake for 25 to 30 minutes.

Rhoda Gould
Parkland, Florida

FILLED BROWNIES

Yield: 32

1 (14-ounce) package light caramels
½ cup plus ⅓ cup evaporated milk,
  divided
1 (18½-ounce) package German
  chocolate cake mix

¾ cup margarine, melted
1 (6-ounce) package semisweet
  chocolate morsels
1 cup pecan or walnut pieces

- In top of double boiler over hot water, melt caramels with ½ cup milk; stir until smooth.
- Preheat oven to 350°.
- In large mixing bowl, combine cake mix, ⅓ cup milk and margarine. Press ½ of mixture into greased and floured 13x9x2-inch baking pan.
- Bake for 8 minutes.
- Sprinkle chocolate morsels over baked crust. Spread caramel mixture and nuts over chocolate morsels. Crumble remaining dough and sprinkle over caramel-nut layer.
- Bake for 18 to 20 minutes. Cool slightly. Chill for about 30 minutes to firm caramel. Cut into bars before caramel hardens. Bars may be frozen.

Carole T. Miller
Lake Mary, Florida

LEMON SQUARES

Yield: 24

Crust

¾ cup margarine, softened
½ cup confectioner's sugar

2 cups all-purpose flour
Dash of salt

- Preheat oven to 350°.
- In large mixing bowl, combine margarine, sugar, flour and salt. Using electric mixer at low speed, blend for 3 minutes.
- Press dough into bottom of greased 13x9x2-inch baking pan.
- Bake for 20 minutes.

Filling

4 eggs, beaten
2 cups sugar
1 teaspoon baking powder

½ teaspoon salt
3 tablespoons grated lemon peel
½ cup lemon juice

- In large mixing bowl, combine eggs, sugar, baking powder, salt, peel and juice; mix thoroughly.
- Pour filling over partially baked crust.
- Bake for 25 to 30 minutes. Cool in pan. Squares may be frozen.

Barbara Moritz
North Miami Beach, Florida

EASY TIME COMPANY SQUARES

Yield: 20 to 24

1½ cups sugar
1 cup margarine, softened
4 eggs
1 teaspoon vanilla

2 cups all-purpose flour
1 (20-ounce) can fruit pie filling
Confectioner's sugar

- Preheat oven to 350°.
- In large mixing bowl, cream sugar and margarine until smooth. Add eggs, 1 at a time, beating after each addition. Blend in vanilla and flour.
- Spread batter in greased 15x10x1-inch jellyroll pan. Use knife tip to score into 20 or 24 squares. Place 1 tablespoon pie filling in center of each square.
- Bake for 40 minutes.
- Sprinkle with confectioner's sugar. Squares may be frozen.

Shirley Gelfand
Delray Beach, Florida

LEMON CHEESE BARS

Yield: 32

Crust

1 (18½-ounce) package pudding-added
  yellow cake mix

1 egg
⅓ cup vegetable oil

- Preheat oven to 350°.
- In large mixing bowl, combine cake mix, egg and oil; mix until crumbly.
- Reserving 1 cup crumbs, press remainder in bottom of ungreased 13x9x2-inch baking pan.
- Bake for 15 minutes.

Filling

1 (8-ounce) package cream cheese,
  softened
⅓ cup sugar

1 egg
1 teaspoon lemon juice

- In medium-sized mixing bowl, combine cheese, sugar, egg and lemon juice; beat until light and smooth.
- Spread filling over partially baked crust; sprinkle with reserved crumbs.
- Bake for 15 minutes. Cool before cutting into bars.

Shirley Grossman
Tamarac, Florida

SCOTCH TOFFEE BARS

Yield: 24

⅓ cup melted butter
2 cups oatmeal, uncooked
½ cup firmly-packed brown sugar
¼ cup dark corn syrup
½ teaspoon salt

1½ teaspoons vanilla
1 (6-ounce) package semisweet
  chocolate morsels, melted
¼ cup chopped nuts

- Preheat oven to 450°.
- In large mixing bowl, pour butter over oatmeal; mix well.
- Stir in brown sugar, syrup, salt and vanilla; mix thoroughly.
- Press mixture into greased 11x7x2-inch baking pan.
- Bake for 12 minutes. Cool.
- Spread melted chocolate over crust; sprinkle with nuts. Chill before cutting into bars.

Miriam Weisberg
Lake Worth, Florida

OLD WORLD RASPBERRY BARS

Yield: 16

Crust

1¼ cups all-purpose flour   ½ cup butter or margarine
⅓ cup sugar

- Preheat oven to 350°.
- In medium-sized mixing bowl, combine flour and sugar. Cut in margarine. Press crumbs into 8x8x2-inch baking pan.
- Bake for 25 minutes.

Filling

½ cup raspberry jam   ¼ teaspoon baking powder
1 cup chopped raisins   1 teaspoon salt
2 eggs, lightly beaten   1 teaspoon grated orange peel
¾ cup firmly-packed brown sugar   1 teaspoon vanilla
¼ cup all-purpose flour   1 cup chopped nuts

- Spread jam on partially baked crust. Sprinkle raisins over jam.
- In medium-sized mixing bowl, combine eggs, brown sugar, flour, baking powder, salt, peel, vanilla and nuts; mix well. Spread batter over jam layer.
- Bake for 25 minutes or until filling is firm. Use knife to separate from sides of pan; cool in pan before cutting into bars or squares. Sprinkle with confectioner's sugar, if desired.

Donna Breiner
Tampa, Florida

TEACUP CAKES

Yield: 24

Pastry

1 (3-ounce) package cream cheese,
softened

½ cup butter, softened
1 cup all-purpose flour

- In medium-sized mixing bowl, blend cream cheese, butter and flour until smooth. Chill overnight.

Filling

1 egg
¾ cup firmly-packed brown sugar
1 tablespoon butter, softened

1 teaspoon vanilla
Pinch of salt
⅔ cup chopped walnuts

- In medium-sized mixing bowl, combine egg, brown sugar, butter, vanilla and salt; beat until smooth.
- Divide pastry into 24 balls. Press dough into bottom and sides of cups of miniature muffin pans.
- Preheat oven to 325°.
- Sprinkle ½ of nuts in dough-lined cups, pour teaspoon of filling over nuts and top with remaining nuts.
- Bake for 35 minutes or until crust is lightly browned. Cool in pans 5 minutes before removing. Cakes may be frozen.

Irma Rosenzweig
Orlando, Florida

SUGAR GLAZED WALNUTS

Yield: 1 pound

½ cup butter
1 cup firmly-packed brown sugar

1 teaspoon ground cinnamon
4 cups walnut halves

- In 1½-quart microwave-safe casserole, melt butter on high (100%) for 1 to 1½ minutes.
- Stir in brown sugar and cinnamon; cook on high for 2 minutes.
- Add nuts, stirring to coat; cook on high for 3 to 5 minutes.
- Spread glazed nuts on waxed paper. Cool slightly.
- Serve warm or cold.

Arlene Gelber
Boca Raton, Florida

CRUNCHY PECANS

Yield: 1 pound

½ cup lightly salted butter or
  margarine
2 egg whites, at room temperature
Pinch of salt

1 cup sugar
1 pound large pecan halves
Salt

- Preheat oven to 325°.
- Melt butter in 15x10x1-inch jellyroll pan in oven.
- In medium-sized mixing bowl, beat egg whites with salt until stiff. Gradually add sugar, beating thoroughly. Fold in pecans.
- Carefully spread pecans on butter-covered pan.
- Bake for 30 minutes, gently stirring every 10 minutes. Pecans will separate. Do not overbake or pecans will become bitter.
- Sprinkle lightly with salt. Cool. Store in airtight container. Do not freeze.

Dottie Stevens
Sarasota, Florida

APPLE-CRANBERRY CRISP

Serves: 12 to 16

8 apples, peeled and sliced
2 cups uncooked cranberries
½ cup honey
½ teaspoon ground cinnamon
½ cup butter, softened
½ cup firmly-packed brown sugar

¾ cup oatmeal, uncooked
¾ cup all-purpose flour
¼ cup powdered milk
¼ cup wheat germ
¾ cup pecans, chopped

- In large mixing bowl, combine apples, cranberries, honey and cinnamon. Spoon into 13x9x2-inch baking pan.
- Preheat oven to 350°.
- In same mixing bowl, cream butter and brown sugar until smooth. Stir in oatmeal, flour, powdered milk, wheat germ and pecans. Sprinkle mixture over fruit.
- Bake for 1 hour.
- Serve warm.

Judith Leon
Atlanta, Georgia

FRUIT CRISP

Serves: 8 to 10

1 cup corn flakes
6 peaches, apples, plums or
  combination, sliced
1 cup sifted all-purpose flour
¾ cup sugar

1 teaspoon baking powder
1 egg or 2 egg whites
⅓ cup melted butter or margarine
Ground cinnamon

- Sprinkle corn flakes in bottom of buttered 2-quart casserole.
- Arrange fruit on flakes.
- Preheat oven to 350°.
- In small mixing bowl, combine flour, sugar, baking powder and egg; mix with fork until crumbly. Spoon over fruit.
- Pour butter over crumb topping and sprinkle with cinnamon.
- Bake for 30 to 40 minutes.
- Serve warm.

Anita Kessler
Boca Raton, Florida

CRANBERRY-APPLE CASSEROLE

Serves: 6 to 8

1 cup oatmeal, uncooked
½ cup all-purpose flour
1 cup firmly-packed brown sugar
½ cup margarine, melted

1 (16-ounce) can apple slices
1 (16-ounce) can whole cranberry
  sauce
1 teaspoon ground cinnamon

- Preheat oven to 350°.
- In medium-sized mixing bowl, combine oatmeal, flour, brown sugar and margarine; mix until crumbly.
- Layer apples and cranberry sauce in 12x8x2-inch baking dish. Sprinkle with crumb mixture, then cinnamon.
- Bake, uncovered, for 45 minutes.
- Serve warm.

Bunnie Taratoot
Dunwoody, Georgia

BAKED FRUIT COMPOTE

Serves: 10 to 12

1 (6-ounce) can frozen orange juice concentrate, thawed
2 tablespoons cornstarch
3 tablespoons pineapple juice
1 teaspoon ground cinnamon
4 large baking apples, peeled and thinly sliced

3 bananas, sliced diagonally
1 (29-ounce) can sliced peaches, drained
1 (20-ounce) can pineapple slices, drained
Maraschino cherries

- Preheat oven to 325°.
- In small mixing bowl, combine orange juice, cornstarch, pineapple juice and cinnamon.
- In buttered 3-quart casserole, layer apples, bananas, peaches and pineapple, sprinkling each with juice mixture. Place cherries in center of pineapple rings of the top layer. Sprinkle with remaining juice.
- Bake, uncovered, for 1 hour. Compote may be assembled a day in advance, baked for 45 minutes, stored overnight in refrigerator and reheated before serving. Compote should not be frozen.

Hilda Messinger
North Miami, Florida

PETIT COEUR A LA CRÈME

Serves: 4

1 (3-ounce) package cream cheese, softened
¼ cup sour cream
1 tablespoon confectioner's sugar

⅛ teaspoon salt
Cognac or fruit brandy
2 cups fresh or stewed fruit

- In small mixing bowl, beat cream cheese and sour cream together until smooth. Add sugar and salt; mix well.
- Beat in cognac or brandy a few drops at a time, using up to 2 teaspoons.
- Serve with fruit.

Harriet Cramer
West Palm Beach, Florida

EASIEST PEACH KUCHEN

Serves: 8

2 cups all-purpose flour
¼ teaspoon baking powder
¼ cup sugar, divided
½ cup margarine
12 canned peach halves, drained

1 teaspoon ground cinnamon
2 egg yolks
1 (8-ounce) carton sour cream or
    substitute

- Preheat oven to 400°.
- In medium-sized mixing bowl, sift flour, baking powder and 2 tablespoons sugar together. Using pastry blender or 2 table knives, cut in margarine until fine crumbs form.
- Press crumbs into bottom and on sides of 9-inch pie plate. Arrange peaches on crust, cut sides up. Sprinkle with cinnamon and 2 tablespoons sugar.
- Bake for 15 minutes.
- In small mixing bowl, blend egg yolks and sour cream. Pour over peaches.
- Bake for 30 minutes or until crust is lightly browned.
- Serve warm.

Bettina Janney
Coconut Creek, Florida

BANANA SPLIT CAKE

Serves: 16

16 graham crackers, crushed
3 tablespoons lite margarine, melted
2 cups water-packed pineapple, well
    drained
1 banana, sliced
1 cup strawberries, sliced

1 (6-serving) package sugar-free
    instant chocolate pudding mix
2 cups skim milk
2 cups lite whipped topping
Chopped dry-roasted unsalted peanuts
    (optional)

- In small mixing bowl, combine crackers and margarine. Press crumbs into 13x9x2-inch baking pan prepared with non-stick vegetable spray.
- Fold fruit into pudding prepared according to package directions but using 2 instead of 3 cups skim milk. Spread pudding-fruit mixture over crust in pan. Chill until firm.
- Spread whipped topping over pudding. Sprinkle with nuts.
- Serve cold. Cake may be prepared in advance and stored in refrigerator.

Flo Don
Sarasota, Florida

HEAVENLY HASH CAKE

Serves: 36

Cake

1 cup butter, softened
¼ cup cocoa
2 cups sugar
4 eggs, beaten

1½ cups all-purpose flour
1 cup chopped nuts
1 (10-ounce) package miniature
marshmallows

- Preheat oven to 350°.
- In large mixing bowl, cream butter, cocoa and sugar until smooth. Beat in eggs. Add flour and nuts; mix well.
- Pour batter into greased 13x9x2-inch baking pan.
- Bake for 30 to 35 minutes. Immediately spread marshmallows on hot cake.

Topping

¼ cup cocoa
½ cup butter
1 (16-ounce) package confectioner's
sugar

¼ cup evaporated milk

- In heavy 1½-quart saucepan over medium heat, combine all topping ingredients. Cook, stirring often, until well blended.
- Pour topping over marshmallows on cake.
- Serve warm.

Susan Harberg Lack
Atlanta, Georgia

LEMON CRÈME

Serves: 10

1 (3-ounce) package lemon gelatin
1 cup boiling water
1 pint vanilla ice cream, softened

½ cup fresh lemon juice
½ cup cold water

- In glass serving bowl, dissolve gelatin in boiling water. Stir in ice cream, lemon juice and cold water.
- With rotary beater, beat for about 6 minutes until frothy and blended.
- Chill. Crème may be stored in refrigerator several days.

Muriel Shindler
Sarasota, Florida

LEMON MOUSSE WITH RASPBERRY SAUCE

Serves: 8

Mousse

2 eggs, separated
1½ cups milk, divided
2 tablespoons unflavored gelatin
¾ cup plus 2 teaspoons sugar, divided

Zest of 4 lemons, chopped
Juice of 4 lemons
2 cups whipping cream, whipped

- In top of double boiler, beat yolks with 1 cup milk.
- In small saucepan, soften gelatin in ½ cup milk; dissolve over low heat and cool. Stir gelatin into yolk mixture.
- Add ¾ cup sugar to yolk mixture. Over simmering water, heat mixture, stirring constantly, for about 5 minutes or until slightly thickened.
- Stir in zest and juice. Pour mixture into large bowl; let cool until consistency of soft custard.
- In medium-sized bowl, beat egg whites with 2 teaspoons sugar until stiff. Fold cream into whites, then fold into lemon mixture.
- Pour mousse into 2½-quart soufflé dish prepared with non-stick vegetable spray. Chill overnight.

Sauce

1 cup fresh or 2 (10-ounce) packages
  frozen raspberries
¼ cup sugar

2 tablespoons lemon juice
1½ tablespoons light rum

- In saucepan, cook fresh raspberries with 1 tablespoon water; drain, reserving liquid. If using frozen raspberries, thaw, drain and reserve liquid.
- Using food processor, combine raspberries, sugar, lemon juice and rum; process to purée consistency. Strain seeds; thin with reserved liquid.
- Unmold chilled mousse on serving dish. Spoon sauce over and around mousse.
- Serve cold.

Erika Brodsky
Boca Raton, Florida

BEST EVER CHOCOLATE MOUSSE

Serves: 4

1 (6-ounce) package semi-sweet
chocolate morsels
3 tablespoons hot strong coffee

3 eggs, separated
1 teaspoon vanilla
1 tablespoon rum

- Using food processor or blender, chop chocolate morsels for 20 seconds. Add coffee and process for 20 seconds; add egg yolks and process for 20 seconds; add vanilla and rum and process for 20 seconds.
- In small mixing bowl, beat egg whites until stiff. Fold into chocolate mixture until no white shows.
- Pour mixture into glass casserole or soufflé dish. Chill for 3 hours or overnight.
- Serve cold, garnished with whipped cream and shaved chocolate if desired.

Anita B. Hoffman
Jensen Beach, Florida

FLAN

Serves: 12

1 cup sugar
4 eggs
1 (14-ounce) can sweetened
condensed milk

1 can water
2 tablespoons vanilla

- In small skillet over high heat, bring sugar to a boil to carmelize, stirring constantly. Immediately pour into 9x5x3-inch loaf pan, covering bottom and sides. Cool.
- Preheat oven to 350°.
- Using electric blender, combine eggs, milk, water and vanilla; blend until smooth. Pour into sugar coated loaf pan. Cover with aluminum foil. Place pan in large baking pan filled with 1 inch water.
- Bake for 1 to 1¼ hours or until firm. Cool and store in refrigerator, removing just before serving. Use knife to separate flan from sides of pan; invert on serving dish. Flan may be prepared a day in advance.

Eileen Hazan Ginzberg
North Miami Beach, Florida

LEE'S FAMOUS PUDDING DESSERT

Serves: 4 to 6

Crust

1 cup all-purpose flour
½ cup margarine, melted

½ cup chopped nuts

- Preheat oven to 350°.
- In small mixing bowl, combine flour and margarine. Blend in nuts.
- Press mixture into bottom of 9-inch round or 12x8x2-inch baking pan.
- Bake for 20 minutes or until lightly browned. Cool.

Filling

1 (12-ounce) carton frozen non-dairy
   whipped topping, thawed, divided
1 (8-ounce) package cream cheese,
   softened
1 cup confectioner's sugar

2 (3¾-ounce) packages instant
   pudding mix
2 cups milk
½ cup chopped nuts

- In large mixing bowl, combine ½ of whipped topping, cream cheese and sugar; mix until smooth. Spread over baked cooled crust.
- In medium-sized mixing bowl, mix pudding with milk. Pour over whipped layer.
- Spread remaining whipped topping over pudding layer. Sprinkle with nuts.
- Serve chilled. Dessert may be prepared in advance and stored, covered, in refrigerator or frozen.

Leona Fuss
Port St. Lucie, Florida

OLD FASHIONED NEW ENGLAND BREAD PUDDING

Serves: 6

½ (16-ounce) loaf white bread, slightly stale
¾ cup raisins
Boiling water
3 eggs, beaten
¾ cup sugar

2 teaspoons vanilla
⅛ teaspoon salt
1 teaspoon ground cinnamon
¼ teaspoon ground nutmeg
4 cups milk

- Preheat oven to 325°.
- Tear bread into ½-inch pieces and place in ungreased 3-quart casserole.
- In small mixing bowl, pour boiling water over raisins; drain.
- In medium-sized mixing bowl, combine eggs, sugar, vanilla, salt, cinnamon and nutmeg. Add milk and beat well.
- Mix raisins with bread in casserole. Pour milk mixture over bread and raisins.
- Bake for about 1 hour or until table knife inserted halfway between center and edge of casserole comes out clean.
- Serve warm, at room temperature or cold. Store in refrigerator.

Frani Imbruno
Sarasota, Florida

BAKED PINEAPPLE CASSEROLE

Serves: 8

⅓ cup butter or margarine, softened
½ cup sugar
4 eggs, beaten

1 (20-ounce) can crushed pineapple, drained
5 slices white bread, cubed

- Preheat oven to 350°.
- In large mixing bowl, cream butter and sugar until smooth. Blend in eggs.
- Stir in pineapple and fold in bread cubes. Pour mixture into greased 1½-quart casserole.
- Bake, uncovered, for 1 hour.
- Serve warm or cold.

Sylvia Herzog
Boca Raton, Florida

GRAHAM CRACKER-VANILLA DESSERT

Serves: 12

2 (3¾-ounce) packages French vanilla instant pudding mix
3 cups milk
1 (8-ounce) carton frozen non-dairy whipped topping, thawed
Graham crackers

2 (1-ounce) packets melted chocolate
1½ cups confectioner's sugar
2 tablespoons light corn syrup
1 tablespoon vanilla
2 tablespoons margarine, softened
1 to 2 tablespoons hot water

- In medium-sized mixing bowl, combine pudding mix and milk. Using electric mixer, beat for 5 minutes. Fold in whipped topping.
- Line bottom of buttered 13x9x2-inch baking pan with graham cracker squares. Spread ½ of pudding over crackers, add layer of crackers, spread pudding over crackers and top with layer of crackers.
- In small mixing bowl, combine chocolate, confectioner's sugar, syrup, vanilla, margarine and hot water; beat until smooth. Spread frosting over cracker layer.

Shirley Grossman
Tamarac, Florida

BLINTZ SOUFFLÉ

Serves: 8

8 frozen blintzes
½ cup butter or margarine, melted
¾ cup orange juice

7 eggs
⅓ cup sugar
1 teaspoon vanilla

- Preheat oven to 350°.
- Place blintzes in 10x8x2-inch baking dish.
- Pour butter over blintzes, turning to coat on all sides.
- In electric blender container, combine orange juice, eggs, sugar and vanilla; blend until smooth. Pour over blintzes.
- Bake for 40 minutes.
- Do not prepare in advance.

Evelyn Glick
North Miami Beach, Florida

PRETZEL DESSERT PIE

Serves: 16

Crust

2 cups crushed pretzels
¾ cup butter

3 tablespoons sugar

- Preheat oven to 400°.
- In medium-sized mixing bowl, combine pretzels, butter and sugar. Press mixture into bottom of 13x9x2-inch baking pan.
- Bake for 8 minutes. Cool for 25 minutes.

Filling

1 (6-ounce) package strawberry gelatin
2 cups boiling water
2 (10-ounce) packages frozen strawberries, partially thawed
1 (8-ounce) package cream cheese, softened

1 cup sugar
1 (12-ounce) carton non-dairy whipped topping, thawed

- In large mixing bowl, dissolve gelatin in boiling water. Add strawberries and chill for 10 minutes.
- In large mixing bowl, combine cheese and sugar; cream until smooth. Fold in whipped topping. Spread cheese mixture over pretzel crust.
- Pour partially set strawberry mixture over cheese layer.
- Chill until served.

Marlyn Wolman
Orlando, Florida

TART CRANBERRY MOLD

Serves: 12

1 (3-ounce) package lemon or apple gelatin
½ cup boiling water
1 (16-ounce) can smooth or whole cranberry sauce

⅔ cup drained crushed pineapple
½ to ¾ cup walnut halves
Dash of nutmeg (optional)
1 (8-ounce) carton sour cream (optional)

- In large mixing bowl, dissolve gelatin in boiling water; mix well.
- Add cranberry sauce to gelatin, blending thoroughly. Stir in pineapple, walnuts, nutmeg and sour cream. Pour into 5-cup mold. Chill overnight.
- Invert on serving plate. Serve cold.

Leona Fuss
Port St. Lucie, Florida

BLUEBERRY-GRAPE MOLD

Serves: 12

1 (16-ounce) bottle grape juice
2 (3-ounce) packages black raspberry, grape or raspberry gelatin

1 (16-ounce) carton sour cream
1 (16-ounce) can blueberries, drained

- Grease 6- or 8-cup mold; float in sink filled with ice water until ready to fill.
- In 1-quart saucepan, bring grape juice to a boil. Add gelatin and stir until dissolved. Pour into large mixing bowl and chill until thickened.
- Using electric mixer, whip gelatin for 5 to 7 minutes or until foamy. At low speed, fold in sour cream. Fold blueberries into gelatin mixture by hand.
- Pour into prepared mold. Chill overnight.
- Unmold on serving plate and serve immediately.

Sue Rosenbluth
Largo, Florida

COTTAGE CHEESE GELATIN MOLD

Serves: 8

1 (3-ounce) package strawberry or lime gelatin
2½ cups boiling water, divided
1 (6-ounce) package lemon gelatin
1 (20-ounce) can crushed pineapple, drained with juice reserved

1 cup small curd cottage cheese
1 (8-ounce) carton frozen non-dairy whipped topping, thawed
1 cup chopped nuts

- In small mixing bowl, dissolve strawberry gelatin in 1½ cups boiling water. Pour into 8- or 10-cup mold. Chill.
- In large mixing bowl, dissolve lemon gelatin in 1 cup boiling water; add 1 cup reserved pineapple juice. Chill until partially firm.
- Add cottage cheese, whipped topping, pineapple and nuts, mixing after each addition. Pour into mold. Chill until firm.
- Invert on serving plate. Serve cold.

Anne Gaynor
Tamarac, Florida

STRAWBERRY MOLD

Serves: 8 to 10

3 (3-ounce) packages strawberry
  gelatin
2½ cups water, divided
3 (6-ounce) packages frozen
  strawberries, thawed

1 (8-ounce) carton sour cream
1 pint vanilla ice cream, softened

- In 2-quart saucepan, combine gelatin and 1½ cups water; bring to a boil and stir until gelatin is dissolved.
- Place strawberries in colander; reserve juice. Press strawberries through colander.
- Add 1 cup strawberry juice with 1 cup water to gelatin. Stir in strawberry pulp, sour cream and ice cream. Mix with rotary beater until creamy. Pour into 8-cup mold. Chill overnight.
- Unmold on serving plate. Serve cold.

Ann E. Logan
Miami, Florida

STRAWBERRY NUT MOLD

Serves: 6 to 8

2 (3-ounce) packages strawberry
  gelatin
1 cup boiling water
2 (6-ounce) packages frozen
  strawberries, thawed

1 (20-ounce) can crushed pineapple,
  drained
3 medium bananas, mashed
1 cup coarsely chopped nuts
1 (16-ounce) carton sour cream

- In 3-quart saucepan, dissolve gelatin in boiling water.
- Fold in strawberries with juice, pineapple, bananas and nuts. Pour ½ of mixture into 12x8x2-inch baking dish. Chill for 1½ hours or until firm. Keep remainder of mixture at room temperature.
- Spread sour cream over firm gelatin. Carefully spoon remaining gelatin mixture over sour cream layer. Chill until firm.
- Cut into squares. Serve cold.

Boni Tye Raitt
Fort Myers, Florida

BUTTERSCOTCH WALNUT ICE CREAM

Serves: 8 to 10

2 tablespoons butter or margarine
¼ cup firmly-packed brown sugar
1 tablespoon light corn syrup
½ cup chopped walnuts

3 eggs, separated
1 teaspoon vanilla extract
1 tablespoon confectioner's sugar
1 cup whipping cream

- In 1-quart saucepan, melt butter. Stir in sugar, syrup and walnuts; bring to a boil, then cook for 2 to 3 minutes or until golden brown. Remove from heat.
- Slowly add walnut mixture to egg yolks in small mixing bowl, stirring constantly. Add vanilla.
- In medium-sized mixing bowl, beat egg whites until firm peaks form. Whisk in confectioner's sugar, 1 teaspoon at a time, beating after each addition.
- In medium-sized mixing bowl, whip cream until soft peaks form. Add with egg yolk mixture to egg whites, using metal spoon to gently blend.
- Pour mixture into 9-inch springform pan prepared with non-stick vegetable spray. Freeze overnight.
- Release pan sides, place on serving plate and garnish with piped whipped cream and whole walnuts, if desired.

Lorraine Watkins
Atlanta, Georgia

HALVAH "ICE CREAM"

(Parve)

Serves: 4 to 6

3 eggs, separated
⅓ cup sugar
1 (8-ounce) carton frozen non-dairy
whipped topping, thawed

1 (6-ounce) package marble halvah

- In large mixing bowl, beat egg yolks with sugar until creamy. Fold whipped topping into yolk mixture.
- In medium-sized mixing bowl, beat egg whites until stiff. Fold into egg yolk mixture.
- Chop halvah. Add ⅔ to egg mixture, reserving remainder for topping.
- Pour mixture into freezer-proof serving dish. Sprinkle with reserved halvah. Freeze.
- Serve frozen.

Helen Stanley
Atlanta, Georgia

INDEX

Women's American ORT, Southeast District
2101 East Hallandale Beach Boulevard Suite 301
Hallandale, Florida 33009

Please send me _____ copies of **Chef's EscORT**....... $15.00 each $ _____
    Plus postage and handling .... $ 2.50 each $ _____
    Florida residents add sales tax .... $ 1.05 each $ _____
Enclosed is a check or money order for .... Total $ _____

Name: _____
Address: _____
City: _____ State: _____ Zip: _____

(Please make checks payable to **Women's American ORT**)
Sending a copy of **Chef's EscORT** to an old or new friend? See reverse side for details.

Women's American ORT, Southeast District
2101 East Hallandale Beach Boulevard Suite 301
Hallandale, Florida 33009

Please send me _____ copies of **Chef's EscORT**....... $15.00 each $ _____
    Plus postage and handling .... $ 2.50 each $ _____
    Florida residents add sales tax .... $ 1.05 each $ _____
Enclosed is a check or money order for .... Total $ _____

Name: _____
Address: _____
City: _____ State: _____ Zip: _____

(Please make checks payable to **Women's American ORT**)
Sending a copy of **Chef's EscORT** to an old or new friend? See reverse side for details.

Women's American ORT, Southeast District
2101 East Hallandale Beach Boulevard Suite 301
Hallandale, Florida 33009

Please send me _____ copies of **Chef's EscORT**....... $15.00 each $ _____
    Plus postage and handling .... $ 2.50 each $ _____
    Florida residents add sales tax .... $ 1.05 each $ _____
Enclosed is a check or money order for .... Total $ _____

Name: _____
Address: _____
City: _____ State: _____ Zip: _____

(Please make checks payable to **Women's American ORT**)
Sending a copy of **Chef's EscORT** to an old or new friend? See reverse side for details.

Unless otherwise specified, all books will be sent to the address on the order form. If you wish books sent to other addresses, please specify below and enclose your gift card(s) with this order.

Send to: _____

Address: _____

City: _____ State: _____ Zip: _____

Send to: _____

Address: _____

City: _____ State: _____ Zip: _____

List additional names on a separate sheet of paper; please include your name.

Unless otherwise specified, all books will be sent to the address on the order form. If you wish books sent to other addresses, please specify below and enclose your gift card(s) with this order.

Send to: _____

Address: _____

City: _____ State: _____ Zip: _____

Send to: _____

Address: _____

City: _____ State: _____ Zip: _____

List additional names on a separate sheet of paper; please include your name.

Unless otherwise specified, all books will be sent to the address on the order form. If you wish books sent to other addresses, please specify below and enclose your gift card(s) with this order.

Send to: _____

Address: _____

City: _____ State: _____ Zip: _____

Send to: _____

Address: _____

City: _____ State: _____ Zip: _____

List additional names on a separate sheet of paper; please include your name.